Educational Leadership as a Culturally-Constructed Practice

This edited book collection disrupts received notions of educational leadership, culture and diversity as currently portrayed in practice and theory. It draws on compelling studies of educational leadership from the global north and south, as well as from a range of ethnic, religious and gendered perspectives and critical research approaches. In so doing, the book powerfully challenges contemporary leadership discourses of diversity that reproduce essentialising leadership practices, binary divisions and asymmetrical power relations. The various chapters contest and move beyond exhortations for leadership in increasingly diverse societies, revealing through their rich portraits of the hybidity of leadership practice the shallowness of diversity discourses that are framed as something 'we' (the culturally homogenous leader) do to (heterogenous) 'others'.

The volume is more than critique. Instead it offers readers new directions and possibilities through which to understand, theorise and practise educational leadership in the 21st century. In portraying leading as a "relational practice in contexts of cultural hybridity" (Blackmore, this volume), it extends critical theories for and of leadership practice, examining the intersectionality between leadership and a range of social categories, and challenging notions of leadership as a singular construct. Compelling research narratives reveal educational leadership practice as nuanced, temporal, site-specific and prefigured by traditions and cultural understandings that reach beyond a simplification of educational leadership as understood through unitary lenses of race, gender or ethnicity.

This book is essential reading for academics and students of educational leadership and management, as well as administrators.

Jane Wilkinson is an Associate Professor of Educational Leadership in the Faculty of Education, Monash University and Associate Dean, Graduate Research.

Laurette Bristol is the Director-Academic Services at UWI School of Business and Applied Studies Ltd (UWI-ROYTEC – www.roytec.edu), Trinidad and Tobago, West Indies.

Routledge Research in Education

For a full list of titles in this series, please visit www.routledge.com

186 **Transnationalism, Education and Empowerment:**
The latent legacies of empire
Niranjan Casinader

187 **Reflective Practice**
Voices from the Field
Edited by Roger Barnard and Jonathon Ryan

188 **Citizenship Education in America**
A Historical Perspective
Iftikhar Ahmad

189 **Transformative Learning and Teaching in Physical Education**
Edited by Malcolm Thorburn

190 **Teaching young learners in a superdiverse world**
Multimodal approaches and perspectives
Edited by Heather Lotherington & Cheryl Paige

191 **History, Theory and Practice of Philosophy for Children**
International Perspectives
Edited by Saeed Naji and Rosnani Hashim

192 **Teacher Professional Knowledge and Development for Reflective and Inclusive Practices**
Edited by Ismail Hussein Amzat and Nena P. Valdez

193 **Contemplative and artful openings**
Researching women and teaching
Susan Casey Walsh

194 **Educational Leadership as a Culturally-Constructed Practice**
New Directions and Possibilities
Edited by Jane Wilkinson and Laurette Bristol

Educational Leadership as a Culturally-Constructed Practice

New Directions and Possibilities

Edited by
Jane Wilkinson and
Laurette Bristol

LONDON AND NEW YORK

First published 2018
by Routledge
2 Park Square, Milton Park, Abingdon, Oxon OX14 4RN

and by Routledge
711 Third Avenue, New York, NY 10017

Routledge is an imprint of the Taylor & Francis Group, an informa business

© 2018 selection and editorial matter, Jane Wilkinson and Laurette Bristol; individual chapters, the contributors

The right of Jane Wilkinson and Laurette Bristol to be identified as the authors of the editorial material, and of the authors for their individual chapters, has been asserted in accordance with sections 77 and 78 of the Copyright, Designs and Patents Act 1988.

All rights reserved. No part of this book may be reprinted or reproduced or utilised in any form or by any electronic, mechanical, or other means, now known or hereafter invented, including photocopying and recording, or in any information storage or retrieval system, without permission in writing from the publishers.

Trademark notice: Product or corporate names may be trademarks or registered trademarks, and are used only for identification and explanation without intent to infringe.

British Library Cataloguing-in-Publication Data
A catalogue record for this book is available from the British Library

Library of Congress Cataloging-in-Publication Data
A catalog record for this book has been requested

ISBN: 978-1-138-91531-2 (hbk)
ISBN: 978-1-315-69030-8 (ebk)

Typeset in Galliard
by Apex CoVantage, LLC

Contents

List of contributors	vii
Acknowledgements	xii
Introduction	1
JANE WILKINSON AND LAURETTE BRISTOL	
1 **The unexamined constructions of educational leadership**	7
JANE WILKINSON AND LAURETTE BRISTOL	
2 **Beyond culture as ethnicity: Interrogating the empirical sites for leading scholarship**	23
LAURETTE BRISTOL AND JANE WILKINSON	
3 **The role of ethical practices in pursuing socially just leadership**	40
AMANDA KEDDIE AND RICHARD NIESCHE	
4 **"We're going to call our kids 'African Aussies'": Leading for diversity in regional Australia**	54
JANE WILKINSON	
5 **Is she in the wrong place? Exploring the intersections of gender, religion, culture and leadership**	75
SAEEDA SHAH	
6 **Exploring the successful school leadership literature in China**	95
QIAN HAIYAN, ALLAN WALKER AND LI JIACHENG	
7 **Indigenist holistic educational leadership**	118
ZANE MA RHEA	

8 Communicating research: A challenge of context 137
LAUNCELOT BROWN, LAURETTE BRISTOL AND TALIA ESNARD

9 Practice traditions of researching educational leadership across national contexts 152
JANE WILKINSON, KARIN RÖNNERMAN, LAURETTE BRISTOL AND PETRI SALO

10 Conduct un/becoming: Discipline in the context of educational leadership research 171
VONZELL AGOSTO AND ZORKA KARANXHA

11 Left out: Gender and feminism in the educational leadership curriculum 189
MICHELLE D. YOUNG, CATHERINE MARSHALL AND TORRIE EDWARDS

12 Commentary: Leadership as a relational practice in contexts of cultural hybridity 208
JILL BLACKMORE

Index 217

Contributors

Vonzell Agosto's research agenda engages theories of social oppression in connection with concepts of curriculum and leadership. Her primary line of inquiry explores how educators conceptualise and operationalise curriculum in the contexts of teaching, leading and learning. This line of inquiry attends to the preparation of educators, administrators and youth, and their experiences within and influence on educational contexts being (more or less) oppressive, especially in regard to culture, race, gender and dis/ability.

Jill Blackmore is Alfred Deakin Professor in the Faculty of Arts and Education, Deakin University, and former Director of the Centre for Research in Educational Futures and Innovation and Fellow of the Academy of Social Sciences Australia. Her research interests include, from a feminist perspective: globalisation, education policy and governance; international and intercultural education; educational restructuring, leadership and organisational change; spatial redesign and innovative pedagogies; teachers' and academics' work, all with a focus on equity. Recent higher education research has focused on disengagement with and lack of diversity in leadership, international education and graduate employability. Her research has focused in particular on the re/constitution of the social relations of gender in and through education in the early 21st century. Publications include J. Blackmore (2016) *Critical perspectives on educational leadership: Nancy Fraser*, Routledge; Blackmore, J. Sanchez, M. and Sawers, N. (Eds.) (2017) *Globalised re/gendering of the academy and leadership*, Routledge; Arber, R.; Blackmore, J. and Vongalis, Macrow, A. (Eds.) (2014) *Mobile teachers and curriculum in international schooling*, Rotterdam: Sense.

Laurette Bristol is the Director-Academic Services at UWI School of Business and Applied Studies Ltd (UWI-ROYTEC – www.roytec.edu), Trinidad and Tobago, West Indies. Her research focuses broadly on in-service teacher education for educational transformation. Her empirical projects revolve around postcolonial perspectives in education and the educational practices enacted amongst teachers and prefigured by conditions internal and external to the educational community (leading, professional learning and mentoring). She can be reached at laurettebristol@gmail.com.

Launcelot Brown is a Professor and Chair in the Department of Educational Foundations and Leadership at Duquesne University. He is a former teacher, special educator and principal of a school for students with emotional and behavioural difficulties, and a school for deaf children. He has served on many national educational boards in Trinidad and Tobago, including the National Advisory Committee on Special Education. His research interests are in the area of school leadership and school effectiveness. Recently he has turned his attention to national assessment and teachers' use of assessment data. He served as an Associate Editor for the journal *Educational Measurement: Issues and Practice* from 2006 to 2009.

Torrie Edwards is a doctoral student in Education at the University of North Carolina – Chapel Hill. Her program focuses on policy, leadership and school improvement. Specifically, her research interests are in the intersection of politics and education, language and discourse and issues of gender equity in education policy.

Talia Esnard is a sociologist attached to the Department of Behavioral Sciences, Faculty of Social Sciences, the University of the West Indies (UWI). Her research interests centre on issues affecting Caribbean women who work within educational and entrepreneurial spheres. Some of her work has been published in the *Journal of Asian Academy of Management*, *NASPA Journal about Women in Higher Education*, *Journal of the Motherhood Initiative*, *Mentoring & Tutoring: Partnership in Learning*, *Caribbean Curriculum*, *Journal of Educational Administration and History* as well as *Women, Gender & Families of Color*.

Qian Haiyan is an Assistant Professor in the Department of Education Policy and Leadership at The Education University of Hong Kong. Her research interests include education leadership and school principalship in China and influence of the social and cultural context on schooling across Chinese societies. Her studies in these fields emphasise building indigenous understandings about how Chinese school leaders develop teachers, promote learning and teaching and improve schools. She can be reached at hqian@eduhk.hk.

Li Jiacheng is a researcher at the Institute of Schooling Reform and Development and a professor in the Department of Education Science at the East China Normal University, Shanghai. He is the author of *Caring for life: School reform in China* (2006), *Student development in everyday classroom life* (2015) and the co-author of *School leadership reform in China* (2007), *School life and student development* (2009) and *Manual for school-family collaboration* (2016). He can be reached at jcli@dem.ecnu.edu.cn.

Amanda Keddie is a Professor of Education within the Research for Educational Impact (REDI) Strategic Research Centre at Deakin University. Her published work examines the broad gamut of schooling processes, practices and conditions that can impact on the pursuit of social justice in schools including student identities, teacher identities, pedagogy, curriculum, leadership, school structures, policy agendas and socio-political trends. Her recent books are *Leadership, ethics and schooling for social justice* (2016), *The politics of difference in schools* (2017) and *Supporting and educating young Muslim women: Stories from Australia and the UK* (in press).

Zorka Karanxha's research agenda focuses on educational leadership policies that influence marginalised communities through continued investigation of two interwoven conceptual strands: (1) social justice leadership praxis to reduce educational inequities, and (2) social justice leadership to reduce inequities in legal education policy and policy implementation. Her research focuses on educational leadership preparation, education law, school discipline and charter schools. Dr. Karanxha has published her research in many journals including *Educational Administration Quarterly*, *Journal of School Leadership*, *Journal of Research in Leadership Education* and *Journal of Special Education Leadership*.

Zane Ma Rhea has worked with Indigenous people over the last 35 years in various capacities. She is recognised internationally for her expertise in comparative education and leadership development using a rights-based framework, focusing on organisational change management, professional development and the recognition and preservation of Indigenous knowledge in mainstream organisations through meaningful partnerships with Indigenous families and communities. She teaches, researches and supervises across Indigenous education, leadership, and teacher education in early years and primary-level programs at Monash University, focusing on cross-curricula and cross-cultural comparative and international studies in organisational development.

Catherine Marshall is Distinguished Professor of Educational Leadership and Policy at the University of North Carolina. Her scholarly agendas combine gender issues and politics. Books include *Designing qualitative research*, *Reframing educational politics*, *Feminist critical policy analysis*, *Leadership for social justice* and *Activist educator*. Dr. Marshall has led the American Educational Research Association Politics of Education Association and Division L, Politics and Policy. Awards include the Willystine Goodsell Award for Research on Women, Politics of Education Association Bailey Award for "Shaping the Intellectual and Research Agendas of the Field" and the University Council for Educational Administration's Campbell Award for "Lifetime Contributions to the Leadership Field".

Richard Niesche is a Senior Lecturer in the School of Education at the University of New South Wales, Sydney, Australia. He has worked as a teacher in Queensland and New South Wales at both primary and secondary levels. His research interests include educational leadership, the principalship and social justice. His particular research focus is to use critical perspectives in educational leadership to examine the work of school principals in disadvantaged schools and how they can work towards achieving more socially just outcomes.

He has published his research in a range of peer-reviewed journals and is the author of a number of books including *Foucault and educational leadership: Disciplining the principal* (Routledge, 2011) and *Deconstructing educational leadership: Derrida and Lyotard* (Routledge, 2013). His most recent book is *Leadership, ethics and schooling for social justice*, co-authored with Dr. Amanda Keddie (Routledge, 2016).

Karin Rönnerman is Professor of Education at the Department of Education and Special Education, The University of Gothenburg, Gothenburg, Sweden. Professor Rönnerman's main research focus is action research and teacher professional development. She is specifically interested in how leadership is generated by taking part in action research. She is the Swedish coordinator of the international Pedagogy, Education and Praxis (PEP) research network. Her most recent book co-edited with Petri Salo is *Lost in practice: Transforming educational action research* (2014).

Petri Salo is Professor of Adult Education and Dean at the Faculty of Education and Welfare Studies, Åbo Akademi University, Vaasa, Finland. Petri researches and teaches in adult education and action research, as well as school development and school leadership. He is the national coordinator of the Nordic Network in Action Research as well as the international coordinator of the Pedagogy, Education and Praxis research network. He is a co-editor of *Nurturing praxis: Action research in partnerships between school and university in a Nordic light* (Rotterdam: Sense Publishers, 2008) and *Lost in practice: Transforming Nordic educational action research* (Rotterdam: Sense Publishers, 2014).

Saeeda Shah is currently working at the School of Education, University of Leicester, teaching masters and doctoral programmes. She is Director PhD and Member, International Strategy Forum. She is also visiting Professor of Education at the University of Derby (UK). Previously, she has worked in higher education in Pakistan in senior leadership positions. Her research interests include educational leadership with a focus on diversity, gender, cultural and belief systems, power issues, social justice and Islamic philosophy of education. She is on editorial boards of many journals. Saeeda is recognised as an international authority in her field of expertise and has published widely in highly prestigious journals. She is invited for keynotes and lectures internationally and has also presented her work at international conferences in many parts of the world. She has also been actively involved in the voluntary sector in Britain since 1995 and has participated in the United Nation's Human Rights Commission's sessions in relation to her work for human rights, particularly for the rights of women and youth.

Allan Walker is Joseph Lau Chair Professor of International Educational Leadership, Dean of the Faculty of Education and Human Development and Director of The Joseph Lau Luen Hung Charitable Trust Asia Pacific Centre for Leadership and Change at The Education University of Hong Kong. Allan's research interests include the impact of culture on educational leadership and school organisation; school leadership in South East Asia, particularly China; leadership development; leading international schools and values and educational leadership. He has published widely and is currently editor of the *Journal of Educational Administration*. He can be reached at adwalker@eduhk.hk.

Jane Wilkinson is an Associate Professor of Educational Leadership in the Faculty of Education, Monash University and Associate Dean, Graduate Research. Jane's main research and teaching interests are in the areas of educational leadership for social justice and practice theory (feminist, Bourdieuian and practical philosophy), gender and leadership and refugee education. She has conducted extensive research with women leaders of diverse ethnic backgrounds in the university sector and with young refugee students and schools in regional Australia. Jane's publications include *Professional development: Education for all as praxis* (with Bristol and Ponte) (Routledge, 2016); *Changing practices, changing education* (2014) (with Kemmis, Edwards-Groves, Hardy, Grootenboer and Bristol) (Springer, Singapore) and *Travelling towards a mirage? Gender, leadership and higher education* (with Fitzgerald) (Post Pressed, 2010). Jane is co editor of the Journal of Educational Administration and History (JEAH).

Michelle D. Young, PhD, is the Executive Director of the University Council for Educational Administration and a professor of leadership at the University of Virginia. Dr. Young's scholarship focuses on the preparation and practice of educational leaders and seeks to understand how leaders and policies can ensure equitable and quality experiences for all school community members. She is the recipient of the William J. Davis award for the most outstanding article published in a volume of the *Educational Administration Quarterly*. Most recently she edited, with Gary Crow, the second edition of the *Handbook of research on the education of school leaders*.

Acknowledgements

To the local and international colleagues who generously provided their time and expertise to read drafts of chapters and provide critical feedback for improvement, we say a very appreciative thank you.

We especially acknowledge the school leaders and educational leadership researchers whose practice stories give form to the substance of this edited collection. This book is for you! We hope that you find the chapters within to be an expression of the social and cultural dynamism, which prefigure and give shape to your site-based educational leadership and educational leadership research practices.

To our family members: Peter, Sarah, Shirley, Rosita, Louren, Laurel, Junior, Jovica, Issa, Izaiah and Laurissa. Thank you for your patience, encouragement and love.

Jane would like to dedicate this book to her Mum, who believed in the power of education and who showed what it is possible for women to achieve, despite adverse circumstances. May she rest in peace.

Laurette dedicates this work to her mother, who taught her that a good education would open the doors often closed to young Black women from single-parent homes. I pray that she carries on teaching the value of education to her grandchildren.

Introduction

Jane Wilkinson and Laurette Bristol

> *There has been for a number of years a certain cachet or attractiveness to being a woman and of minority background for universities. On the negative side, the very things that make you attractive are then the things that for some people irritate, grate or are attributes of an outsider. You're carrying an extra burden on top of the outsiderness that women bring … in a place, particularly in management, that's dominated by Anglo men.*
> (Simone, senior academic in an Australian university)

Introduction

In 2015 a storm of controversy erupted over the release of *Go Set a Watchman*, a book by the North American author Harper Lee. In Lee's book, the main character, heroic white father figure and lawyer Atticus Finch is portrayed as a racist and defender of segregation in the American South of the 1950s. This is in sharp contrast to his characterisation in Lee's immensely popular previous book, *To Kill A Mockingbird*, where Finch is characterised through his adoring daughter's eyes as a heroic figure bravely defending an African-American male against charges of rape of a white woman. Much of the media reporting centred on the storm of controversy and disillusionment reportedly experienced by many North American readers in response to Lee's new book and its portrayal of Finch. As one reviewer of the book lamented, "Hey Boo(hoo): Wish I'd not read Harper Lee's new book". Less widely reported was the reception of the book by African-American readers, generations of whom may have read it as a text in segregated classrooms in the US.

The quotation which begins this chapter is from research conducted by one of the authors with senior women from different ethnic and class backgrounds who held major leadership roles in Australian universities in the early 2000s (Wilkinson, 2007, 2008, 2009). Simone's quotation suggests that to be a female leader from a non-Anglo background in the predominantly Anglo-Australian milieu of university management is precarious and risky business. It can operate as a form of distinction for Australian universities, keen to parade their equity credentials to an increasingly diverse student market. Alternatively, it may become a form of symbolic violence for individuals such as Simone who experience themselves as "outsiders within" academic management (Anderson & Williams, 2001).

Simone's quotation captures the symbolic value of her subject location, where her diversity carries "a certain cachet" – but also its inherent difficulties – which stretch beyond her gender to encompass her socioeconomic status and her non-Anglo-Australian ethnicity, "an extra burden".

The sense of betrayal experienced by many North American readers to Harper Lee's re-presentation of Atticus Finch as a fallen and flawed white male hero and Simone's bruising confrontations with Anglo-Australian masculinities of academic leadership suggest the enduring and deep-seated nature of dominant mythologies of leadership, drawn from the media, popular culture and a nation's histories. These mythologies, coupled with existing organisational and familial structures and cultures, inform and constitute "dominant institutional and populist notions of leadership" (Blackmore, 2010, p. 50). Implicit within these notions of leadership is the threat of material and deleterious consequences for those who do not fit within dominant paradigms.

Simone's remarks connote the symbolic and material power of leadership as a culturally constructed phenomenon, which is gendered, raced, sexualised and classed. They hint at how representations and understandings of educational leadership in Australia and other Anglophone nations are largely premised on a subject location of leadership as a white and masculinist practice – a taken-for-granted and un-interrogated centre (Moreton-Robinson, 2000; Wilkinson, 2007). Yet understandings of leadership which disrupt this dominant centre remain silenced or marginalised in mainstream scholarship. This is despite an increasing body of literature challenging dominant approaches to educational leadership as a universal, decontextualised and depoliticised organisational practice, underpinned by instrumentalist notions of effectiveness and improvement (e.g., Blackmore & Sachs, 2007; Bristol, 2014; Bristol, Esnard, & Brown, 2015; Brooks, 2012; Esnard, Bristol, & Brown, 2013; Fuller, 2015; Niesche & Keddie, 2016; Theoharis & Scanlan, 2015; Wilkinson & Eacott, 2013; Wrigley, Thomson, & Lingard, 2012). This latter approach critiques how mainstream scholarship overlooks the ways in which leadership subjectivities are racialised, classed, gendered and sexualised – constructed and informed by discourses, organisations and systems which form the leadership subject of which they speak (Parker, 2005, as cited in Blackmore, 2010, p. 46). This refusal to critically interrogate how asymmetrical power relations are produced and reproduced through leadership practice, scholarship and research approaches has had major and deleterious material impacts. For example, it has perpetuated unjust outcomes in schools for students from various equity groups (Smyth, 2011) and discouraged a diversity of leaders and forms of leadership in educational settings such as schools and universities (Watterson, 2015).

Hence, a crucial aspect of the political project which underpins this edited collection is deconstructing leadership constructions as they are played out in educational sites, and understanding and interrogating their constitutive, symbolic and material effects on how educational leadership is theorised, represented and practised. We ask: Whose knowledges and practices are rendered visible and whose knowledges and practices are marginalised and ploughed under through particular kinds of representational and theoretical practices and approaches? In so doing, our book aims to challenge educational leadership scholars to interrogate dominant trends within practice and research that assume leadership as operating from a uni-dimensional, apolitical and neutral centre. Instead, it foregrounds the multi-dimensional nature of cultural sites for leadership practice.

The book utilises the construct of *culture* as an interrogative lens in two ways. Firstly, at the level of leadership practice, it utilises sites as the ontological lens through which to examine the culturally specific contexts in which educational leadership practices are enacted. Secondly, at the level of leadership research, the book explores some of the challenges and opportunities which arise when different theoretical frameworks are used to examine and re-present culturally specific leadership practices. In particular, it examines the thorny issue of representation and how educational leadership researchers can both re-present stakeholders in ways that are 'true' to the culture/s being represented, whilst simultaneously recognising that they are employing theoretical lenses which necessarily occlude or silence particular aspects of culturally specific leadership practices.

The organisation of the book

The cases in this edited collection consider the implications for leadership practices and the empirical forms scholarship in the field might take in order to represent leading practices in culturally responsive ways. The collection argues for a form of leadership inquiry that is bounded and contextualised by more than race, gender or ethnicity. The book's main objectives are to interrogate and extend the scholarship examining leadership as a culturally situated practice. In so doing, it challenges existing bodies of research in three ways. Firstly, it challenges cross-cultural and multi-ethnic approaches to leadership practice and research, which continue to perpetuate unexamined constructions of culturally inclusive leadership practices as an unproblematic binary, primarily focused on what (frequently white, male) leaders 'do' to (generally non-white) 'others'. Secondly, it extends critical theories *for* and *of* leadership practice. Most frequently these approaches examine leadership and a particular category (e.g., ethnicity, gender, socioeconomic status) from a unitary approach. Rarer still is scholarship which examines the intersectionality between leadership and a range of social categories, that is, which examines, for example, how leadership operates as a raced, gendered and classed construct. Finally, the book extends critical leadership research approaches by interrogating the frequently unexamined assumptions underlying the employment of different theoretical frameworks to examine leadership practice. It asks, how are these theoretical lens employed by researchers in ways that may enable and/or constrain particular aspects of culturally specific leading practices?

Chapters 1and 2 set the broad parameters of the debate. Chapter 1 examines the 'cultural turn' in educational leadership. It interrogates the epistemological, methodological and ontological constructions of mainstream educational leadership scholarship and practice. It surveys theoretical frameworks and research approaches which are challenging dominant paradigms of educational leadership, located in unexamined constructions of the unitary white masculinist leadership subject. Chapter 2 examines the relationship between culture and the empirical sites *of* and *for* leadership inquiry and scholarship. As such, the fundamental question it examines is: How does the application of theoretical concepts and methodological practices in culturally varying empirical sites serve to subjugate alternative understandings, practices and inquiry into leadership?

Chapters 3–7 are illustrative of cases that take as their lens the notion of leading practices as located in culturally specific sites. Chapter 3 employs a Foucauldian perspective to highlight the need for a nuanced approach to understanding the dynamics of leadership for social justice and the ways in which leaders work on themselves and others to enable social justice in education. Chapter 4 raises concerns about school leadership for diversity and the ways it is represented, embodied and enacted through research, policy and practice. Chapter 5 explores the question of how gender and leadership are shaped at the intersections of diverse social factors and, in so doing, prefigures women's leadership as a form of gender-transgressive performance. Chapter 6 analyses the landscape of successful school leadership in China and the ways in which educational reform in China is being influenced by both Western and Asian ideas. Chapter 7 employs an Indigenist perspective to interrogate leadership change and the building of respectful collaborative partnerships between educators as they seek to respond to the educational needs of the site. Chapters 8–11 consider the impact of leadership research employing theories which originate outside the cultural contexts in which they are applied. These chapters examine the implications for the representation of participants and practices and the re-presentation of leading realities. Chapter 8 exposes leadership research practices in communicating research on educational leadership and the cultural challenge this poses to the social context. Chapter 9 challenges the homogenising and taken-for-granted researcher assumptions which underpin the choice of methods employed in the field of leadership research in schools. This is examined across differing national contexts when deploying similar theoretical tools. Chapter 10 confronts leading and researching from the perspective of participants'/students' interactions with school-based leadership and research as the authors (researchers) engaged with youth as co-participants. Chapter 11 interrogates the knowledge content of principal preparation programmes in the US and the ways in which these knowledges and the methods used serve the development of gender equity in education. Chapter 12 by Jill Blackmore comments and critiques the ideas and conclusions outlined in Chapters 1–11. It draws together the key ideas in the book and considers the implications for leadership practices and the empirical forms scholarship in the field might take in order to represent leading practices in culturally responsive ways.

In assembling this collection, we draw on our experiential positions as critical educational leadership scholars in positions of authority in our higher education institutions – organisations which nonetheless remain constructed on naturalised premises of white masculinist authority. Jane is an Associate Professor of Educational Leadership at Monash University, Australia and Associate Dean, Graduate Research. Her early experiences as a female secondary deputy principal from a working-class, Anglo/Eastern European Jewish background in a region dominated by Anglo-Australian male principals had a profoundly politicising impact on her, leading to her adoption of a critical feminist stance. Laurette is the Director of Academic Services at University of West Indies School of Business and Applied Studies Ltd (UWI-ROYTEC) and a former post-doctoral researcher and lecturer at Charles Sturt University, Australia. Her early career experiences as a Black female academic from the Caribbean operating outside home in the UK and Australia led to her adoption of a postcolonialist stance as she considers the persistent historical and contemporaneous impact of colonialism on the assumption and consumption of leadership discourses in small developing nation states like Trinidad and Tobago. We evoke our positionality then, not as an introspective or self-aggrandising response as individuals but to position this work and our own locations within it as part of a "politics of location that make core issues and ideas the basis for dialogue and collaboration, disagreement and debate" (Mirza & Joseph, 2013, p. 84). As such, the book forms part of a method of "feminist global praxis" which we hope will inspire and "enable political action" (Mirza & Joseph, 2013, p. 84).

Like us, the authors in the book put their positionality on the line, as they consider and in some cases reconsider their constructions of leadership discourses, practices, preparation and research. Leadership is a messy encounter with people in space and time, with history as past and as being made in the moment, and with policy change imperatives as navigations of the dynamics of international imperatives and localised social justice agendas. We hope that in reading this book the audience is challenged to reimagine alternative forms of leadership practice, leadership research and leadership understandings as an opportunity of contact and context.

References

Anderson, P., & Williams, J. (Eds.). (2001). *Identity and difference in higher education: 'Outsiders within'*. Aldershot, Hampshire: Ashgate Publishing Limited.

Blackmore, J. (2010). 'The other within': Race/gender disruptions to the professional learning of white educational leaders. *International Journal of Leadership in Education: Theory and Practice, 13*(1), 45–61. doi:10.1080/13603120903242931

Blackmore, J., & Sachs, J. (2007). *Performing and reforming leaders: Gender, educational restructuring, and organizational change*. Albany, NY: State University of New York Press.

Bristol, L. (2014). Leading-for-inclusion: Transforming action through talk. *International Journal of Inclusive Education, 19*(8), 1–19. doi:http://dx.doi.org/10.1080/13603116.2014.971078.

Bristol, L., Esnard, T., & Brown, L. (2015). In the shadow/ from the shadow: The principal as a reflective practitioner. *Journal of Cases in Educational Leadership (JCEL)*, 215–227. Retrieved from http://jel.sagepub.com/content/current

Brooks, J. (2012). *Black school, white school: Racism and (mis)leadership*. New York: Teachers College, Columbia University.

Esnard, F., Bristol, L., & Brown, L. (2013). Women as educational leaders: Emotional neutrality and psychic duality. In D. J. Davis & C. Chaney (Eds.), *Black women in leadership: Their historical and contemporary contribution* (pp. 74–90). New York: Peter Lang. ISBN: 978-1-4331-1682-7

Fuller, K. (2015). *Gender, identity and educational leadership*. London: Bloomsbury.
Lee, H. (2010). *To kill a mockingbird*. New York: Grand Central Publishing.
Lee, H. (2015). *Go set a watchman*. New York: HarperCollins.
Mirza, H. S., & Joseph, C. (2013). *Black and postcolonial feminisms in new times: Researching educational inequalities*. London: Routledge.
Moreton-Robinson, A. (2000). *Talkin' up to the white woman: Indigenous women and feminism*. Brisbane, Queensland: University of Queensland Press.
Niesche, R., & Keddie, A. (2016). *Leadership, ethics and schooling for social justice*. Abingdon, Oxon: Routledge.
Smyth, J. (2011). The *disaster* of the 'self-managing school' – genesis, trajectory, undisclosed agenda, and effects. *Journal of Educational Administration and History*, *43*(2), 95–117. doi:http://dx.doi.org/10.1080/00220620.2011.560253
Theoharis, G., & Scanlan, M. (2015). *Leadership for increasingly diverse schools*. New York: Routledge.
Watterson, B. (2015). *Environmental scan: Principal preparation programs*. Prepared for the Australian Institute for Teaching and School Leadership [AITSL], Melbourne.
Wilkinson, J. (2007). But what do we know about women? Feminist scholarship for/about women academic leaders. *New Zealand Journal of Educational Leadership*, *22*(2), 13–21.
Wilkinson, J. (2008). Good intentions are not enough: A critical examination of diversity and educational leadership scholarship. *Journal of Educational Administration and History*, *41*(2), 101–112.
Wilkinson, J. (2009). A tale of two women leaders: Diversity policies and practices in enterprise universities. *The Australian Educational Researcher*, *36*(2), 39–54.
Wilkinson, J., & Eacott, S. (2013). Outsiders within? Deconstructing the educational administration scholar. *International Journal of Leadership in Education*, *16*(2), 191–204.
Wrigley, T., Thomson, P., & Lingard, B. (2012). *Changing schools: Alternative ways to make a world of difference*. Abingdon, Oxon: Routledge.

1 The unexamined constructions of educational leadership

Jane Wilkinson and Laurette Bristol

Introduction

Mainstream approaches in educational leadership have ignored the influence of societal culture and the culturally specific contexts or sites within which education takes place (Dimmock & Walker, 2005). This lack of examination of the cultural specificity in which educational settings are embedded reveals educational leadership scholarship's historical silence in surfacing the issues of politics and power which lie at the heart of leadership practice. In this chapter, we attempt to go some way to redressing this imbalance, through sketching some key threads of an emerging body of educational leadership scholarship and research approaches arising from what has been labelled a "cultural turn" in education leadership (Blackmore, 2010, p. 48). Due to word length limitations, this sketch is by its very nature a limited and non-exhaustive account. Nonetheless, it highlights a rich and growing body of scholarship in the field that raises serious questions about the applicability and currency of dominant accounts of educational leadership scholarship and practice. The scholarship we examine challenges prevailing discourses shaping and influencing contemporary accounts of educational leadership. It raises questions about the relationship between what we know about educational leadership (epistemology), how we have come to know it (methodology) and the nature of leadership (ontology) across educational sites. As such, it interrogates the epistemological, methodological and ontological constructions of educational leadership in scholarship and practice – an interrogation which is developed further in Chapter 2 of this volume.

In this first chapter we provide a sketch of theoretical frameworks and research approaches which are currently challenging dominant paradigms of educational leadership located in unexamined constructions of the unitary white masculinist leadership subject. We do so as part of a broader challenge to traditional tropes of leadership within educational administration, a challenge which resides in a growing understanding of the implications of educational leadership as a cultural construct. One aspect of this growing understanding is the useful case that has been made by Blackmore (2010) for what has been termed a "cultural turn" in educational leadership scholarship. Her argument for such a turn is based on the emergence of critical theories originating from postcolonial, Black, Indigenous and feminist bodies of scholarship, which have arisen from and/or connect up to a range of contemporary human rights and other civil and social movements (Blackmore, 2010). These movements, Blackmore contends, include Indigenous demands for recognitive justice (Fraser, 2008), which have gained increasing momentum in nation states such as Australia, North and South America and New Zealand over the past two to three decades. They include a shift towards "super diversity", that is, significantly higher levels of population diversity (Vertovec, 2007), which have placed greater demands on predominantly white principals in Anglophone school settings. These movements also include an increasing volume of research examining women's experiences of leadership in developing nations. Finally, they encompass literature which examines the clash of values arising from the largely unproblematised importation of Western leadership models to Asian, Middle Eastern and African education settings – an importation which operates as a form of epistemic imperialism and violence (c.f., Spivak, 1988).

The diverse trajectories sketched by Blackmore (2010) that make up this "cultural turn" encompass a range of subjugated knowledges about leadership. However, when these subjugated knowledges are explored in leadership research, they are frequently engaged with through a single social category. For example, leadership is constructed as gendered – as opposed to considerations of the intersections between various categories – such as the relationship between gender, age, socioeconomic status and ethnicity and their impact on leading practices. This intersectionality (the location of culture) is also a space of subjugated knowledges in the field of educational leadership. Such knowledges and approaches remain fringe-dwellers on the body politic of mainstream approaches to educational leadership. Nonetheless, as explicated in this chapter, we argue that they raise serious questions about the utility, generalisability and applicability of dominant leadership models, both in terms of their content, their research approaches and their general applicability.

Before turning to a sketch of this emerging body of leadership literature located within notions of a "cultural turn", however, we need to elucidate how we are employing the term "culture". We define culture as signifying the '"glue" that binds people together through a shared and common understanding of an accepted way of life that is distinguishable from other groups" (Giddens, 1989, as cited in Dimmock & Walker, 2005, p. 8). In so doing, we stress culture as a process (not a fixed or stable entity or 'given'), and recognise it as a highly contested concept. Moreover, we focus on culture as incorporating the "more recent and contemporary changes and additions" that have occurred in the social sites in which this and the subsequent book chapters are located (Dimmock &Walker, 2005, pp. 8–9). We tease out this conceptualisation of culture further in Chapter 2.

Towards a cultural turn in educational leadership scholarship

Examining Indigenous bodies of literature

In relation to the first trajectory of educational leadership noted by Blackmore (2010) as part of a turn towards culture, i.e., demands for reconciliation between

Indigenous and non-Indigenous peoples, a clear thread which emerges is a reframing of leadership as power *with* the human and material world. Brunner (2005, p. 126) has labelled this a "synergistic, co-active, collective melding of common being or action" (Brunner, 2005, p. 126). This understanding of power is in contrast to more traditional notions of wielding power *over* others, in which power becomes a form of "dominance, control, authority and influence" (Brunner, 2005, p. 126). Instead, leadership amongst Indigenous scholars is reframed as a participatory, community-based, holistic and interconnected process (Coyhis, 1995, as cited in Benham & Murakami-Ramalho, 2010, p. 78).

There are some parallels here between the concept of power *with* and Robert Greenleaf's (2002) notions of servant leadership. In the latter, there is a focus on the growth and well-being of humans and their communities. However, what makes the trajectory amongst Indigenous scholars of leadership particularly distinct, as opposed to the more generic concept of Greenleaf's, is its insistence on the specific Indigenous cultural contexts and local ways of knowing and understanding the world from which leadership derives. For instance, Benham and Murakami-Ramalho's model of a "community of leadership" is grounded in critical analysis of interviews with Indigenous Hawaiian educational leaders (2010). These forms of leadership, they argue, may be "derived from the local protocols of exchange among communities of indigenous peoples", which in turn underpin "stories from which principles of leadership can be elicited which encompass spirituality" (Benham & Murakami-Ramalho, 2010, p. 79). The four principles include the concept of Ha, the "breath of life . . . that links all persons, past, present, and future", and the notion of place, in which "land, sky, and sea'" are "fundamentally pedagogical" (Benham & Murakami-Ramalho, 2010, p. 81). Thus, they challenge Western notions of formal institutions such as schooling and universities as the sole repositories of valued learning. Instead, they foreground the importance of learning within the lifeworld of community and earth. The model includes the principles of the "sacredness of relations and mana" and "the concept of individual generosity and collective action" (Benham & Murakami-Ramalho, 2010, p. 81). It thus challenges traditional epistemologies of Western leadership as a unidirectional, hierarchical and culturally neutral property of individuals. Instead, it posits an "epistemology of engaging in leadership through which one must understand the context, history, and relations of indigenous peoples within their community, and across diverse or dissimilar communities over time" (Benham & Murakami-Ramalho, 2010, p. 82). Importantly, the research approaches we are highlighting are not essentialising attempts to derive unitary models of Indigenous leadership. Rather, they open up epistemological, methodological and onotolgical spaces through which to "pose questions and to speak back to some of the troubling narratives that do not fully account for Indigenous . . . ways of knowing, acting, and leading" (Fitzgerald, 2010, p. 103).

Another thread underpinning Indigenous reframing of educational leadership is that leading and managing Indigenous education in a postcolonial world involves reconceptualising learning as part an ecological continuum. Yolnu philosophy in East Arnhem Land, Australia terms this approach "two ways/both ways" teaching and learning (Ma Rhea, 2015, p. 25). Rather than an instrumentalist focus on learning as a series of formal, narrowly measured outcomes, learning in school sites becomes part of an ecological "process of knowledge production" in which two different cultures work together, aiming for a "dynamic . . . continuous striving for a balanced environment" (Ma Rhea, 2015, p. 25; c.f., Ma Rhea, this volume). This perspective of learning demands a very different epistemology of leadership. It entails a move away from hierarchical and linear understandings of educational leadership in which schooling is managed by non-Indigenous leaders, towards a

> fractal approach using an Indigenist, rights-based approach underpinned by theories of complex adaptivity and social exchange, where Indigenous and non-indigenous people can work in equal partnership to lead and manage the improvement in the education of Indigenous children.
>
> (Ma Rhea, 2015, p. 173)

Importantly, Ma Rhea (2015) warns against simplistic assumptions that employment of Indigenous educational administrators will in and of itself disrupt the colonial mindset of educational administrators. Instead she argues that both Indigenous and non-Indigenous administrators should demonstrate an *Indigenist* approach. This would include non-Indigenous settlers undertaking

> antiracist work with non-indigenous people . . . cultural awareness workshops . . . and working within organisations that are controlled by non-indigenous settlers to effect changes that acknowledge and respect Indigenous people's rights, histories, cultures and languages.
>
> (Ma Rhea, 2015, p. 154)

A final thread which characterises much Indigenous research and writing on educational leadership is the critical role played by Indigenous women as researchers, educators and leaders. Much of this research takes an explicitly feminist stance, for Indigenous women leaders are frequently forced to confront gendered racism in their leadership roles, be it from outside their communities or from within (White, 2010). For instance, Lisa Udel (2001) has argued that Native American women regard "motherwork" as being a critical part of the politically activist role they must play in order to ensure the survival and flourishing of their communities. In Australia, there has been an extraordinary growth in the numbers of Indigenous women leaders emerging in a whole range of spheres, including politics and education (Baker, Garngulkpuy, & Guthadjaka, 2014). For Indigenous women leaders in remote Australian communities, leadership involves consultation with elders and achieving community consensus about decisions; that is, as leaders they "speak for their community, not themselves" (Baker et al., 2014, p. 39). The growth in remote Indigenous Australian women leaders disrupts stereotypes of Indigenous cultures as frozen in time. It is argued that as women have become increasingly well-educated, fathers have recognised their potential by choosing their daughters to become clan leaders – a recent development in the past 30 years (Baker et al., 2014, p. 41). While recognising the paternalistic origins of their ascension to leadership – it is the father who chooses – research on the models of leadership the women are enacting is derived from the women's words, their community's philosophy and processes, rather than imposing Western theories and paradigms (Baker et al., 2014).

Leading ethnically diverse schools

A second trajectory of educational leadership outlined by Blackmore (2010) as part of a turn towards culture is the demand on educational administrators to lead and manage increasingly ethnically diverse student populations (see, for example, Brooks, 2012; Shields, Larocque, & Oberg, 2002; Theoharis & Scanlan; Wilkinson, Forsman, & Langat, 2013; Wilkinson, in this volume). This movement is encompassed under a range of terms, including culturally responsive leadership, "culturally proficient leadership, culturally relevant leadership, culture-based leadership, cultural competency, multicultural leadership, and leadership for diversity" (Johnson, 2007, p. 148). Drawing on culturally responsive pedagogy and with overlaps with leadership for social justice, culturally responsive leadership "involves those leadership philosophies, practices and policies that create inclusive schooling environments for students and families from ethnically and culturally diverse backgrounds" (Johnson, 2007, p. 148). Applied Critical Leadership (ACL) is another emergent response whose roots derive from critical pedagogy and critical race theory. It is "grounded in practices that are framed by social justice and educational equity wherein leadership results from both professional practice and leaders' embodied lived experiences" (Santamaria & Santamaria, 2015, p. 26). As a strengths-based model, ACL attempts to capture the "essence of the complex roles self-described diverse leaders play as they toggle between the reality of being members of historically underrepresentend and often disenfranchised social groups" while simultaneously attempting to "provide effective leadership in various educational settings" (Santamaría & Santamaría, 2015, p. xii).

The Australian Professional Standard for Principals recognises the increasing complexity of this role when it notes that principals must "embrace inclusion and help build a culture of high expectations that takes account of the richness and diversity of the wider school community and the education systems and sectors" (Australian Institute for Teaching and School Leadership, 2015, p. 19). It also notes that principals must "foster understanding and reconciliation with Indigenous cultures" (Australian Institute for Teaching and School Leadership, 2015, p. 19). Yet, there are contradictions here. Despite the increasing ethnic diversity of Australia and its educational settings, diversity and inclusion in the Standard remains a property of the student 'other' – something which the principal must lead, direct, "embrace" and respond to. Unlike in ACL approaches to educational leadership, the assumption in the Standard is that principals are raced (gendered and classed) within normative constructions of whiteness and masculinity (Santamaría & Santamaría, 2015, p. xii). The dominance of white, masculinist approaches to educational leadership remains intact, with no call for increasing diversity in leaders or leadership practices. Moreover, the Standard is silent in regard to re-imagining different forms of leadership, such as the different epistemology demanded of leadership when learning is constructed as "two ways/both ways", as noted in the previous section on Indigenous research for/with educational leadership. Hence, literature which challenges the privilege which whiteness, masculinity and/or heteronormativity confers on educational leadership still remains uncommon, albeit with some exceptions (c.f., Blackmore, 2010; Hernandez & Fraynd, 2015; Koschoreck, 2005; Niesche & Keddie, 2013; Wilkinson, in this volume). Moreover, despite a concomitant increase in students' ethnic diversity in universities, there does not appear to have been a parallel focus or sense of urgency on how educational leaders in universities should lead diverse student populations or the models and practices of leadership that are adopted at this level. Rather such considerations have tended to be confined to considerations of higher education pedagogy, whereas university leadership remains principally focused around research, change management or increasing institutional sources of funding.[1]

Rarely is there an explicit connection made between the need to respond to increasing student diversity and the largely monocultural teaching and leadership profile dominating the compulsory and post-compulsory educational sectors of Australian and other Anglophone nations such as England and Canada. Exceptions to this myopia include Allard and Santoro's examination of teacher education students' constructions of class and ethnicity (2006) and Wilkinson's critique of the centrality of whiteness underpinning educational leadership scholarship (2009). While there is some recognition in research that educational leaders and leadership need to become more diverse (c.f., Lumby with Coleman, 2007), this recognition tends to remain the responsibility of diverse others, thus 'whitewashing' out of the picture dominant epistemologies of white masculinity as the naturalised and uninterrogated centre of leadership.

Female leaders in economically developing nations

A third trajectory of educational leadership as part of the turn towards culture is the experiences of mainly "female leaders in economically developing, often faith-based, nation states, and how women struggle with their own professional and personal aspirations within their own cultural and religious contexts" (Blackmore, 2010, p. 49). This literature encompasses a range of perspectives that challenge previously unexamined constructions of educational leadership as culturally neutral and apolitical. For instance, the recent publication of two special themed issues of *Educational Management and Leadership*: *Educational Leadership in Africa* and *Leading Schools in Contexts of Multiple Deprivation in South Africa* includes a number of articles examining the intersection of gender and ethnicity through the lens of females leading schools and higher education in South Africa (c.f., Diko, 2014; Faulkner, 2015; Lumby, 2015; Naidoo & Perumal, 2014) and sub-Saharan Africa (Turner Johnson, 2014).

Alternatively, Saeeda Shah has examined the experiences of Pakistani female heads of girls-only colleges through the lens of gender, ethnicity and faith (2010; Shah, this volume). She argues that a major gap in conceptualisations of leadership from a cultural perspective is the significance of religion and in this case, how Muslim societies conceive of educational leadership, particularly as it interplays with gender and ethnicity. A crucial point that Shah raises and which underpins this book is that culture is not solely about ethnicity but about how other social categories such as religion and gender intersect with ethnicity. As such, Shah notes that "how a particular society perceives and constructs educational leadership is influenced by the dominant cultural and belief systems prevailing in that society or community" (2010, p. 29). Educational leadership for the women leaders of Shah's study necessitated a complex balancing act between family and professional responsibilities in the face of all the challenges posed in a "feudal, patriarchal, segregated society". To some extent, they resolved the paradox of a "public activity such as educational leadership in a segregated society . . . by re-inventing the . . . [college] . . . site as 'family' and re-locating it within the domestic" (Shah, 2010, p. 36; c.f., Shah, this volume).

Cross-cultural value systems

A fourth trajectory of educational leadership as part of a turn towards culture is the increasing emergence of "*cross-cultural value systems* with the importation/ imposition of Western school models into Asian, Middle Eastern, Caribbean and African contexts, raising issues for school leaders" (Blackmore, 2010, p. 49). Clive Dimmock and Allan Walker's work in this area has been pivotal in exploring differences between educational leadership and management in diverse cultures and challenging the hegemonic nature of Anglophone educational leadership scholarship.

The hegemony of Anglophone leadership scholarship has occluded understandings of educational leadership as a "culturally bounded process . . . subject to the cultural traditions and values of the society in which it is exercised. . . [and] thus manifest[ing] . . . itself in different ways in different settings" (Dimmock & Walker, 2005, p. 1). Part of this silencing work includes leaving out of the debates scholarship from large/small geographical spaces which may be viewed as having little of value to contribute. It also may involve including such contributions but in such a way that they remain tokenistic or marginal to the 'main game' (e.g., chapters from non-English nations may be placed last in an edited book or handbook section).

Despite the recognition of leadership as a "culturally bounded process", educational leadership debates continue to be ethnocentric, framed on individualistic assumptions which assume a "false universalism" that does not take into account the "particularities of the local cultural context that it influences and shapes" (Dimmock & Walker, 2005, pp. 1, 205). Nor do these debates interrogate the relevance of models such as transformational, distributed leadership, school effectiveness and teacher appraisal in "societies whose cultural and power relations assume a totally different configuration from more egalitarian 'western' countries" or "in schools in Western cultures where diverse conditions may throw... [these concepts]... into serious question" (Dimmock & Walker, 2005, pp. 1, 164; c.f., Haiyan, Jiacheng & Walker, this volume).

The meaning of leadership varies depending on the societal culture in which it resides. For Anglophone nations, dominant discourses construct leadership as a form of techné, a largely instrumentalist set of technical skills which can be learned, rather than as a praxis-oriented, pedagogical practice situated within the site-specific lifeworld of educational sites (Kemmis et al., 2014; cf., Wilkinson, this volume). Alternatively, in China, leadership is seen as a "process of influencing behaviours and modelling... 'desirable' behaviours" (Dimmock & Walker, 2005, p. 15). Much of the power of leadership in Chinese culture rests on patriarchal notions and Confucian ideals, and thus "functions within that value system" (Tung 2003; Wong, 2001 as cited in Shah, 2010, p. 30). In contrast, in Muslim societies, the link between religion and knowledge creates a "discourse of educational leadership, which elevates it to a sacred duty of the highest order" (Shah, 2010, p. 31). Shah's study of female Pakistani Muslim university leaders reveals them as caught between competing gendered discourses around "what it means to be a 'good' Muslim" woman – to "uphold the honour of the family and community" through remaining invisible, leaving more visible roles that are seen as male domains such as finances to male accountants in the schools (Shah, 2010, pp. 36, 39; cf. Shah, this volume).

A number of gaps emerge in the research on cross-cultural value-systems in educational leadership. Much of the research tends to remain situated within Li's (2012) four-stage framework for indigenous research. This framework encompasses "basic exploitation" (Li, 2012), that is, an initial stage in which there is uncritical transplantation of Western theories into local indigenous contexts. It may encompass stage two, what Li (2012) has labelled "advanced exploitation", that is, a "multi-context, comparative research with the potential to discover one or more novel local constructs" that suggest possibilities for modifying existing Western theories (Eacott & Asuga, 2014). Moreover, culture in research on cross-cultural values systems is frequently read as a codeword for ethnicity, with leadership diversity largely being limited to ethnic differences. There is little acknowledgement of how social relations of power firmly underpin relations of gender, ethnicity, religion and other social categories within differing national contexts. Yet, as the preceding research on female leaders in developing nations and Indigenous leadership research reveals, our ways of knowing about and doing leadership vary greatly, depending on leaders' subject locations within these varying social relations of power. Collard and Reynolds' survey of leadership, culture and gender in education note this gap when they contend that there is a need for

> more sophisticated and fine-grained approaches to research questions... if we are to adequately explain differences between gender groups... we will also inevitably be drawn towards enriched understandings of culture regarding such elements as race, class and sexuality.
>
> (2005, p. 204)

Understanding the significant differences in how leadership may be understood *across* differing nation states is one thing. However, there are also major omissions in educational leadership scholarship when it comes to understanding the viability and applicability of Western theoretical concepts such as distributed or transformational leadership in differing national contexts and in nations which have highly diverse student cohorts (Dimmock & Walker, 2005). Hence, there have been significant gaps in the literature regarding how cultural differences may be understood *within* nations, particularly when it comes to these increasingly diverse student populations (Blackmore, 2010; Dimmock & Walker, 2005). However, research strands such as culturally responsive leadership and applied critical leadership are beginning to fill these gaps. Importantly, the latter approach in particular derives from socially critical theories of pedagogy and thus is more cognisant of how social relations of power underpin dominant educational leadership practices.

Finally, despite an increasing emphasis in literature on cross-cultural value systems research on how leadership may be read, understood and practised, this body of literature largely omits reference to and examination of how "whiteness as a privileged signifier has become global" and how English has become the lingua franca of knowledge capitalism (Blackmore, 2010, p. 49; Leonardo, 2004, p. 117). Thus, the adoption of more socially critical theoretical tools would greatly benefit this leadership trajectory. Otherwise, the danger is that new orthodoxies of educational leadership emerge that refuse to interrogate the social relations of power, politics and privilege that underpin educational leadership practices and its approaches.

Examining theoretical frameworks and research approaches within educational leadership as a culturally constructed practice

If we are to accept that educational leadership is in essence "a social and cultural process . . . an interactive . . . interdependent . . . and culture-bound activity" (Dimmock & Walker, 2005, p. 79), a number of questions and critiques subsequently arise in regard to the research approaches and theoretical frameworks that still dominate contemporary leadership research. One of the major critiques is that educational leadership as a discipline remains firmly gripped by functionalist and positivist or logical empiricist paradigms (c.f. Lakomski, 2005), thus revealing its roots in the scientific management principles of the early 20th century.

The latest iterations of school effectiveness and school improvement, for instance, require that schools in the Australian state of Queensland draw on system-generated data as part of "an unrelenting focus on improved student achievement" (Queensland Department of Education, Training and Employment, 2011). In this iteration, the role of the principal has shifted from the entrepreneur and manager of the 1990s to a re-emergence of the principal as instructional leader.[2] The data on Queensland schools is largely quantitative in nature, derived from national assessments of literacy and numeracy, Year 12 results and research about student effect sizes (Hattie, 2009). There is little or no questioning of what kinds of evidence should constitute the data to which schools must respond, or of the subsequent narrowing of what constitutes effective educational practice. Approaches which include qualitative research, critical theories of practice, considerations of teacher and leadership praxis, of practitioner-led research and of educators as activist researchers appear to have been swept aside in Australian states as principals' work is increasingly steered at a distance through high-stakes assessment and ac/counting by numbers (Lingard & McGregor, 2013).[3] Nor is there a questioning of the site-specific nature of the cultural contexts in which leadership practices are located and to which they must respond. Rather, there is a normative assumption of a generic approach to leading school improvement, underpinned by neoliberal principles of quantification and accountability that re-inscribe the very inequities that the school improvement agenda is aiming to ameliorate.

Cross-cultural values systems approaches have critiqued the field, arguing that the ethnocentric grip in which its current models and theories are located means that educational leadership and management "as a field of study and research has failed to keep pace with current events leading to the internationalising and globalising of policy and practice societies" (Dimmock & Walker, 2005, p. 205). Subsequently, unlike other related fields such as management, educational leadership "has failed to develop models, frameworks, methodologies and analytical tools by which to understand these dramatic changes and their effects on school leadership and schooling in different societies" (Dimmock & Walker, 2005, p. 205). Ron Heck's investigation of the issues that underpin school research across cultures (2002) similarly argued that there was a need for comparative studies which could "give insights into the assumptions, structures, process, and outcomes of educational systems", particularly as societies "become more culturally diverse and globally interdependent' (p. 79). He contended that the field of educational administration "lacks cross-cultural models, theoretical frameworks, and taxonomies for comparing schools and school systems internationally" (Heck, 2002, p 79). In making comparisons of school leadership across cultural settings, Heck noted that the researcher "runs the risk of decontextualizing the leadership norms, values, or behaviours from the wider contextual setting. Yet, the notion of generalization (or transfer) of phenomena across settings is at the center of comparative work" (Heck, 2002, p. 89). Heck also questioned taken-for-granted educational leadership models such as instructional and transformational approaches, arguing that they were "likely too limited to adequately explain the diversity of school leadership practices in a global setting" (2002, p. 92). The desire for cross-comparative taxonomies, models and frameworks through which schools and systems can be compared is a fundamental basis on which such cross-cultural values systems in educational leadership research resides. Yet the insistence that comparative studies achieve cross-cultural validity is highly problematic, for it raises a conundrum: How can researchers on the one hand argue for recognition of the importance of context when it comes to understanding how various approaches to leadership may or may not be valid depending on the culture, and yet on the other hand, insist on the importance of the "transfer . . . of phenomena across settings"?[4] Furthermore, the positivist and functionalist desire to produce comparative models, taxonomies and frameworks means that there is a real danger of glossing over and neutralising the very cultural nuances and social relations of power that the studies are attempting to elicit.

David Stephen's more recent examination of the role of culture in conducting research in educational leadership and management asserts that culture must be foregrounded in what is being studied and through the research design (2012, p. 47). He poses a series of helpful questions that should be addressed in order to carry out "high quality, culturally appropriate research", be it within one's nation state or without (Stephens, 2012, p. 51). Yet, despite a recognition that researchers need to examine their own positionality when conducting such research (Stephens, 2012), culture still appears in his chapter to be the unexamined property of the participant non-white, non-masculine 'other'. This lack of an examination of one's own subject location as a white male frequently based in educational administration departments of universities in the global south (Connell, 2007) reinforces a similar lack of reflexivity in the cross-cultural scholarship of other researchers in this field.

Indigenous feminist scholarship such as that of Linda Tuhiwai Smith's (1999) drew attention to how the very nature and processes of research are based on Western constructs of what counts as knowledge, with research and European colonialism being inextricably linked. She argued that the "system of classification and . . . representation" that underlies the search for such models, taxonomies and frameworks helps to "determine what counts as real" with subsequent dire implications for Indigenous peoples (Tuhiwai Smith, 1999, p. 44). An examination of leadership and Aboriginal education in contemporary education in Canada contends that an additive approach of relying on Aboriginal educators for change will not get to the bottom of fundamental questions such as "who decides or speaks for Aboriginal knowledge" and "what methodology do we employ to talk about the 'other'?" (Battiste, 2005, p. 155). Moreover, as Fitzgerald argues in her study of New Zealand and Australian Indigenous women leaders in relation to educational leadership research and theorising, "we cannot adopt a 'one size fits all' approach to philosophy, practice and knowledge for/about educational leadership" (Fitzgerald, 2010, p. 100). The consequences will be a reproduction of the dominant (white) status quo. She also notes that there is still an "underpinning assumption . . . that Indigenous leaders can and should acquire the same knowledge, skills and abilities as their White colleagues", thus locating them in a deficit position (Fitzgerald, 2010, p. 101).

Rather, as White (2010) notes in her study of Indigenous women's leadership in Australia, some Indigenous researchers are drawing on "Indigenous knowledge and spirituality frameworks" and new research approaches that are alternate to these research traditions. Benham and Murakami-Ramalho's (2010) model of a "community of leadership" grounded in Indigenous Hawaian principles of breath, place, sacredness of relations and generosity of individual and collective actions is one example of this form of knowledge. As they contend:

> The model posits a view or an *epistemology of engaging in leadership* through which one must understand the context, history, and relations of indigenous peoples within their community, and across diverse or dissimilar communities over time.

Feminist critical approaches to educational leadership, "rooted in post-positivism", have critiqued the gender-neutral assumptions underpinning dominant forms of educational leadership research. They have employed a range of research approaches and methods, including discourse analysis, in order to

> move beyond mere descriptions of women leaders' experiences and consider such things as intrasubjectivity, heteronormativity, and the social construction of multiple forms of masculinity and femininity.
> (Collard & Reynolds, 2005, p. xv)

However, these approaches, along with others such as postcolonialism are still largely excluded due to the colonisation of the field by functionalist and positivist or logical empiricist approaches. The latter approaches are based on an assumption of an external reality that is mirrored in the production of "an authoritative text". Consequently, these "'masks of validity' . . . continue to function as a barrier in the production of knowledge" (Koschoreck, 2005, p. 144; Scheurich, 1997). For instance, the overwhelming heteronormativity of educational administration scholarship excludes

> lesbian students, teachers, administrators and . . . researchers in educational research accounts . . . it surely matters that only heterosexual or faux-heterosexual people are usually welcome to do school-based educational research.
> (Koschoreck, 2005, p. 144)

Conclusion

As this sketch of theoretical frameworks and research approaches suggests, an emerging stream of critical theory drawing on postcolonial, Black, Indigenous and feminist critical scholarship is interrogating educational leadership and administration theory and paradigms as culturally neutral and apolitical. It reveals that these unexamined constructions of research and theory unproblematically signify leadership as a white, masculinist practice. This representation undermines the enactment of more site-based, culturally appropriate leading practices, where leaders are equipped to respond to the dynamic profiles of schools (Bristol, 2014). Chapters 3 to 11 of this volume extend these critical leadership research approaches by interrogating the frequently unexamined assumptions underlying the employment of different theoretical frameworks to examine leadership practice. The chapters examine how specific theoretical lenses are employed by researchers in ways that may enable and/or occlude particular aspects of culturally specific leading practices. Before doing so, however, we first examine the relationship between culture and the empirical sites *of* and *for* leadership inquiry and scholarship.

Notes

1 We would like to acknowledge and thank the anonymous reviewer who drew our attention to this point.
2 We would like to acknowledge and thank an earlier anonymous reviewer for raising this point.
3 There have been some attempts to broaden the measuring sticks by which students' learning is understood and assessed. For example, Victoria's *Framework for Improving School Outcomes* (2016) places a strong emphasis on schools building links to communities as part of a more holistic understanding of student learning and well-being. However, the predominant mode of assessment remains largely focussed on a narrow set of quantifiable indicators.
4 We would like to acknowledge and thank an earlier anonymous reviewer for raising this point.

References

Allard, A. C., & Santoro, N. (2006). Troubling identities: Teacher education students' constructions of class and ethnicity. *Cambridge Journal of Education, 36*(1), 115–129.

Australian Institute for Teaching and School Leadership Limited. (2015). *Australian professional standard and the leadership profiles.* Retrieved from www.aitsl.edu.au/docs/default-source/school-leadership/australian-professional-standard-for-principals-and-the-leadership-profiles.pdf?sfvrsn=8

Baker, G., Garngulkpuy, J., & Guthadjaka, K. (2014). Guthadjaka and Garŋgulkpuy: Indigenous women leaders in Yolngu, Australia-wide and international contexts. In J. Damousi, K. Rubenstein, & M. Tomsic (Eds.), *Diversity in leadership: Australian women, past and present* (pp. 39–52).Canberra: ANU Press, The Australian National University.

Battiste, M. (2005). Leadership and aboriginal education in contemporary education: Narratives of cognitive imperialism reconciling with decolonization. In J. Collard & C. Reynolds (Eds.), *Leadership, gender and culture in education: Male and female perspectives* (pp. 150–156). Berkshire, Maidenhead: Open University Press.

Benham, M., & Murakami-Ramalho, E. (2010). Engaging in educational leadership: The generosity of spirit. *International Journal of Leadership in Education: Theory and Practice, 13*(1), 7–25. doi:10.1080/13603120903242907

Billott, J., Goddard, T., & Cranston, N. (2007). How principals manage ethnocultural diversity: Learnings from three countries. *International Studies in Educational Administration, 35*(2), 3–19.

Blackmore, J. (2010). 'The other within': Race/gender disruptions to the professional learning of white educational leader. *International Journal of Leadership in Education: Theory and Practice, 13*(1), 45–61. doi:10.1080/13603120903242931

Bristol, L. (2014). Leading-for-inclusion: Transforming action through teacher talk. *International Journal of Inclusive Education*, 19(8), 802–820. doi:10.1080/1360 3116.2014.971078

Brooks, J. S. (2012). *Black school, white school: Racism and educational (mis)leadership*. New York: Teachers' College Press.

Brunner, C. (2005). Women performing the superintendency: Problematizing the normative alignment of conceptions of power and constructions of gender. In J. Collard & C. Reynolds (Eds.), *Leadership, gender and culture in education: Male and female perspectives* (pp. 121–135). Berkshire, Maidenhead: Open University Press.

Bush, T. (2014). Special themed issue on educational leadership in Africa: Building the knowledge base. *Educational Management Administration and Leadership*, 42(6), 787–791. doi:10.1177/1741143214549135

Collard, J., & Reynolds, C. (2005). Introduction. In J. Collard & C. Reynolds (Eds.), *Leadership, gender and culture in education: Male and female perspectives* (pp. xv–xxi). Berkshire, Maidenhead: Open University Press.

Connell, R. (2007). *Southern theory: The global dynamics of knowledge in social science*. Crows Nest: Allen & Unwin.

Diko, N. (2014). Women in educational leadership: The case of Hope High School in the Eastern Cape Province, South Africa. *Educational Management Administration & Leadership*, 42(6), 825–834.

Dimmock, C., & Walker, A. (2005). *Educational leadership: Culture and diversity*. London: Sage.

Eacott, S., & Asuga, G. (2014). School leadership preparation and development in Africa: A critical insight. *Educational Management Administration & Leadership*, 42(6), 919–934.

Faulkner, C. (2015). Women's experiences of principalship in two South African high schools in multiply deprived rural areas: A life history approach. *Educational Management Administration & Leadership*, 43(3), 418–432.

Fitzgerald, T. (2010). Spaces in-between: Indigenous women leaders speak back to dominant discourses and practices in educational leadership. *International Journal of Leadership in Education: Theory and Practice*, 13(1), 93–105. doi:10.1080/13603120903242923

Greenleaf, R. (2002). *Servant leadership: A journey into the nature of legitimate power and greatness* (25th anniversary ed.). New York: Paulist Press.

Hattie, J. (2009). *Visible learning: A synthesis of over 800 meta-analyses relating to achievement*. London: Routledge.

Heck, R. (2002). Issues in the investigation of school leadership across cultures. In A. Walker & C. Dimmock (Eds.), *School leadership and administration: Adopting a cultural perspective* (pp. 77–100). New York: Routledge Falmer.

Hernandez, F., & Fraynd, D. (2015). Inclusive leadership and lesbian, gay, bisexual, transgendered, and questioning students. In G. Theoharis & M. Scanlan (Eds.), *Leadership for increasingly diverse schools* (pp. 101–118). New York: Routledge.

Johnson, L. (2007). Rethinking successful school leadership in challenging U.S. schools: Culturally responsive practices in school-community relationships. *International Studies in Educational Administration*, 35(3), 49–57.

Johnson, L. (2014). Culturally responsive leadership for community empowerment. *Multicultural Education Review*, 6(2), 145–170. doi:10.14328/MER.2014.09. 30.145

Kemmis, S., Wilkinson, J., Edwards-Groves, C., Hardy, I., Grootenboer, P., & Bristol, L. (2014). *Changing practices, changing education*. Singapore: Springer.

Koschoreck, J. W. (2005). Transgressing heteronormativity in educational administration. In J. Collard & C. Reynolds (Eds.), *Leadership, gender and culture in education: Male and female perspectives* (pp. 143–149). Berkshire, Maidenhead: Open University Press.

Lakomski, G. (2005). *Managing without leadership: Towards a theory of organizational functioning*. Amsterdam: Elsevier.

Leonardo, Z. (2004). The worlds of white folk: Critical pedagogy, whiteness studies and globalisation discourse. In G. Ladson-Billings & D. Gillborn (Eds.), *The RoutledgeFalmer reader in multicultural education* (pp. 117–136). London: RoutledgeFalmer.

Li, P. P. (2012). Towards an integrative framework of indigenous research: The geocentric implications of Yin-Yang balance. *Asia Pacific Journal of Management, 29*(4), 849–872.

Lingard, B., & McGregor, G. (2013). High stakes assessment and new curricula: A Queensland case of competing tensions in curriculum development. In M. Priestley & G. Biesta (Eds.), *Reinventing the curriculum: New trends in curriculum policy and practice* (pp. 207–228). London: Bloomsbury.

Lumby, J., with Coleman, M. (2007). *Leadership and diversity: Challenging theory and practice in education*. London: Sage.

Ma Rhea, Z. (2015). *Leading and managing Indigenous education in the postcolonial world*. Abingdon, Oxon: Routledge.

Maringe, F., & Moletsane, R. (2015). Special Issue: Leading schools in contexts of multiple deprivation in South Africa: Mapping some conceptual, contextual and research dimensions. *Educational Management Administration and Leadership, 43*(3), 347–362.

Naidoo, B., & Perumal, J. (2014). Female principals leading disadvantaged schools in Johannesburg, South Africa. *Educational Management Administration & Leadership, 42*(6), 808–824.

Niesche, R., & Keddie, A. (2013). Issues of Indigenous representation: White advocacy and the complexities of ethical leadership. *International Journal of Qualitative Studies in Education, 27*(4), 509–526. doi:10.1080/09518398.2013.771223

Queensland Department of Education, Training and Employment. (2011). *United in our pursuit of excellence*. Retrieved from http://education.qld.gov.au/projects/educationviews/news-views/2011/jul/united-in-pursuit-110727.html

Santamaria, L. J., & Santamaria, A. P. (2015). Counteracting educational injustice with applied critical leadership: Culturally responsive practices promoting sustainable change. *International Journal of Multicultural Education, 17*(1), 22–41.

Scheurich, J. J. (1997). *Research method in the postmodern*. London: Falmer Press.

Shah, S. (2010). Re-thinking educational leadership: Exploring the impact of cultural and belief systems. *International Journal of Leadership in Education: Theory and Practice, 13*(1), 27–44. doi:10.1080/13603120903244879

Shields, C. M., Larocque, L. J., & Oberg, S. L. (2002). A dialogue about race and ethnicity in education: Struggling to understand issues in cross-cultural leadership. *Journal of School Leadership, 12*(2), 116–137.

Spivak, G. C. (1988). Can the subaltern speak? In C. Nelson & L. Grossberg (Eds.), *Marxism and the interpretation of culture* (pp. 271–313). Urbana, IL: University of Illinois Press.

Stephens, D. (2012). The role of culture in conducting and interpreting research. In M. Briggs, M. Coleman, & M. Morrison (Eds.), *Research methods in educational leadership and management* (pp. 46–60). Los Angeles, CA: Sage.

Theoharis, G., & Scanlan, M. (2015). *Leadership for increasingly diverse schools.* New York: Routledge.

Tuhiwai Smith, L. (1999). *Decolonising methodologies: Research and Indigenous peoples.* London: Zed Books.

Turner Johnson, A. (2014). Performing and defying gender: An exploration of the lived experiences of women higher education administrators in sub-Saharan Africa. *Educational Management Administration & Leadership, 42*(6), 835–850.

Udel, L. J. (2001). Revision and resistance: The politics of Native women's motherwork. *Frontiers, 22*(2), 50–51.

Vertovec, S. (2007). Super-diversity and its implications. *Ethnic and Racial Studies, 30*(6), 1024–1054. doi:10.1080/01419870701599465

Victorian State Government. (2016). *Fact sheet: Framework for improving school outcomes.* Retrieved from www.education.vic.gov.au/Documents/about/education-state/outcomes.pdf

White, N. (2010). Indigenous Australian women's leadership: Stayin' strong against the post-colonial tide. *International Journal of Leadership in Education: Theory and Practice, 131,* 7–25. doi:10.1080/13603120903242907

Wilkinson, J. (2009). Good intentions are not enough: A critical examination of diversity and educational leadership scholarship. *Journal of Educational Administration and History, 41*(2), 101–112.

Wilkinson, J. (2016). Leading for social justice: Examining educational leading through a practice lens. In K. Mahony, S. Francisco, & S. Kemmis (Eds.), *Exploring practices through the lens of practice architectures.* Singapore: Springer International.

Wilkinson, J., Forsman, L., & Langat, K. (2013). Multiplicity in the making: Towards a praxis-oriented approach to professional development. *Professional Development in Education, 39*(4), 488–512.

2 Beyond culture as ethnicity
Interrogating the empirical sites for leading scholarship

Laurette Bristol and Jane Wilkinson

Introduction

Leadership is under scrutiny. As a practice and as a concept it is being subjected to rigorous forms of deconstruction that can be associated with a form of crisis *of* and *in* leadership. This predicament is aligned with international imperatives for educational reform around school improvement; enhanced educational quality and outcomes; the need for increased social mobility, access and social justice; and closing the opportunity gaps, for example, between people of varying social classes, ethnicity and gender. As this struggle for sense making in leadership and leading ensues, the field like others in the educational arena is beginning to experience a cultural turn (Jacobs & Spillman, 2005), one that is "signalled principally by a shift of interest from structure to agency and from explanation to hermeneutics" (Clammer, 2005, p. 109).

Whereas in Chapter 1 we considered the epistemic and theoretical gaps/silences in the leadership field, here we will proffer an analysis that will consider the relationship between culture and the empirical sites *of* and *for* leadership inquiry and scholarship. As such, the fundamental question to be answered here is: How does the application of theoretical concepts and methodological practices in culturally varying empirical sites serve to subjugate alternative understandings, practices and inquiry into leadership?

We acknowledge that inquiry into leadership informs the development of professional knowledge and we recognise that historically:

> not only has professional knowledge proved itself to be unconsolidated, cultural knowledge is also not communicated sufficiently adequately to be effective in learning cultures, structure decisions, and working processes.
> (Robak, 2014, p. 62 *sic*)

Too often the cultural knowledge related to leadership is fragmented and subjugated. We argue that subjugated knowledges operate in the dimension of traditions and cultures – of the 'othered' – where concepts such as ethnicity are understood as a property of non-white realities.

When subjugated knowledges are explored in leadership research, they are frequently engaged through a single social category, i.e., leadership as gendered, as opposed to considerations of the intersections between various categories, e.g., the relationship between gender, age, socioeconomic status and ethnicity and their impact on leadership practices. Lumby and Foskett (2011) in their critique of the engagement of culture and education suggest that this need for cultural simplification is a tool used in the process of sense making as we come to terms with the state of the human condition exercised in social spheres. Contrary to this involuntary need for the over-simplification of the social world we will argue, as in the vein of Lumby and Foskett (2011), for an understanding of culture in leading, where cultural understandings influence leadership practices in such a way that culture is located in the complex intersectionalities of the leadership field.

The argument that we will construct moves through four phases. First, we examine understandings of subjugated knowledges as an element of the relationship between culture and power. Second, we interrogate how culture is applied as an organisational mechanism geared towards the improvement of outcomes for those considered to members of a subjugated or disempowered population. Here we explore the opportunities and challenges embedded in rising movements of culturally sensitive leading in its varying forms, where leading is responsive to the particularities of context (Davis, Krieg, & Smith, 2015; Hultman, 2001; Schratz, 2009). Third, we construct an argument of intersectionality. This is a reaction to responsive educational leadership, one that is beyond the notion of culture as coloured/ethnic or culture as unitary. Fourth, we highlight the empirical and methodological implications of culturally sensitive leadership research.

The point of this chapter is to examine what emerges when culture is oriented as a legitimatised reality. We consider the lessons to be learnt about leadership practices and research when culture becomes the lens through which deliberations of leadership quality are undertaken. Taken from the view of intersectionality (between culture as socially constructed and leadership as practised within socially constructed sites), leading should become fashioned as a set of humanising and democratic relationships amongst people in organisations in time and place, and re-defined as a notion of 'power with' rather than 'power over'.

Subjugated knowledges: Education, leadership and power

As we engage with this debate, we must first come to a shared understanding of how we construct a relationship between knowledge and power, which originates with and through knowledge [c.f., Freire, 1993; Foucault, 1995]. 'Knowing' offers access to a world that is often designed by others with the power (knowledge) to influence the flow of knowledge to others. Knowledge, whatever its form, provides a meaning and purpose to life. Meaning – and how it comes to be shared and represented over time – provides social stability and access through the creation of social orders (e.g., forms of acting, speaking, eating, living and socialising), some of which over time become hegemonic and normalised. Coupled with political and economic imperatives, normalised social orders gradually begin to regulate the meanings given to social reality as those with power maintain their hold on power. Any knowledge construed as located *outside of* or *on the periphery of* the normalised social order is often experienced as a subjugated knowledge, that is knowledge emerging from any social group historically, politically and economically situated as without power or with less power (Foucault, 1980, as cited in Bozaleck, 2007, p. 56). The idea of 'subjugated knowledges' highlights the importance of subject locations within processes and systems of power and the ways in which these systems of power render 'other' social groups not centrally located within particular systems of power. For Spivak (1988), the conceptualisation of subjugated knowledges provided an "account of how an explanation and narrative of reality was established as the normative one" (p. 76). Subjugated knowledges are then caught up in dialectical relationships with hegemonic knowledges and thus cannot be explained in the absence of hegemonic knowledges. For Freire, "the oppressed can overcome the contradiction in which they are caught only when this perception enlists them in the struggle to free themselves" (1993, p. 31). The same is true for groups occupying subjugated subject locations. It is an awareness of one's condition as subjugated that triggers an ideological struggle for freedom, and a struggle for equality of value amongst a range of equally rated ideologies despite origin-perceived authority and historical maturity.

For Hartman DSW (2000), who wrote about the relationship between the social worker and client, subjugation is often perpetuated through relationships and is made just only when

> we enter into a collaborative search for meaning with [others] and listen to their voices their narratives, and their constructions of reality . . . we must attend to difference, to particularity, the contradictory, the paradoxical . . . direct practice must be built on local knowledge.
>
> (pp. 21–22)

While Hartman DSW recognises the need for a state of openness in relationships, a practice of domination occurs through acts of silencing (e.g., not listening, not acknowledging, not recognising, not valuing, seeking unity and disregarding difference). Practices of power have formidable social justice implications for education and more so for leadership practices. For Humphry (2014) there is value in the conversational "pause", creating the space for

> educators to challenge commonly held understandings of young people who have been educationally displaced [moving them] from operating in a debilitating, powerless silence to a silence that can resist and question and ultimately challenge and replace the dominance of deficit knowledges for the support of disadvantaged.
>
> (p. 497)

Bristol (2014) adds to the debate on the interplay between silence and presence engineered through conversation and relationships by suggesting that in educational contexts, teacher talk has the potential to promote forms of *leading-for-inclusion* that

> summon . . . inclusion as a medium for interrogating existing practices of leading that appear to be oriented towards inclusion. In doing so, leading-for-inclusion becomes a lived reality of negotiation rather than the rhetoric of political promotion.
>
> (p. 2)

When applied to a practice of leadership, subjugated knowledge is manifested through "the centralized political, economic, and institutional regimes that produce privileged knowledges, but also with their exercise of power in the capillaries as they flow out and are practices at the local level" in schools (Hartman DSW, 2000, p. 20).

Hegemonic leadership ideas prevail by making obscure, silent and irrelevant the experiences, ideas and conditions of leaders in subjugated subject locations. Thus, it is appropriate that the notion of culture in leadership be extended beyond the social narratives of race and include experiences of class, gender, religion, sexual orientation and nationhood, to name but a few (Parker, 2010). Given global movements these are fast becoming spaces of subjugated knowledges. An interrogation of subjugated knowledges in leadership brings to the forefront the "power-knowledge critique [and] enables a new kind of research program" that allows us access to the "power-knowledge effects [and] the kind of human relations and social systems that it creates" (Marginson, 1997, p. 224 *sic*). Inquiry into educational leadership and leading practices that is "culturally ethical" (Bristol, 2010, 2012 a, 2012b) demands then a form of engagement that apprehends culture as an organising feature of educational leadership.

Culture as an organising mechanism for leadership

Leadership research often examines the relationship between one social category (at most two) and leadership, i.e., between being Black and the effects/experience of leadership or the experience of Black women in leadership (e.g., Davis & Chaney, 2013). Others have used culture as an ontological and epistemological framework for making sense of how leadership arises or comes into being in relation with others in contexts: promoting possibilities of collaboration to create a socially just school ethos (Brooks & Miles, 2010; Lumby & Foskett, 2011); fostering socially just pedagogy (Brooks & Miles, 2008); building cultural competence and asset-based approaches to leading (Nelson & Guerra, 2014); and being responsive to the dynamism of schools in order to ensure school improvement and student outcomes (Johnson, 2014). More recently, cultural positioning: the interactions between leadership frameworks and culture (Jogulu & Ferkins, 2012); culturally responsive leading (Johnson, 2014); leading-for-inclusion (Bristol, 2014); leadership for social justice (Liasidou & Antoniou, 2015); and inclusion for leadership (Angelides, Antoniou, & Charalambous, 2010) have been called into being to respond to global concerns.

These concerns revolve around a range of 'wicked' problems such as: the provision of equal opportunities in education; reducing the educational gap between white students and non-white students; and the impact of civil and political unrest on migration patterns and on the dynamic nature of students and the complexity of schools. This cultural turn in leadership policy and research is oriented towards the need to improve the academic outcomes of students. It explicitly connects leading practices to student outcomes and the quality of educational experiences in schools.

As the phenomenon of globalisation makes the experience of difference a real-time certainty, notions of culture, diversity and difference are called into spaces that have been previously homogenous. As difference struggles for equality, education and leadership are caught up in cultural dramas manifested across dynamic contexts. Often these "deep racial, cultural, and identity problems are manifested in the complex struggles for equitable education in various contexts" (Hickling-Hudson, Darder, & Mayo, 2012, p. xi). This is an indication of the challenge posed for research on leading and leadership. It also indicates how in the leadership research arena the narrative of culture can be used as an organising mechanism or interrogative lens through which the everyday of leading and leadership is made sense of at an institutional level.

In Chapter 1, we defined culture as the "'glue' that binds people together through a shared and common understanding of an accepted way of life that is distinguishable from other groups" (Giddens, 1989, as cited in Dimmock & Walker, 2005, p. 8). Here we will develop this position further by borrowing from the work of Clammer (2005), who suggests that culture is not simply a universalising structure. Rather he proposes that we should think of culture as

> narrative rather than as structure, not in the deconstructionist sense of a 'text' outside which there is no other reality, but in the sense of an ever-evolving and constantly edited response to a very insistent reality constantly impinging on the human subject.
>
> (p. 111)

For Clammer (2005) assuming this position on culture as more than structure, as more than an abstract means of distinguishing one group from another through shared and common understandings, locates people at the heart of the process in the constant making and re-making of culture. These are people with "emotions and values, who suffer and seek meaning in their suffering, and who seek continually to expand their capacities and range of experiences" (Clammer, 2005, p. 111). Adopting this position ensures that culture is conceptualised as dynamic and negotiated rather than closed and abstract. It is the interpretive and subjective nature of culture that makes it contested and problematic.

The challenge of culture is its endemic connection to hegemonic constructs of identity (the value, purpose and socio-historical role given to an individual or segment of the society). In so doing it gives a summative, absolute and singular form and sense to a person or individual as Black, as white or Asian. When culture is mistakenly recognised as a unitary construct, the gradations in the happenings of people sharing a common subject location are subsumed into the identity of the group. Here lies its inherent paradox particularly when applied to the field of leadership. We will unpack this paradox using our own stories as examples.

Both Jane and I are women. At one time we lived in the same town, on the same street and worked at the same institution, in the same department and our offices were adjacent to each other. We shared a similar societal (Australian) and organisational culture and were able to connect to each other through common work and research experiences. However, our understandings of our shared societal and organisational culture were located in more than one social category such as our gender. This is because we occupied fundamentally different subject locations.

I was a Black/Creole, Catholic, Trinbagonian,[1] from a low socioeconomic background and a migrant worker in Australia. Jane was a Jewish, atheist Australian from a working-class background. We are both world travellers, but our markers for class originate from the predominant discourses of our national geographic backgrounds. Our sense of our culture and ourselves is not defined by our race or some classic notion of ethnicity; rather it is defined in the intersubjectivities of the variance of our shifting identities and our professional and geopolitical locations. The same is true for all leaders and leadership researchers, yet this variance is not often expressed or reflected in the field.

As we engage in this debate it is important to make a distinction between organisational culture and societal culture. Here we will position organisational culture as "the way we do things around here" (Krapfl & Kruja, 2015, p. 36). The way things are done in different social sites organises educational institutions and leadership practices such that the practice of education and leading, though manifesting differently, becomes recognisable within sites and across sites. Speaking specifically to the organisational culture in schools, Lahtero and Risku (2012) suggest that the organisational

> culture of a school is considered to consist of the network of the common symbols and meanings, through which the members of the school organisation interpret their experiences and which thus direct their actions. . . . It is a product of the meaning and interpretation processes which constitute themselves through the symbols.
>
> (p. 527)

Like societal culture, organisational culture is socially constructed through relationships; it is dynamic and comes into being in the interpretation of experience. Organisational cultures are learned and continuously reproduced as professionals move in and out of the institution. Dimmock and Walker (2005) make an important distinction between societal culture and organisational culture:

> [S]ocietal cultures differ mostly at the level of basic values, while organisational cultures differ mostly at the level of more superficial practices, as

reflected in the recognition of particular heroes, symbols and rituals . . . This allows organisational cultures to be managed and changed whereas societal cultures are more enduring and change gradually over long time periods, if at all.

(Dimmock & Walker, 2005, p. 32)

It is this marker of societal culture as enduring and less resistant to change that makes an engagement with it through research challenging, as often educational policies change faster than the societal cultures they attempt to respond to. This rapidity of change results in a clash that poses a challenge to educational development and the practices of leaders in schools.

Organisational culture is often referred to as the climate or ethos of an institution and is shaped by the dynamics of individual personalities (Dimmock & Walker, 2000). Beyond personality however, Hargreaves (1995, as cited in Ainscow and Sandill, 2010, p.406), suggests that in schools, culture "can be seen as having a reality-defining function, enabling those within an institution to make sense of themselves" (p. 406). Going further to include geopolitical locations and their impact on organisational culture, Khan and Afzal (2011) suggest that:

> All countries have their own interpretation of organisational culture which reflects their mode of thinking, acting, beliefs, practices, behavior, environment, and hosts of other inter-linked factors. Thus, culture has different connotations in different societies and so does its impact on organizations and their development.
>
> (p. 1389)

As societal culture is complex, so too is organisational culture, and as such when culture is invoked in leadership and leading, it should call into being an interrogation of paradox, contradiction and difference in experience. Often times, however, the need for simplification and clarified explanations serves to flatten and make one- or two-dimensional the complex arena that is culture. Dimmock and Walker (2000) caution that:

> The challenge for researchers is whether a more comprehensive definition of societal culture than those typically used in other fields is useful, necessary or desirable when studying educational leadership. Such a challenge raises both conceptual and methodological components.
>
> (p. 112)

As we engage in leadership through a cultural framework there is need for caution; such an approach has implications for the ways in which culture in leadership is conceptualised and the ways in which leadership in varying cultural contexts is investigated.

Arguing the case of diversity, Ahmed (2009) warns, "when race equality becomes a performance indicator [located in bodies] you know you are in trouble" (p. 42). Like diversity, when the cultural turn in leadership becomes a performance indicator, which suggests a set collection of actions and possibilities that are legislated through policy, it has the potential to limit opportunities and obscure challenges to social justice within cultures and across cultures. This it does through what Ahmed (2009) refers to as "'image management': diversity work is about generating the 'right image', and correcting the wrong one" (p. 45). The conclusion can then be drawn that there is no right, absolute or complete image of difference as expressed through culture. Culture is nuanced; it is organised and symbolic. Yet its dynamic and negotiated features allow it to escape predictability and universality, although it can be argued that it retains some elements of national predictability. Despite this, culture invoked as an organising mechanism for leadership and leading relationships attains a nuanced difference when implicated within organisational cultures.

Beyond the notion of culture as coloured/ethnic or culture as unitary

Given the cultural turn that now surrounds educational leadership research and policy, what then are the implications for the development of leadership practices and how are these to be navigated in the face of subjugated knowledges? Most often within the field of leadership research, the knowledge of the oppressed (subjugated) is coloured and made sense of through an ethnic framework which is closely connected to bounded understandings of culture. As indicated earlier, we seek to expand the boundaries of culture further to include social categories other than race, colour or ethnicity.

Taking up the notion of the 'othered' in leadership research, the question arises: How does leadership inquiry take into consideration the experiences of those most often 'othered', displaced and subjugated through traditionally hegemonic (successful leadership traits as being closely aligned to socially normalised masculine personality types) and emerging hegemonic debates in educational leadership? Here we want to speak about the ways in which some of the new culturally sensitive debates can actually work to silence more complex cultural occurrences in the arena through their non-engagement with complex understandings of social phenomena. This silencing occurs through the need to provide a description of the field, rather than an account for the narratives/experiences of leadership in the field.

The *cultural turn* in the leadership field, whilst critical, is also polemical and must be addressed with judiciousness, lest it be reduced to rhetorical posturings aimed at soothing culturists and those clamouring for inclusive voice. Culture in leadership operates under three major structural paradigms: the first as a form of institutional or school culture/ethos, the second as relating to context and the peculiarities of the educational site, and the third as a disposition of relating with 'others,' irrespective of colour/race/ethnicity, recognising and valuing difference. Leadership inquiry that is framed by cultural sensitivities then needs to be always attentive to the ways in which these structural paradigms can become a performance indicator in the face of imperatives for measured improvements in schools and the learning outcomes of students. The cultural turn must be ever vigilant against *cultural instrumentalism*, where culture is called into being as a tokenistic means of checking for the correctness of the particular political movement.

Protection from cultural instrumentalism in leadership research comes only through a full embrace of the experience of culture as kaleidoscopic and multifaceted. Thus, thinking about leadership and culture must move beyond culture as a unitary or binary opposite force where leadership/leading is measured against more than being Black, being white, being Asian or being female. The relationship between leadership and culture must begin to reflect the full complexity of social phenomena, such that the understanding of leadership and the doing of leading is measured against, for example, the realities of being a Black, single, female Catholic leader in a rural small island setting in the Caribbean; being a Jewish, LGBT male middle management leader in Russia; or being a first-generation Asian female early career leader in a private elite school in a southern state in the US. While these are examples based on the complexity of an individual experience, as cultural complexities they go beyond the notion of culture as coloured/ethnic or unitary. For examples of cultural complexities operating at scaled social levels, we need to turn to the modes of inquiry necessary for and appropriate to representing and re-presenting the relationship between leadership and culture as moving beyond a unitary social category. This brings to mind the methodological implications for a cultural turn in leadership research.

A cultural turn to leadership research

Employing a more culturally sensitive lens to inquire into leadership begs the consideration of the question of: *In whose interest?* This question is above and beyond the moral-cultural imperative and the need to secure social access and equality. It requires a response to the question of how does culturally sensitive leadership research serve the sustainable development of education and the improvement of student outcomes in schools? *Of what use is culture to leadership research and leadership education?* This line of thinking is critical given the advice provided by Gunter and Fitzgerald (2008, p. 273) that "if we want to develop educational leadership then we need to frame it, debate it and conceptualise it" against a background of cultural complexity. Thus, a move towards a consideration of the empirical and methodological implications of culture in leadership research provides a way of conceptualising the leadership field as it responds to the global conditionalities of difference and dynamism.

Singh (2006) characterises these global conditionalities as sites of interaction, or "contact zones" where various cultural identities and power relations meet and are "reconstructed and renegotiated in everyday interactions" (p. 2). Positioning education and schools as non-neutral spaces, she openly acknowledges her cultural-political impact on the space as a researcher/messenger:

> As the *messenger* who travelled to the place of schools, and took responsibility for re-presenting the concerns of teachers, community members and

students, I cannot occupy an objective, neutral place. Rather, I am implicated in the non-neutral practices of schooling institutions – firstly in my position as political delegate writing on behalf of those who do not have the resources to write in such forums, and secondly through the depictions (images, messages) that I convey through such writing.

(p. 3)

Reading the leadership field and the practices of leaders in schools through a cultural lens requires two recognitions: first, the challenge of "theoretical transferability" and second, a recognition of researcher stance. It is in the exploration of these that we are able to articulate the ways in which leadership research must begin to serve the sustainable development of education and the improvement of student outcomes in schools.

The challenge of transferability and the recognition of researcher stance

In noting that "culture influences many of the values that underline leadership theories and styles" (Owusu, Kalipeni, Awortwi, & Kiiru, 2015, p. 6), the authors raise the question of cultural transferability and the ways in which theories designed and normalised in one cultural context are then used to measure the performance and experiences of leaders in a varying cultural context. When this practice uncritically occurs, it re-inscribes the memory of research as a dirty word (Smith, 1999), e.g., when colonisers employed research as a measured justification for the dehumanising and child-like positioning of the colonised. As Wee Pin Goh (2009) reminds us, theoretical transferability is only acceptable when there is a "degree of similarities between cultures" (p. 324) and when educational leadership theories, policies and practices are transferred in a manner that is "culturally contextual or sensitive" (p. 339). Moreover, Wee Pin Goh (2009, p. 325) contends that cultural transferability becomes a challenge because all educational leadership theories are in fact "culture-bound". The author goes on to observe that "It is thus alarming that some Western-based theories, which may be normative or prescriptive, continue to be introduced into contexts that do not take into account cultural difference" (p. 338). Therefore, in the application of leadership theory to practice, researchers and leaders should continuously interrogate the cultural assumptions of theory and the constraints that may be made manifest in the social field (Wee Pin Goh, 2009).

These preceding points suggest that research that is culturally sensitive is research "which incorporates into its design and implementation the historical context, and cultural experiences, norms, values, beliefs, and behaviours of a distinct ethnic or cultural group" (Burnette, Sanders, Butcher, & Rand, 2014, p. 365 *sic*). In doing research with Indigenous communities, Burnette et al. (2014) recommend that adopting a cultural stance contributes to the value of the study and "yields information better able to address pressing problems of . . . communities" (p. 379). It is thus critical that the researcher explicitly occupies the subject location of political ambassador. They carry a significant moral-cultural obligation to represent the field (Bristol, De Four-Babb, Esnard, Lavia, & Perez, 2012) and re-present the experiences of leaders in the field, as well as navigate the surrounding social-cultural arena with participants. In adapting a cultural stance the researcher does not have the privilege of standing objectively apart. This introduces the second challenge: that of researcher stance.

We define researcher stance as the sets of cultural assumptions that the researcher brings to the field of study. Some writers such as Wee Pin Goh (2009) suggest that the researcher must be able to suspend his/her cultural assumptions and remain in a state of openness in order to fully apprehend the multifaceted dimensions of the field under investigation. This is not easy work. It requires that the researcher and the leader must be ready to face his or her own demons in relation to their assumptions and beliefs that have been inculcated in them from the moment of their birth. These are beliefs and assumptions that shape the ways in which they ask questions, interface with the members in the site, make sense of the information that they are receiving from the site and go on to represent the site. The researcher and leader must be prepared to make sense of their own ontological positioning and then put this aside in order to understand the realities of other leaders and teachers, even when these realities are diametrically opposed to their own.

Undertaking this process is enabled by the eclectic use of research methods that allow for a contrapuntal interaction between the tools, the information being elicited from the field through the various tools, and the researcher's interaction with the participants in the field. The key purpose of inquiry designed in this way is to provide an account of: (1) the researcher's stance and declaration of bias; (2) the realities of the participants in the field and how these go on to enable and constrain particular forms of practices; and (3) the intersubjective relationship between the ontological realties of researchers and participants (leaders); and (4) how in the nexus of this relationship, new understandings of leading practices emerge. For this to occur

> future studies should continue to investigate relationships between culture and educational leadership from various angles in order to arrive at more accurate and clearer understanding of these two very important aspects in education.
>
> (Wee Pin Goh, 2009, p. 339)

Undertaking culturally sensitive leadership research, though advocated by some significant interlocutors in the field such as Dimmock and Walker (2000, 2005) and Gunter and Fitzgerald (2008), is still not yet normalised by universities and research funding agencies. This situation serves to suspend the development of a more strategic research relationship between culture and leadership. This complex political reality is addressed by Burnette et al. (2014), who note that

> despite its benefits, working in a culturally sensitive way requires increased attention, planning, resources, and even time to conduct research. Fluidity

and flexibility is necessary, and researchers who choose to work in this way should not be penalized by research and publishing institutions.

(pp. 379–380)

The cultural turn in leadership research challenges normativity, deconstructs mainstream subject locations for leadership, illuminates hegemonic ideologies and practices and makes possible a third space of leadership in the intersectionalities of relationships, social sites and political experiences. Further, it requires political will on the part of the researchers, accrediting institutions and research funding agencies. For these stakeholders the values found in this will are located in the public interest of the educational communities that they serve across the educational leadership continuum. Sustainable educational development and improved student outcomes will never be fully realised in the absence of a cultural perspective, one that goes beyond the divides of race and colour to incorporate the range of social categories that more appropriately reflects social life.

Conclusion

In recent times educational leadership has attracted significant attention as education systems are now preoccupied with guaranteeing educational outcomes through strategic school improvement initiatives. This plan is constantly challenged by the changing dynamics of the compositions of schools. Globalisation and all of its effects continues to bring dissimilar cultures into contact and, depending on the particularities of social conditions, forces them to assimilate, collaborate or engage in selective isolation as they respond to the vagaries of difference. As education systems respond to increasingly globalised societies, educational leaders across the world are being increasingly "responsibilised" (Lingard, 2014), positioned at the centre of a fulcrum around which school success and societal development is oriented and balanced.

In this chapter, we have engaged with the challenge of *culture in leadership*, a turn of phrase that is as ambiguous as it is clear, as it can refer to the cultural categories that the leader occupies (class, race, gender, ethnicity), as well as to the culture that the leader in his or her practice of leading interacts with, that is, both societal and organisational culture. We have reflected upon the challenge of culture in leadership through a consideration of the empirical and methodological implications of culture in leadership. We have attempted to craft a response to the question: *How does the application of hegemonic theoretical concepts and methodological practices in culturally varying empirical sites serve to subjugate alternative understandings, practices and inquiry into leadership?* While the answer to this question will be exemplified through the anthological collection of articles in this edited book, for our purposes here we will begin to indicate the ways in which culture as a social narrative provides empirical fodder for the conceptualisation of leadership practices.

The challenge of culture in leadership is its propensity to be a reference point for unitary social constructs such as race or some other single social category.

Culture is not unitary; it can be viewed from at least three perspectives: the individual, the social and the intersubjective dimensions where the individual comes into encounter with the social in the organisation of schools and in the wider community. This makes the narrative of culture slippery. Constructions of leadership and leading operating in hard-to-define discursive spaces therefore require an alternative response to their conceptualisation and materialisation, particularly in educational landscapes that require a more socially just orientation towards educational outcomes.

We have proposed an argument for responsive leadership research. We suggest that there are lessons to be learned about leadership practices and leadership research when culture becomes the lens through which deliberations of leadership quality and leading effectively are undertaken. When culture, i.e., societal culture as the umbrella for organisational culture, becomes the lens through which leadership practices are made sense of, there is potential for leaders to develop sets of humanising and democratic relationships amongst people in organisations in time and place, with leadership being re-defined as a notion of 'power with' rather than 'power over'. The implications of this approach are that school improvement initiatives driven by culturally sensitive educational leaders and researchers can be re-oriented as critical forms of communicative action that value relationships and the perspectives of those involved in the practice community.

The challenge of culture in leadership is the need for sensitivity and a critical awareness of the historical sensitivities of oppression. This is a sensitivity that is beyond the stamp of political correctness; it is not a sensitivity of image management. Rather it requires a disposition for leadership criticality that is open to conversation that is vulnerable to the interrogation of socio-historical understandings and the peculiarities of social experiences constructed in complex political and economic arrangements. This is particularly so when it comes to the role that educational leaders play in the promotion of educational access, the management of educational outcomes and the drama of school improvement initiatives for social advancement.

When applied to understanding and practising leading, a consideration of subjugated knowledges provides the empirical space for us to consider: particular notions of leading (what it is), the manifestation of leading (how it is engaged), the purpose of leading (what it is for), and how over time and in particular spaces, these philosophical and ontological positionings have become normalised as forms of grand narratives. These are narratives that, given their canonical nature, influence and in some cases determine how leadership is understood across cultures (or geopolitical spaces) and how leading and leadership is researched across cultures. This occurs in the absence of a consideration of culture in and of itself and of the ways in which culture also influences theorisation and forms of inquiry into leadership.

As we engage with the challenge of culture in leadership we are left to face a fundamental question: Of what use is culture to leadership research and leadership education? We are called to re-examine the ways in which we can deploy cultural understandings to arrive at new ways of interrogating leadership practices across geopolitical spaces. We are called to arrive at new responses to key questions such as: What is leading across social cultures? How is it experienced across social cultures? How is it constructed across social cultures? How is it researched and theorised across social cultures? We hope that the chapters that follow assist in responding to these questions, opening up dialogical spaces to explore culturally sensitive responses to these crucial questions.

Note

1 Dialectic reference for a person who is a citizen of the Republic of Trinidad and Tobago.

References

Ahmed, S. (2009). Embodying diversity: Problems and paradoxes for Black feminists. *Race Ethnicity and Education, 12*(1), 41–52. doi:10.1080/13613320802650931

Ainscow, M., & Sandill, A. (2010). Developing inclusive education systems: The role of organisational cultures and leadership. *International Journal of Inclusive Education, 14*(4), 401–416. doi:10.1080/13603110802504903

Angelides, P., Antoniou, E., & Charalambous, C. (2010). Making sense of inclusion for leadership and schooling: A case study from Cyprus. *International Journal of Leadership in Education, 13*(3), 319–334. doi:10.1080/13603120902759539.

Bristol, L. (2010). Practicing betwixt oppression and subversion: Plantation pedagogy as a legacy of plantation economy in Trinidad and Tobago. *Power and Education, 2*(2), 167–182. Retrieved from www.wwwords.co.uk/power/content/pdfs/2/issue2_2.asp#5

Bristol, L. (2012a). *Plantation pedagogy: A postcolonial and global perspective.* New York: Peter Lang. ISBN: 978-1-4331-1715-2

Bristol, L. (2012b). Postcolonial thought: A theoretical and methodological means for thinking through culturally ethical research. In J. Lavia & S. Mahlomaholo (Eds.), *Culture, education and community: Expressions of postcolonial imaginations* (pp. 15–32). New York: Palgrave Macmillian. ISBN: 978-0-230-33825-8.

Bristol, L. (2014). Leading-for-inclusion: Transforming action through teacher talk. *International Journal of Inclusive Education, 19*(8), 802–820. doi:10.1080/13603116.2014.971078

Bristol, L., De Four-Babb, J., Esnard, T., Lavia, J., & Perez, L. (2012). Comparative collaboration: A transgressive academic practice of being and becoming. In J. Lavia & S. Mahlomaholo (Eds.), *Culture, education and community: Expressions of postcolonial imaginations* (pp. 235–254). New York: Palgrave Macmillian. ISBN: 978-0-230-33825-8.

Brooks, J. S., & Miles, M. T. (2008). From scientific management to social justice . . . and back again? Pedagogical shifts in the study and practice of educational leadership. In A. H. Normore (Ed.), *Leadership for social justice: Promoting equity and excellence through inquiry and reflective practice* (pp. 97–112). Charlotte, NC: Information Age Publishing.

Brooks, J. S., & Miles, M. T. (2010). The social and cultural dynamics of school leadership: Classic concepts and cutting-edge possibilities. In S. D. Horsford (Ed.),

New perspectives in educational leadership: Exploring social, political, and community contexts and meaning (pp. 7–28). New York: Peter Lang Publishing.

Burnette, C. E., Sanders, S., Butcher, H. K., & Rand, J. T. (2014). A toolkit for ethical and culturally sensitive research: An application with indigenous communities. *Ethics and Social Welfare*, 8(4), 364–382. doi:10.1080/17496535.2014.885987

Clammer, J. (2005). Culture, development, and social theory: On cultural studies and the place of culture in development. *The Asia Pacific Journal of Anthropology*, 6(2), 100–119. doi:10.1080/14442210500168218.

Davis, D. J., & Chaney, C. (2013). Introducing Black women in leadership: Their historical and contemporary contributions. In D. J. Davis & C. Chaney (Eds.), *Black women in Leadership: Their historical and contemporary contribution* (pp. 3–6). New York: Peter Lang. ISBN: 978-1-4331-1682-7.

Davis, K., Krieg, S., & Smith, K. (2015). Leading otherwise: Using a feminist-poststructuralist and postcolonial lens to create alternative spaces for early childhood educational leaders. *International Journal of Leadership in Education*, 18(2), 131–148. doi:10.1080/13603124.2014.943296.

Dimmock, C., & Walker, A. (2000). Societal culture and school leadership charting the way ahead. *Asia Pacific Journal of Education*, 20(2), 110–116. doi:10.1080/02188791.2000.10600187

Dimmock, C., & Walker, A. (2005). *Educational leadership: Culture and diversity*. London: Sage publications.

Foucault, M. (1980). Power/knowledge: Selected interviews and other writings 1972–1977. In Bozalek, V. (2007). Power as resistance: Using students' subjugated knowledges to inform the Social Work curriculum, in *Enhancing higher education, theory and scholarship*, Proceedings of the 30th HERDSA annual conference, Adelaide, July 8–11, 2007 (pp. 52–61). ISBN: 0 908557 71 X.

Foucault, M. (1995 [1975]). *Discipline and punish: The birth of the prison* (A. Sheridan, Trans.). New York: Vintage Books.

Freire, P. (1993). *Pedagogy of the oppressed*. London: Penguin Books.

Gunter, H. M., & Fitzgerald, T. (2008). The future of leadership research? *School Leadership & Management*, 28(3), 261–279. doi:10.1080/13632430802145902

Hartman DSW, A. (2000). In search of subjugated knowledge. *Journal of Feminist Family Therapy*, 11(4), 19–23. doi:10. 1300/J086v11no4_03

Hickling-Hudson, A., Darder, A., & Mayo, P. (2012). Series editors preface. In J. Lavia & S. Mahlomaholo (Eds.), *Culture, education, and community: Expressions of the postcolonial imagination* (pp. ix–xii). New York: Palgrave Macmillian. ISBN: 978-0-230-33825-8.

Hultman, G. (2001). Leading cultures: A study of 'acting in context' and the creation of meaning in school leaders' work activities. *International Journal of Leadership in Education*, 4(2) 137–148. doi:10.1080/13603120110035059.

Humphry, N. (2014). Disrupting deficit: The power of 'the pause' in resisting the dominance of deficit knowledges in education. *International Journal of Inclusive Education*, 18(5), 484–499.

Jacobs, M., & Spillman, L. (2005). Cultural sociology at the crossroads of the discipline. *Poetics*, 33(1), 1–14.

Jogulu, U., & Ferkins, L. (2012). Leadership and culture in Asia: The case of Malaysia. *Asia Pacific Business Review*, 18(4), 531–549. doi:10.1080/13602381.2012.690301.

Johnson, L. (2014). Culturally responsive leadership for community empowerment. *Multicultural Education Review*, 6(2), 145–170.

Kemmis, S., Wilkinson, J., Edwards-Groves, C., Hardy, I., Grootenboer, P., & Bristol, L. (2014). *Changing practices, changing education*. Singapore: Springer.

Khan, M. A., & Afzal, H. (2011). High level of education builds up strong relationship between organizational culture and organization performance in Pakistan. *The International Journal of Human Resource Management, 22*(7), 1387–1400. doi:10.1080/09585192.2011.561955

Krapfl, J. E., & Kruja, B. (2015). Leadership and culture. *Journal of Organizational Behavior Management, 35*(1–2), 28–43. doi:10.1080/01608061.2015.1031431.

Lahtero, T. J., & Risku, M. (2012). Symbolic leadership and leadership culture in one unified comprehensive school in Finland. *School Leadership & Management: Formerly School Organisation, 32*(5), 523–535. doi:10.1080/13632434.2012.724669

Liasidou, A., & Antoniou, A. (2015). Head teachers' leadership for social justice and inclusion. *School Leadership & Management, 35*(4), 347–364. doi:10.1080/13632434.2015.1010499.

Lingard, B. (2014). A "systemless system": Responsibilising schools, principals and teachers. Paper given as part of the symposium: *The dismantling of public education systems: Implications for educational leadership scholarship and issues of social justice*. Annual conference of the Australian Association of Research in Education (AARE) and New Zealand Association of Research in Education (NZARE). Queensland University of Technology, Kelvin Grove Campus, Brisbane: Queensland, 30 November–4 December.

Lumby, J., & Foskett, N. (2011). Power, risk and the utility: Interpreting the landscape of culture in educational leadership. *The University Council for Educational Administration, 47*(3), 446–461. doi:10.1177/0013161X11400187

Marginson, S. (1997). Subjects and subjugation: The economics of education as power-knowledge. *Discourse: Studies in the Cultural Politics of Education, 18*(2), 215–227. doi:10.1080/0159630970180204

Nelson, S. W., & Guerra, P. L. (2014). Educator beliefs and cultural knowledge: Implications for school improvement efforts. *Educational Administration Quarterly, 50*(1), 67–95.

Owusu, F., Kalipeni, E., Awortwi, N., & Kiiru, J. M. M. (2015). Building research capacity for African institutions: Confronting the research leadership gap and lessons from African research leaders. *International Journal of Leadership in Education, 20*(2), 220–245. doi:10.1080/13603124.2015.1046497.

Parker, J. (2010). Subjugated knowledges and dedisciplinarity in a cultural studies pedagogy. In R. G. Kristensen & R. M. Claycomb (Eds.), *Writing against the curriculum: Ant – disciplinarity in the writing and cultural studies classroom* (pp. 35–56). New York: Rowman & Littlefield Publishers, Inc.

Robak, S. (2014). 'Culture programs,' cultural differences, knowledge resources, and their impacts on learning cultures in transnational enterprises in China. *European Education, 46*(4), 61–81. doi:10.1080/10564934.2014.995552.

Schratz, M. (2009). Leading and learning as a transcultural experience: A visual account. *International Journal of Leadership in Education, 12*(3), 283–296. doi:10.1080/13603120802699298.

Singh, P. (2006). Urban education, cultural diversity and poverty: A case study of globalization: Brisbane, Australia. In J. Kincheloe & K. Hayes (Eds.), *Metropedagogy: Power, justice, and the urban classroom* (pp. 133–146). Rotterdam, The Netherlands: Sense Publishers.

Smith, L. T. (1999). *Decolonizing methodologies: Research and indigenous peoples.* London: Zed Books.

Spivak, G. (1888). Can the subaltern speak? In C. Nelson & L. Grossberg (Eds.), *Marxism and the interpretation of culture* (pp. 66–111). Basingstoke: Macmillan Education.

Wee Pin Goh, J. (2009). 'Parallel leadership in an "unparallel" world' – cultural constraints on the transferability of Western educational leadership theories across cultures. *International Journal of Leadership in Education, 12*(4), 319–345. doi:10.1080/13603120902980796.

3 The role of ethical practices in pursuing socially just leadership

Amanda Keddie and Richard Niesche

Introduction

> So, I think I've really [only] been able to define social justice for me as a person in the last seven months, for the first time in my career really. And maybe that's a sad indictment on the opportunities I've had in life.
> — "Carol"

> In a sense we all have a mission statement, which is to prepare our students for the next stage in their lives, but for us that is recognising that . . . to get a job, to be a worthy and productive member of society, to have an identity, to have choices involves success in exams.
> — "Jenny"

These two quotes begin to point to the complexities of leadership for social justice in two very different school contexts. Carol is the principal of a secondary school in a very poor urban area of Australia. Jenny is the head teacher of a large secondary school in outer London. In the excerpt from Carol she is referring to the processes at her school over the last seven months that have prompted her to question the privilege of her white middle-class Western background (like that of many principals, head teachers and teachers in Western contexts). These processes highlight for Carol how the 'opportunities' in her life arising from this privilege have sheltered her from the vastly complex and challenging circumstances of working in a very disadvantaged part of Australia. This then becomes a 'call to arms' for Carol as she recognises the highly political and risky work that she needs to do to try to alleviate disadvantage, improve educational outcomes and provide the necessary support for the students in her school. This is the work of leading for social justice. Improving educational outcomes for Jenny in her role as leader of a secondary school is a similar 'call to arms'. She views this agenda (and, in particular, students' success on exams) as a "mission statement" and crucial to "preparing students for the next stage in their lives". Like all school leaders however, Carol and Jenny must navigate and overcome many challenges and barriers in attempting to realise goals for social justice.

We explore some of these challenges in this chapter. In so doing, we highlight the need for a nuanced approach to understanding the complexity of leadership for social justice. In this chapter, through the lenses of some of Michel Foucault's key work around ethics, we provide critical insight into how school leaders might work in more socially just ways. This approach begins from the premise that leadership practices in schools must start from an understanding of the socially, culturally and historically specific site itself, rather than an apolitical understanding of educational leadership as put forward in many models and standards-based approaches (for example, see Blackmore, 2006; Brooks, 2012; Larson & Murtadha, 2006; Khalifa, Gooden, & Davis, 2016; Normore, 2009; Shields, 2010; Theoharis, 2010). Foucault's work, and in particular, his more recent work in the area of ethics, allows us to account for the constructs of power, politics and subjectivity inherent in leadership work and, as we argue, has particular utility for understanding and theorising leadership in schools serving disadvantaged and diverse students.

Issues of social justice and equity in the field of educational leadership have become more salient in recent years. The unprecedented diversity, uncertainty and rapid social change of the contemporary global era are generating new and unfamiliar equity questions and challenges for schools and their leaders (see Blackmore, 2008; Marshall, 2004; Normore, 2008, 2009; Ryan, 2010). Framed by the current audit culture in Western education, equity for schools has become a high-stakes issue. This is perhaps most evident in the urgency around 'closing the gap' in educational outcomes between disadvantaged students and their more advantaged peers. Such 'gap talk' however reflects a highly reductionist and narrow view of equity. It has, as many have argued (see Ball, 2003; Grimaldi, 2012; Lingard, Sellar, & Savage, 2014), rearticulated notions of social justice and equity to performance indicators on national and international standardised tests. In this chapter we engage in a much broader view of social justice. Our explicit engagement with notions of social justice in relation to ethics signals our intention to re-insert these notions back into the discourse of educational leadership at a time when they have been marginalised by highly performative governmental rationalities in many countries around the world (see Furman, 2004). We also wish to highlight that we do not use the term ethics in the way that it has often been used in educational leadership in terms of the concepts of ethical or authentic leadership. While acknowledging the importance of work in these areas, we draw on Foucault's notion of ethics to illustrate how power works to constitute leaders as particular subjects in working towards goals of social justice. Therefore, this is not a model to be prescribed or adopted but rather a way to understand the different ways educational leaders are constituted as subjects.

Amid the performative environment of education systems in many countries around the world, the role of school leaders has vastly changed. Schools' subjection to ever-increasing forms of external and public accountabilities means, on the one hand, that principals and head teachers are under greater surveillance than ever before (and are especially accountable to raising the performance of underachieving and disadvantaged students), while at the same time, schools are more self-managing and autonomous in terms of the devolution of roles that were formerly the responsibility of the state (see Ball & Junemann, 2012; Exley & Ball, 2011; Gunter, 2012). These tensions are significant in shaping how equity is articulated in schools. The equity work of school leaders in the contemporary educational environment is incredibly complex, challenging and demanding. While the number of studies exploring these issues has increased in recent times, we feel there needs to be a richer theoretical engagement, focus and depth to capture this complexity. This is what we attempt to do here.

We refer in this chapter to some of our published work and, in particular, the leadership practices of Carol and Jenny in our book *Leadership, ethics and schooling for social justice* (Niesche & Keddie, 2016). In this book we make transparent the ethical work that leaders take up to address the equity challenges of the present climate. We illuminate the moral imperatives of equity work and the significant role school leadership plays in such work. The book represents voices from two case studies conducted in Australia and England. The Australian case study focused on the practices of Carol, in a suburban government school in Queensland, "Ridgeway" Secondary School, while the English case study focused on the practices of Jenny, the head teacher of "Clementine" Academy, a secondary school in outer London.[1] In this chapter we report on this research as a secondary source and thus we present key findings associated with the leaders' stories in summary form rather than including the original raw data that appears in the book.

These schools are very different in many ways. Ridgeway is a low-performing state secondary school situated in suburban Queensland. It is a relatively small school that caters to a high proportion of very poor students including a relatively large cohort of Indigenous Australian and Polynesian students who are from a broader community that is troubled by violence, crime and culturally driven conflict. The security at Ridgeway is tight, with 24-hour video surveillance cameras dotted about its grounds and two Rottweiler dogs. The Clementine Academy is, by contrast, a high-performing secondary school situated in a London borough. While catering to a diversity of students, many are from so-called "model minority" groups and are thus hard-working and high-achieving. The school's outstanding performance has led to it being given the responsibility of leading a group of 20 schools in their quest for school improvement. It is large and well-resourced with friendly learning huts and relatively minimal security.

While vastly different contextually, socially and indeed geographically, what we highlight in our book are the key points of resonance reflected in the leadership practices that both Carol and Jenny deploy in their efforts to work in more ethical and socially just ways. We highlight these points of resonance in this chapter with reference to some of the tools within Foucault's ethical framework. In understanding the complexities confronting these leaders, we find particular utility in his ideas of advocacy, truth-telling and counter-conduct. The practices capture well the aspects of social justice in the work of these leaders. It is our contention that they capture the processes that work towards social justice through leadership that moves beyond a focus on improving academic results to removing the barriers and structures (whether they be economic, cultural or political) that constrain students' lives and their capacity to participate in the social world on par with others (see Fraser, 2009).

Consistent with the main themes of this collection, our representation of leadership in this chapter highlights, in particular, the significance of: (1) considering how a myriad of contextual factors within and beyond schools impact on how socially just leadership is understood and pursued; and (2) the imperative of a critical theorising that both accounts for the complexity of these factors but also provides a framework through which to think of these factors anew toward more ethically and socially just leadership.

Foucault's ethics

In Foucault's later work his concern was with ethics and the relationship one has with oneself. This work should also be understood as being situated at the intersection of his theorising of subjectivity and power and his analysis of forms of governmentality (Davidson, 2005). This means that there is a clear link between the relationship of the self to itself but also in the governing of others. Foucault refers to ethics as "the considered form that freedom takes when it is informed by reflection" (Foucault, 2000, 284). Elaborating on this, Foucault uses a four-fold ethical framework to designate those aspects of ethical work consisting of various technologies of the self and in the governing of others. Briefly, Foucault (1990, 1992) refers to the four aspects as:

- *Ethical substance*, or the part of oneself or one's behaviour that is to be considered for ethical judgement for the purposes of moral conduct. The leadership practices of principals – the work they undertake to support their community, school, its personnel and students – are practices of ethical substance that can be judged in terms of their moral conduct.
- *Modes of subjection*, or the ways in which individuals are made to think about or recognise their moral obligations. The local communities, students, parents and education authorities themselves form powerful modes of subjection for principals in relation to their ethical and moral articulations of leadership.
- *Forms of elaboration*, or the self-forming activities or practices through which individuals constitute themselves as ethical subjects. There are particular practices that are necessary to transform oneself into an ethical leader who enables social justice.
- *Telos*, or a particular mode of being that is characteristic of an ethical subject. This relates to the kind of principal or leader one aims to be, and the focus/purpose of this leadership in relation to (for the purposes of this chapter) social justice.

This four-fold framework is useful, not for the purposes of characterising or capturing a linear identity formation or prescribed from of best leadership practice, but rather, to examine how individuals constitute themselves as ethical subjects. This framework is useful when considering the work of school leaders as they are implicitly working ethically on themselves and in the governing of their schools. In this chapter we focus in particular on aspects associated with the forms of elaboration that support a socially just telos. The practices that we contend are necessary to transform oneself into an ethical leader who enables social justice within the demands of the current context are practices of truth-telling, advocacy and counter-conduct. We will now examine these in a little more depth.

Forms of elaboration: Truth-telling, advocacy and counter-conduct

We interpret the notions of truth-telling, advocacy and counter-conduct as working within Foucault's framework as forms of elaboration. That is, they are the practices through which the leaders constitute themselves as ethical subjects whose efforts to pursue social justice involve advocating for others and speaking out against or engaging in conduct to counter the injustices of the status quo.

Truth-telling or "parrhesia"

For Foucault truth-telling or "parrhesia" refers to 'free speech' or 'speaking the truth', but more importantly indicates a particular relationship between the speaker and what they say. Engaging in parrhesia as it involves speaking truth to power invariably involves some form of risk and danger. This is because such speaking tends to involve questioning or criticising authority. There is a form of courage attached to truth-telling as there is an element of risk that the speaker is saying something that is dangerous because it is different from what the majority believes or sanctions. It is through the act of parrhesia that a principal will come to know and constitute himself or herself as an ethical subject. There is a relationship between the obligation to speak the truth, the techniques of governmentality and the constitution of the relationship to self, in which the principal is a central actor (Foucault, 2011).

Advocacy

Gary Anderson's notion of "advocacy leadership" (2009) can be conceptualised as a form of elaboration, a form of political subjectivity that exemplifies a key part of the ethical self-formation of the individual. It is a relation that leaders deploy in speaking out for their schools and communities. As a form of elaboration in the pursuit of social justice, such leadership is inherently political and ideological in its focus on advocacy for one's students and communities. This means openly taking up the challenges of advocating for the basic principles of a high-quality and equitable public education for all children and being prepared to take risks in working towards these aims (Anderson, 2009, p. 14). There must be some recognition to working on multiple levels in order to work against forms of discrimination, marginalisation and exclusion of students and community groups. It is very much about openly bringing the political into the leadership arena rather than attempting to take it out, as is often put forward by more traditional and conservative leadership discourses. While such advocacy work is potentially problematic in re-inscribing relations of domination and oppression (as long contended by scholars such as Ellsworth, 1989), advocacy is clearly key to the ethical work of leaders who are interested in pursuing the goals of social justice. It is central to their forms of elaboration, or the work that is done in the process of becoming a political subject.

Counter-conduct

The term governmentality is often referred to as the combination of the terms *government* and *mentality* so as to designate the rationality of government. Furthermore, Foucault regards governmentality as the "conduct of conduct", meaning governments act by implementing particular rationalities and mechanisms by which individuals' conduct is influenced and dictated. One aspect, in particular, that seems to be useful is Foucault's development of his notion of counter-conduct. Moving away from the term "resistance" (and also discarding other terms such as "dissidence", "revolt", "insubordination", etcetera), Foucault develops the term counter-conduct to refer to "the sense of struggle against processes implemented for conducting others" (Foucault, 2007, pp. 200–201).

This notion is useful in conceptualising how school leaders work to counter the modes of subjection that do not align with their ideas of what is important and needed in their schools and communities. The current fascination with neo-liberal forms of governance and accountability, and with competition and choice as some of the key drivers of educational reform, actually works to perpetuate disadvantage and inequality and subsequent deficit discourses of disadvantaged students and communities. We put forward the notion that practices of counter-conduct are necessary to disrupt these powerful discourses in order for school leaders to bring about the desired changes that accompany their particular telos of not only what it means to be a good leader or principal but also what their vision for the school might be. In both cases these goals are closely aligned with principles of social justice and equity rather than compliance to highly hierarchical and performative forms of accountability.

The utility of Foucault's ethical tools in thinking about socially just leadership

As we have mentioned, we are not concerned with articulating or prescribing what constitutes best leadership practice. Rather we are concerned with how educational leaders might better understand and work with the complex and contradictory modes of subjection that shape their practice. We are also concerned with exploring the forms of elaboration that leaders deploy in their work within these modes in their pursuit of social justice. Foucault's four-fold ethical framework provides us with useful tools with which to understand and analyse these processes. In this section of the chapter we provide examples from our research (Niesche & Keddie, 2016) that illustrate the utility of these tools. Referring to the leadership stories and practices of Carol from Ridgeway and Jenny from Clementine we illuminate the ethical work they conduct on themselves and on/with others towards their ideal or telos for leading their schools in socially just ways. Significant to such work are these leaders' responsiveness to the multiple and competing discourses operating within their different contexts. Such specificities of their school contexts shape their pursuit of social justice and the ways in which they engage in advocacy, truth-telling and counter-conduct.

A telos of leading for social justice

Central to how a telos of leading for social justice might be constructed and enacted are matters of context. Subject formation in relation to the type of leader one wishes to be is contingent upon, and inscribed through, the school and community context. The context acts as a mode of subjection but also allows freedom to act according to a particular telos of social justice. For Carol, for example, defining her leadership in relation to social justice necessarily involved responding to the multiple and complex disadvantages confronting students at her current school. As we described earlier, Ridgeway is a highly disadvantaged school that is situated in a deprived area with a high crime rate and high unemployment. The school experiences the social and emotional challenges associated with poverty and a long history of student underachievement on external performance measures. One of the key ways in which Carol is attempting to respond to these challenges is through ensuring her school and students are adequately resourced (socially and emotionally through intensive pastoral care work and academically through extra learning support) to maximise their learning but also to challenge the deficit constructions and low expectations that have undermined her students' school motivation and achievement. This approach, of course, generates tensions and requires Carol to conduct ethical work on herself and others. In relation to student achievement, for example, Carol and the staff at Ridgeway must recognise, and ascribe to, the demands of external modes of subjection, e.g. standardised tests such as the National Assessment Program for Literacy and Numeracy (NAPLAN). They must, to a degree, accept them as indicators of the school's 'success' in educating students. At the same time, Carol and her staff recognise the narrowness of these modes of subjection in: (1) failing to capture the broad pastoral support the school offers students and (2) reinforcing the deficit understandings associated with the school and its students that they are trying to challenge. For Carol and her staff working ethically within these tensions is very difficult and often demoralising. While accepting these parameters, Carol navigates these tensions by never losing sight of the school's emphasis on pastoral care and the significance this plays in supporting the social, emotional *and* learning needs of her students.

For Jenny, the leader of Clementine, issues of context in pursuing a telos of social justice were also central. As we noted earlier, Clementine is a high-performing secondary school charged by the authority of the Department for Education with the responsibility of leading and improving the outcomes of a group of 20 schools through various avenues of professional support. Unlike Ridgeway, it is large and well-resourced. For Clementine working ethically with the other schools in the alliance involves respecting each school's autonomy and fostering collaboration between schools. Important to this telos of leading is Clementine's rejection of an 'expert' or authoritarian style of relating with other schools based on this school's awareness that this would close down, rather than open up, opportunities within the alliance.

As with Carol's view of socially just leadership, the leadership of the alliance was directed towards supporting students to achieve regardless of their background circumstances. Indeed, this was the group's stated 'moral imperative' and was strongly shared by all members. Unlike at Ridgeway, however, there seemed to be a more positive view and take up of external mandates of performance (i.e., exam results). Powerful in shaping leadership behaviour and actions, these modes of subjection were seen by the Clementine alliance as constituting "good" preparation "for the next stage in [students'] lives" (as Jenny explained) in terms of employment credentialing and ensuring students' future access to the labour market. Members of the alliance did express some reservation about the narrowness of these measures in similar ways to Carol. However, as one of the key purposes of the alliance (and evidence it was doing its job) was to raise attainment on these measures, many members looked to the alliance for this very purpose.

Such examples draw attention to the notion of leadership as constantly becoming. The use of the term "becoming" is apt in its recognition of the processes of subject formation rather than focusing on what leaders can be or should do. The formation of subjectivity is an ongoing and endless process of construction, reconstruction and renegotiation of identities that are formed within particular historical, social, economic and cultural contexts, processes and discourses (Ball & Olmedo, 2013; Foucault, 2000). For Carol and Jenny, and evident in the examples, this means that their telos of leadership is in a process of becoming. It is a way of working that is relational and ongoing and that navigates through the particular social circumstances and/or modes of subjection confronting their particular schools. There are of course, as we have begun to suggest, conflicts and tensions associated with this process. As they are relevant to the ideas of advocacy, truth-telling and counter-conduct, these conflicts and tensions are the focus of the next section.

Advocacy, truth-telling and counter-conduct

At both Ridgeway and Clementine there were many ongoing tensions associated with navigating through the multifarious and difficult terrain of the current climate, and especially, the demands of the audit culture. Such tensions were related to Carol and Jenny maintaining their ethically driven telos of leadership and social justice within broader modes of subjection that threatened to undermine this ethical work. Leaders in both of these contexts were acutely aware of the high stakes of their work environments. For Carol and Jenny poor leadership performance (i.e., their schools not reaching expected external targets) could mean demotion or a termination of their contracts. Such external and very public accountabilities not only reduced Ridgeway and Clementine and the work of its leaders to auditable commodities to be quantified, assessed and compared (and possibly found wanting), but they also disciplined Carol and Jenny to fit the profile of the ideal neoliberal subject. As is well recognised, governmentality in its neoliberal form makes conducting others through the subject's own conduct one of its primary goals (Dardot & Laval, 2013; Foucault, 2007). Carol and Jenny certainly governed their own conduct. Indeed, they were "self-responsibilising" in this regard, i.e., they positioned themselves within the broader modes of neoliberal subjection shaping their schools and their work as autonomous, self-determined and self-sustaining subjects who are solely responsible for successfully working within its parameters (see Shamir, 2008).

This positioning, of course, does not mean uncritically accepting these parameters as what constitutes good schooling. But it does allocate responsibility for working ethically within these parameters squarely on the shoulders of school leaders. This is where the significance of ethical or moral leadership within the current environment comes to the fore as crucial in pursuing a social justice agenda in schools that is more than what is narrowly articulated around what is and can be measured. In both school contexts, a strong commitment to advocacy and the practices of truth-telling and counter-conduct were instrumental in this pursuit.

For Carol, the high needs of her students drove her advocacy and her work in becoming a political subject. Circumstances of poverty, including poor housing and health as well as violence and criminality are daily realities for her students. It is these realities that shaped Carol's political advocacy and her efforts to provide the necessary level of care and support for her students so that they can access school and be available to learn. Such level of care and support for Carol is not separate from (but nonetheless crucial to) supporting her students to achieve on the measuring sticks that count – educational performance benchmarks. The great needs of the students act as another important mode of subjection for Carol that, while in tension with other modes of subjection such as external public accountability, are just as potent in shaping her leadership work.

Key to Carol's political subjectivity is challenging the deficit constructions and low expectations that have undermined her students' school motivation and achievement. Her efforts here involve trying to change long-existing perceptions of the community and her students through what she described as "socially checking" herself (as we explained earlier in relation to her opening quote) but also her staff that deficit assumptions are being challenged rather than reproduced. Her role as advocate or political subject is directed to changing a status quo that equates poverty with educational failure. This challenging is evidence of her ethical self-conduct and leadership of others.

A significant part of Carol's advocacy work for her students is evident in her practices of parrhesia or truth-telling. These practices are key to Carol's self-formation as principal and were exemplified in her efforts to improve the circumstances and opportunities of the cohort of Polynesian students at Ridgeway. Here, for example, she spoke out to the Department of Education about the ways in which their modes of policy and governance silenced or missed this group's particular social and education needs (i.e., their nationality and citizenship status in Australia delimited these students' opportunities to access university and healthcare). This is an instance of parrhesia. Such speaking out or truth-telling involved a level of risk for Carol in terms of her employment. Despite this, Carol designates importance to speaking her truth rather than let a status quo that disadvantages her students continue. Another way Carol engaged in counter-conduct against the injustices of the status quo was through silence evident in her deliberately not mentioning or referring to policies and other forms of accountability that she did not agree with or believed did not help her students and local community. For example, Carol refused to engage parents with the *MySchool* website[2] and data. Her reason for this was because the representation of her school in this forum did not capture the complex factors of disadvantage facing students at Ridgeway or provide an accurate evaluation of the effectiveness or quality of the work she and her staff engaged in at the school. In this regard, Carol exercised power in dismissing the relevance of this forum and these data.

Leading as advocacy or political subjectivity for Jenny at Clementine involved supporting other schools in the group. This involved, for example, Clementine taking on an advocacy role to support vulnerable schools, which tended to be underperforming schools (with challenging student demographics) or small (primary) schools that had limited resources and management capacity. Clementine's advocacy or political subjectivity was directed to seeking appropriate financial and professional support for these schools. Jenny's advocacy was also evident in relation to challenging the modes of subjection of external accountability that she saw as inadequate in measuring her school's effectiveness. Jenny, for example, much like Carol's engagement in parrhesia, spoke out to the authorities in the Department for Education against what she saw as the grave inadequacies of the school's recent Office for Standards in Education (Ofsted) inspection in capturing the quality of teaching at the school. She spoke up about the inspection not being "fit for purpose". As with Carol, there was an element of risk in speaking up against the status quo given the deference to Ofsted's authority expected of schools. However, and also similar to Carol's engagement with parrhesia, Jenny designated importance to speaking her truth rather than letting a status quo that misrepresented her school to continue. The contributions of Foucault's theorising of counter-conduct as a key part of the formation of the self as an ethical subject are to be found in these examples.

Conclusion

While worlds apart in many ways, there are clear points of resonance within the leadership practices at Ridgeway State High School and the Clementine alliance. These points of resonance, as illuminated throughout this chapter with reference to the work of Foucault, offer significant insight into how schools might more justly navigate through the multiple and difficult challenges of the present moment. Despite their vastly different contextual and demographic circumstances, leaders in both schools are working towards a telos of socially just leadership that is contextually responsive and a telos of socially just schooling that is committed to improving the educational outcomes of all students. It is clear that pursuing this telos in the current moment is not easy, especially for Carol, who is working within and against the dire conditions of poverty, violence and crime that undermine her students' school participation and engagement. She is trying to support her school and community to think beyond the deficit understandings of her students that strengthen the link between poverty and school/life failure. And she is doing all of this amid broader modes of subjection that seem to thwart her every move, such as external accountability measures that fail to capture crucial elements of the school's social/pastoral care work, and equity policies that fail to include, and thus support, the special needs of her students.

The stakes at both Ridgeway and Clementine in terms of these leaders effectively navigating through such modes of subjection are extremely high – 'poor' leadership performance in both contexts will result in great personal and professional loss. Amid, and perhaps in resistance to these demands, the leadership at Ridgeway and Clementine prioritise ethical ways of working. Leading in these environments is a relational process and thus never fixed or prescriptive as it is always mindful of, and responsive to, context. It is, nevertheless, specific in its social justice agenda or telos. It is firmly directed towards creating the conditions of care and democracy necessary for pursuing better outcomes for all students within the present climate where such conditions are difficult to create. This pursuit, of course, does not mean a rejection of the broader high-stakes environment and the narrow external measures that constitute school effectiveness. In both contexts, for example, the equity significance of students' achievement on these measures is acknowledged. The point is that at Ridgeway and within the Clementine alliance such broader modes of subjection are engaged with critically. This critical engagement, importantly, leads to a strong commitment in both contexts to advocacy and the practices of parrhesia or truth-telling and counter-conduct. This commitment and these practices are seen as instrumental in leading justly and ethically within and against the modes of subjection shaping each of the schools.

The Foucauldian concepts featured in this chapter help us to understand the complex ways in which leaders work on themselves and others. They also open up rather than close down opportunities to conceptualise leadership in different ways from those that are most prevalent within the leadership field. We have purposely chosen to work with Foucault's later work on ethics and the formation of the subject as this body of work has been less fully explored, and it also allows us to demonstrate productive forms of power rather than the still all-too-often examined concepts of discipline and control, or negative aspects of power in education.

In the stories of leadership presented here, this productive use of power is particularly clear in the ways advocacy, truth-telling and counter-conduct are mobilised against the inequities of the broader status quo. For Carol, this is about ensuring that her students are provided with the necessary social and material support so that they are able to access and participate at school and it is about speaking out against dismissive and unfair policy and accountability practices that further marginalise her students and her school. For Jenny, a productive use of power is evident in her provision of the requisite social and material support for 'vulnerable' schools so that they may continue to exist and flourish and is about speaking out against the inadequacies of Ofsted inspections.

Drawing on the concepts of advocacy, truth-telling and counter-conduct is particularly useful in proliferating new lines of thinking in relation to leadership and the *critical* work involved in self-conduct. We have focused on the ongoing processes involved in leaders working on themselves and others in pursuing their telos of social justice through such advocacy work and the productive use of power in this process.

The role of school leaders in contexts like Australia and England has never been more complex and difficult. Whether leading one school or a network of schools, principals and head teachers are confronted with a myriad of new and ever-changing challenges and tensions from the shifting needs of students arising from unprecedented levels of cultural diversity to the shifting expectations and heightened demands of the audit culture. While schools and their leaders are under greater surveillance than ever before, they are also more autonomous and self-managing. Such a context powerfully shapes educational leadership in relation to matters of equity and justice. It has, as we noted earlier, rearticulated social justice and equity priorities in schools to a very narrow focus on what is measured, that is, students' achievement on a limited range of academic outcomes. School leadership must be focused on more than this. If schools are to play a role in transforming the growing inequities of the social world, they must prioritise both the private and public goals of education. They must support social efficiency and social mobility goals while also supporting democracy and citizenship. Such leadership work in the present climate demands an ethical approach that articulates an ideal or telos of leadership that is responsive to context and committed at its core to improving students' educational engagement and outcomes. Such a telos will support leaders to navigate ethically through the many, varied and complex moral codes or modes of subjection that both constrain and enable their work. Such ethical ways of leading demand an engagement with a political subjectivity of truth-telling, counter-conduct and advocacy. This is not to say that these kinds of ethical work are the only practices that need to be engaged in, but we believe they need to form a core part of the ethos of leading schools in the current moment.

It is clear that these leaders are working in socially just ways with an explicit focus on supporting students and communities to overcome disadvantage. How they go about doing this work should give us all some food for thought into the contemporary experience for school leaders and the ways that they grapple with the current constraints of their work, but also the spaces where they can exercise resistance and counter-conduct. We hope that the theoretical tools presented in this chapter provide ways of thinking that can support leaders to adopt a view of social justice that is more than focused on improving academic results. Such leadership, as we have argued, will neither be apolitical or prescriptive. Rather it will understand and be responsive to the myriad of contextual factors shaping schools and their social justice and equity priorities and concerns. It is such understanding and responsiveness that will shape the forms and, indeed, as we have seen from the practices of Carol and Jenny in this chapter, the efficacy of the advocacy, truth-telling and counter-conduct necessary to pursuing social justice in education. We see potential in these tools to extend current thinking about educational leadership in critical but generative ways in their account of the power, politics and subjectivity inherent in leadership work. In particular, we present these tools as supporting education leaders to engage critically and ethically with the challenges of working in diverse and disadvantaged contexts amid the demands of the audit culture towards greater social equity and justice for all.

Notes

1 Please see Niesche and Keddie (2016) for a detailed account of the methodology upon which the stories presented in this chapter are based.
2 The *MySchool* website was introduced by the Australian government in 2010 to provide information about schools and for the purposes of comparing their performance on national standardised tests.

References

Anderson, G. (2009). *Advocacy leadership: Toward a post-reform agenda in education.* London: Routledge.
Ball, S. J. (2003). The teacher's soul and the terrors of performativity. *Journal of Education Policy, 18*(2), 215–228.
Ball, S. J., & Junemann, C. (2012). *Networks, new governance and education.* Bristol: Policy Press.
Ball, S. J., & Olmedo, A. (2013). Care of the self, resistance and subjectivity under neoliberal governmentalities. *Critical Studies in Education, 54*(1), 85–96.
Blackmore, J. (2006). Social justice and the study and practice of leadership in education: A feminist history. *Journal of Educational Administration and History, 38,* 185–200.
Blackmore, J. (2008). Leading educational re-design to sustain socially just schools under conditions of instability. *Journal of Educational Leadership, Policy and Practice, 23*(2), 18–33.
Brooks, J. (2012). *Black school white school: Racism and educational (mis)leadership.* New York: Teachers College Press.
Dardot, P., & Laval, C. (2013). *The new way of the world: On neoliberal society.* London: Verso.
Davidson, A. I. (2005). Ethics as aesthetics. In G. Gutting (Ed.), *The Cambridge companion to Foucault* (2nd ed.). New York: Cambridge University Press.
Ellsworth, E. (1989). Why doesn't this feel empowering? Working through the repressive myths of critical pedagogy. *Harvard Educational Review, 59,* 297–324.

Exley, S., & Ball, S. (2011). Something old, something new . . . understanding conservative education policy. In H. Bochel (Ed.), *The conservative party and social policy* (pp. 97–118). Bristol: Policy Press.

Foucault, M. (1990). *The history of sexuality: Volume 3: The care of the self.* London: Penguin.

Foucault, M. (1992). *The use of pleasure: The history of sexuality: Volume 2.* Harmondsworth, Middlesex: Penguin.

Foucault, M. (2000). The ethics of the concern for self as a practice of freedom. In. P. Rabinow (Ed.), *Essential works of Foucault 1954–1984, volume 1 ethics.* London: Penguin.

Foucault, M. (2007). S*ecurity, territory, population: Lectures at the College de France 1977–1978.* New York: Picador.

Foucault, M. (2011). *The government of self and others: Lectures at the College de France 1982–1983* (F. Gros, Ed., G. Burchill, Trans.). New York: Picador.

Fraser, N. (2009). *Scales of justice: Re-imagining political space in a globalizing world.* New York: Columbia University Press.

Furman, G. C. (2004). The ethic of community. *Journal of Educational Administration, 42*(2), 215–235.

Grimaldi, E. (2012). Neoliberalism and the marginalisation of social justice: The making of an educational policy to combat social exclusion. *International Journal of Inclusive Education, 16*(11), 1131–1154.

Gunter, H. (2012). *Leadership and the reform of education.* Bristol: Policy Press.

Khalifa, M. A., Gooden, M. A., & Davis, J. E. (2016). Culturally responsive school leadership: A synthesis of the literature. *Review of Educational Research, 86*(4), 1–40. doi:10.3102/0034654316630383

Larson, C., & Murtadha, K. (2006). Leadership for social justice. In J. Murphy (Ed.), *Preparing school leaders: An agenda for research and action* (pp. 134–161). Lanham, MD: Rowman & Littlefield.

Lingard, R., Sellar, S., & Savage, G. (2014). Re-articulating social justice as equity in schooling policy: The effects of data and testing infrastructures. *British Journal of Sociology of Education, 35*(5), 710–730.

Marshall, C. (2004). Social justice challenges to educational administration: Introduction to a special issue. *Educational Administration Quarterly, 40*(3), 3–13.

Niesche, R., & Keddie, A. (2016). *Leadership, ethics and schooling for social justice.* London: Routledge.

Normore, A. H. (Ed.). (2008). *Educational leadership for social justice.* Charlotte, NC: Information Age.

Normore, A. H. (2009). Culturally relevant leadership for social justice. In J. Collard & A. H. Normore (Eds.), *Leadership and intercultural dynamics.* Charlotte, NC: Information Age Publishing.

Ryan, J. (2010). Promoting social justice in schools: Principals' political strategies. *International Journal of Leadership in Education, 13*(4), 357–376.

Shamir, R. (2008). The age of responsibilization: On market embedded morality. *Economy and Society, 37*(1), 1–19.

Shields, C. M. (2010). Transformative leadership: Working for equity in diverse contexts. *Educational Administration Quarterly, 46*(4), 558–589.

Theoharis, G. (2010). Disrupting injustice: Principals narrate the strategies they use to improve their schools and advance social justice. *Teachers College Record, 112*(1), 331–373.

4 "We're going to call our kids 'African Aussies'"
Leading for diversity in regional Australia

Jane Wilkinson

Introduction

Australia is one of the most culturally diverse nations in the world with an estimated 28% of its population having been born overseas (Australian Human Rights Commission, 2016). Another 20% of Australians have at least one overseas-born parent and one source estimates that 32% of the Australian population is from a non-Anglo-Celtic background (Australian Human Rights Commission, 2016). As a researcher from a working-class, ethnically mixed background (an Israeli Jewish mother who came to Australia at the age of 20 speaking no English and an Anglo-Celtic Australian father), my own ethnic heritage as a researcher reflects this trend.

The increasingly diverse face of Australia as a nation is mirrored in its regions. Although actual numbers of overseas-born people have not grown as a ratio of its population, the linguistic and cultural diversity of ethnic groups settling in regional and rural Australia has increased markedly as have the countries from which they are drawn (Australian Bureau of Statistics [ABS], 2011). This ethnic diversity has arisen as a result of changes to federal government resettlement policies in the past decade, which aim to settle up to 45% of refugees in regional Australia (Withers & Powall, 2003). The federal government's policy reflects broader international trends in nations such as the UK, US and Canada, in which previously demographically homogenous regions are diversifying due to inflows of immigrants and refugees (Robinson, Andersson, & Musterd, 2003). These shifts in ethnicity provide a sharp contrast to historical constructions of regional and rural Australia as a discursive white landscape (Edgeworth, 2015), that is, an ethnically homogenous landscape in which Indigenous peoples had been positioned as the subaltern 'other'. Such mythologies, rooted in popular culture, ballads and stories have up until recently informed constructions of (white, masculinist) Australian nationhood, identity (Schaffer, 1988; Hage, 1998) and leadership (Sinclair, 1994).

Schools are not isolated from demographic and social trends. As "micropublics" (Ho, 2015) and key socialising agencies of/for young people, schools do not only reflect these shifts. Rather, they can play a crucial role in engendering social cohesion as young people of different backgrounds are forced to deal with one another on a daily basis. Indeed, it is through young people's "daily encounters with cultural difference" in schools that "an organic multiculturalism" may be fostered in their everyday lives (Ho, 2015). It is these kinds of routine, everyday negotiations across cultural difference which can foster intercultural understanding in schools (Ho, 2015) and in everyday learning spaces such as church, youth groups and sport (Wilkinson, & Lloyd, forthcoming; Wilkinson, & Santoro, 2017). However, such outcomes cannot be assumed or taken for granted. Instead, school leaders and leadership practices play a key role in fostering the kinds of necessary conditions for such intercultural understandings to take root and grow (Santamaria & Santamaria, 2015; Wilkinson, 2017). Conversely, school leaders and their practices can produce "miseducation" (Brooks, 2012) and "culturally irrelevant leadership" that stymy intercultural understandings (Brooks, 2009) and perpetuate social and demographic divides.

One of the root causes as to why "culturally irrelevant leadership" (Brooks, 2009) prevails in schools may be due to crucial 'blind spots' in the field of educational research. For instance, a focus on the leading and managing of schools in relation to increasingly diverse student populations emerged in the first decade of this century, often drawing on corporate discourses of diversity in organisational management, as opposed to more transformative notions of diversity based on civil rights. As an analysis of this literature revealed (Wilkinson, 2009), such research rarely connected up to or drew on insights from research which examined the enduring homogeneity of the principalship in terms of ethnic diversity, gender and sexuality. Rather, mainstream research tended to focus on how such diverse populations could be managed and led, drawing on depoliticised and shallow notions of diversity (Wilkinson, 2008). In so doing, it failed to interrogate how and why the increasing diversity of student populations was not reflected in the profile of educational leadership, which remained largely homogenous in terms of gender, as well as linguistically and culturally.

Secondly, a body of critical research drawing on feminist, postcolonial and queer theory has emerged in which schools are examined as raced, gendered and heteronormative institutions (c.f., Theoharis & Scanlan, 2015). Such studies are highly welcome and well overdue. They have the potential to speak back to, and expose, the lacunas in mainstream educational leadership research noted above. However, as Blackmore (2010) notes, less frequently are links made in this more critical body of research between the perpetuation of gendered, raced, heteronormative and other structural barriers in schools on the one hand, and the persistent homogeneity of school leadership on the other hand.

This lack of connection has major implications for how school leadership for/of diversity continues to be researched, understood and practised. For example, the failure of mainstream school leadership scholarship to make links to critical leadership scholarship insights perpetuates the *illusio* of school leadership as a "set of abstract and universal principles" (Brooks, 2010, p. 157), despite the reality that claims to universal principles are coded white (Apple, 2004). In failing to take seriously the cultural specificity and "happeningness" of leading practices (Wilkinson & Kemmis, 2015), such research ignores the reality that leadership is a *social* phenomenon that is "culturally relevant . . . with context-specific political, economic, legal and social dynamics" (Brooks, 2010, p. 157). It perpetuates white masculinities as the "position of privilege" for school principalship, constituted out of the "framing" of non-whites and women as 'other' (Weis, Proweller, & Centrie, 2004, p. 130). This is a "position of privilege" which is revealed in the statistics when it comes to school leaders in Anglophone nations.

Educational leadership as coded white

Despite the linguistic, ethnic and religious heterogeneity of Australia's population which is reflected in our nation's students, a comprehensive study of teaching and leadership staff in Australian government and Catholic and non-government schools reveals an extremely homogenous profile. The teaching profession remains predominantly Anglo-Australian, English-speaking and with a high proportion of females: 80.9% of primary teachers, 58.4% of secondary teachers (McKenzie, Weldon, Rowley, Murphy, & McMillan, 2014, p. xxviii). Despite 28% of the Australian population being born overseas, only 16.4% of primary and 19.2% of secondary teachers in 2011 were born overseas (McKenzie, Weldon, Rowley, Murphy, & McMillan, 2014, p. xxviii). The majority of teachers who were overseas-born were born in the Anglophone nations of the United Kingdom (5.0% primary and 6.0% secondary) and New Zealand (1.5% primary and 1.3% secondary). South Africa represents the third-highest number of overseas-born educators (1.5% primary and 1.3% secondary) (McKenzie, Weldon, Rowley, Murphy, & McMillan, 2014, p. 29).

In 2011, 25% of the Australian population spoke a language other than English (LOTE) at home. In contrast, in 2013, the proportion of teachers and leaders who spoke a LOTE at home was less than half the national average (McKenzie, Weldon, Rowley, Murphy, & McMillan, 2014, p. xxviii). Around 1% of teachers and leaders identified as being of Aboriginal and Torres Strait Islander (ATSI) origin, compared to 3% in the Australian population as a whole (McKenzie, Weldon, Rowley, Murphy, & McMillan, 2014, p. xxviii).

In relation to the principalship, there was even less ethnic, linguistic and gender diversity. Despite some increases in formal leadership representation, females remained under-represented with 65.5% holding leadership positions in primary schools and 48.2% holding leadership positions in secondary schools (McKenzie, Weldon, Rowley, Murphy, & McMillan, 2014, p. xxviii). One area of growth since 2010 was among primary principals where the "proportion who identified as being of ATSI origin increased from near zero to 1.1% in 2013" (McKenzie, Weldon, Rowley, Murphy, & McMillan, 2014, p. xxviii). Primary principals in low socioeconomic status schools (5.0%) were more likely than primary principals in other schools (1.7–1.8%) to speak a language other than English at home, unlike their secondary leader counterparts (McKenzie, Weldon, Rowley, Murphy, & McMillan, 2014, p. 31).

The extreme homogeneity of Australian educational leaders is not a new phenomenon. It is reflected more broadly in the lack of gender and cultural diversity amongst senior leaders in Australian civic institutions including parliament, business and universities (Australian Human Rights Commission, 2016) and in Australian cultural institutions.[1] The pipeline from which we draw principals – the teaching workforce – historically has been overwhelmingly Anglo-Australian, despite an increasing growth in ethnic diversity amongst the Australian population (Allard & Santoro, 2006). A worrying trend reported in the US was that *increasing* diversity in the US amongst school pupils had been matched by a *decreasing* level of ethnic and cultural diversity amongst educators (Ladson-Billings, 2005). Contrary to popular wisdom and 'pipeline' theories of increasing diversity, teaching and school leadership in the early 2000s in the US had become less ethnically and linguistically diverse rather than more diverse.

In relation to Australian teacher education, the breeding ground for future teachers and leaders, Allard and Santoro (2006, pp. 116–117) noted that the predominant focus of awareness raising in relation to diversity was on "developing student teachers' understandings of how gender, ethnicity, 'race' and class shape learner identities . . . how these also shape teachers' identities. . . [was] rarely explored". Allard and Santoro (2006, pp. 116–117) conclude that such an omission:

> leaves subjectivities of teacher education students untouched and unexamined and serves to position school students of non-Anglo and non-middle class status too often as 'problems' to be managed. How teacher education students' identities intersect with those of their potential students is unexamined.

Equally one could argue that a similar situation arises for school leaders in that too often their subjectivities remain "untouched and unexamined", with little or no interrogation of how Anglo-Australian constructions of whiteness, heteronormativity and masculinity intersect with teachers' and students' identities to shape their leadership identities and practices.

The figures in relation to the homogeneity of Australian teachers and school principals reveal a major dissonance between espoused policy and policy-in-use (Walker, 2004). For instance, the Australian Professional Standard for Principals lists what principals are "expected to know, understand and do to achieve in their work" (Australian Institute for Teaching and School Leadership Limited [AITSL], 2016). Principals are expected to

> embrace inclusion and help build a culture of high expectations that takes account of the richness and diversity of the wider school community and the education systems and sectors . . . recognise the multicultural nature of Australia's people . . . foster understanding and reconciliation with Indigenous cultures. . . [and] . . . recognise and use the rich and diverse linguistic and cultural resources in the school community.
>
> (AITSL, 2016)

No reference is made in the Standard to the kinds of critical awareness and consciousness-raising required for principals to achieve these ends, or to the need for the principalship to better reflect the "richness and diversity of the wider school community" they are leading. This is not to suggest that the Standard lacks good intentions, but that there is a crucial silence in terms of the means by which to achieve these intentions. Instead, the figures on the homogeneity of school leadership would suggest that the "embrace of inclusion" may be largely unidirectional.

In this chapter, I draw on a case study of leadership practices in an Australian regional secondary school as the lens through which to examine these 'blind spots' and lacunas, particularly in terms of their impact on/for educational leadership practices. The school had undergone a shift from a largely white Anglo-Australian demographic to a more ethnically diverse student population as a result of an influx of refugee students[2] from a range of African nations. In particular, I examine the complex and fraught terrain of Anglo-Australian leadership advocacy work as the executive attempted to achieve cultural and recognitive justice (Fraser, 2008) for this new demographic. I conclude by examining the implications of such paradoxes and (mis)understandings for school leadership practice and scholarship.

Methods and findings

The chapter draws on a case study conducted in 2009–2010 of a regional high school in New South Wales which had experienced a significant increase in refugee students from a variety of African nations.[3] The 12-month study documented the impact of increasing cultural diversity on school leadership and teachers' pedagogical practices, attitudes and beliefs. It employed semi-structured interviews and focus groups with the school principal and deputy principal, head teachers, English as a Second Language (EAL/D) teachers, teachers from a range of discipline backgrounds, students from both majority (predominantly Anglo-Australian) and minority origins, school counsellors and Learning Support Officers (ethnic). Data were thematically analysed employing NVIVO software package for the purposes of coding, categorising and linking ideas and accurately annotating each transcript.

At the time of the study approximately 5% of Regional High School's students[4] were from Language Backgrounds Other Than English (LBOTE) – the majority of whom were of refugee origin. Most students came from Sudan, but the school also welcomed students from the Congo, Burundi and Sierra Leone. Five per cent of LBOTE students in no way equates to the linguistic and ethnic diversity of many urban-based schools in Australia. However, it represented a significant increase for the school, particularly as these were students who were "highly visible" (Oliver, 2012), both in terms of their non-Anglo-European ancestry and low likelihood of speaking English as a first language.

Four themes emerged in relation to how the school was responding to this changing student demographic and the preconditions that were enabling shifts in educators' practices to occur. These were: the role of leadership in fostering a whole school approach to inclusion; access to appropriate professional development; the increasing diversity of learners in mainstream classrooms; and the enhanced role of EAL/D teachers (Wilkinson & Langat, 2012). Analysis of data suggested that the practices of the executive were particularly crucial in supporting inclusion of the refugee students (Wilkinson & Langat, 2012; Wilkinson, Forsman, & Langat, 2013). Members of the executive modelled a "caring approach" which focused on "possibilities and respect, not on deficits" (Vedoy & Moller, 2007, p. 65). This approach encompassed a range of strategies including: the employment of *discourses* which positioned the diversity of learners and embrace of this diversity as an asset for the school; changes to the *material conditions* for students' learning (e.g., the establishment of an intensive English class where none previously had existed); and attention to the *relational* aspect of student inclusion, through executive staff modelling the importance of reaching out and valuing refugee students (Wilkinson & Langat, 2012). All of these practices modelled a set of "holistic approaches" to refugee education, which in turn have been shown to have positive flow-on effects in reducing refugee students' "vulnerability" and building their "resilience" (Matthews, 2008, p. 40).

However, a number of gaps were also identified in the school's approach to their changing student demographic (Wilkinson & Langat, 2012). These gaps included the need for school leadership to foster conditions for *pedagogical* leadership at the whole school level via a coordinated teaching and learning system (Ferfolja & Naidoo, 2010). Such an approach would focus the learning conditions in the institution as "capabilities-orientated", rather than orientated in its teaching and learning towards lack, deficit and remediation (Ferfolja & Naidoo, 2010). A second gap in the school leadership's approach was that the professional learning practices employed predominantly remained at the level of awareness-raising. However, there were some attempts to raise deeper and more difficult issues about teachers' and leaders' practices in relation to educational access and equity in the school (Wilkinson, 2017). This latter point is explored in more detail below.

As argued in the introduction, the lack of connection within and between critical and mainstream bodies of educational leadership in relation to student diversity and leadership homogeneity has major implications for how school leadership is researched, understood, represented and practised. In the next two sections, I explore these points drawing on two sets of data from the Regional High School study. The first set of data examines responses to interview questions regarding the increasingly diverse student body on the one hand and the lack of diversity amongst teachers and school leadership on the other hand. We were particularly interested in whether interview participants would make links between the two questions. For instance, would the questions provoke reflection on the contradictions between the diversity of the students and the lack of diversity amongst staff? Would educators reflect on what the implications of this situation might be for their own subject locations and educational practices as educators and leaders? The second instance relates to the deputy principal's laudable attempts to secure recognitive justice (Fraser, 2008) for the refugee students in the school through changes in the terminology associated with describing the students. I now turn to an exploration of the first set of data to examine these issues further.

Links between student and teacher/leadership diversity

As part of the interviews and focus groups with school executives, teachers and students, participants were asked:

> (*i*) *Has this increase in ethnic diversity amongst students been reflected in greater teaching and leadership ethnic diversity? What about other forms of diversity such as gender, in particular in relation to leadership?*
> (*ii*) *What do you see as the role of leadership in producing changes to school practices when it comes to this kind of increase in diversity?*

All participants struggled initially to respond to these questions. For instance, after noting the changes to student demographics in terms of gender, linguistic and ethnic diversity, the principal commented in relation to *Question One: Diversity amongst teachers and school executives*:

> Teachers, the split up is more female than male but . . . pretty close. . . . [T]he senior executives, so myself and the two deputies are all male . . . In terms of the ethnic diversity . . . the background is – I won't say it's Anglo Saxon but it's pretty close to it . . . of the senior executive there's neither gender nor ethnic diversity in the three of us, I'm afraid, they're stuck with us.
>
> [W]e still have people who work on staff as learning support officers, ethnic or teachers' aides . . . as they were called who came from an African background but they're not permanent staff . . . it's only really one day a week . . . and that's . . . about funding and stuff, that's one of my big issues.

The principal's ironic response to the first question, "there's neither gender nor ethnic diversity in the three of us, I'm afraid, they're stuck with us" may suggest a level of discomfort about the potentially difficult conversations that often arise as a result of examining issues of recognitive justice. Conversationally he shifts from examining "us" – the senior executive – to "them", the precariously employed, non-Anglo-Australian learning support officers. The links between his privilege/ their lack of privilege are not initially made. Later in the interview, however, he initiates a return to the theme of greater diversity amongst staff. However, the focus remains on teachers, rather than also encompassing the leadership team. He remarks:

> I think certainly the place would be richer for, if we had that greater diversity . . . I mean I'd love to see some young Aboriginal teachers on staff, that would be marvellous. And as time goes on some young teachers from other

backgrounds but . . . staffing . . . it's very hard to pick and choose . . . we're constrained by departmental procedures.

The principal aptly draws attention to the material-economic arrangements that prefigure his agency when it comes to hiring staff (Wilkinson, 2017). His options for staff selection are greatly limited. He is the principal of a government school in which staff selection remains largely in the hands of central office. Secondly, because of the largely ethnically homogenous nature of this regional location, the school attracts predominantly Anglo-Australian staff. As the principal rightly states, it is "very hard to pick and choose".

In relation to Question Two, the role of leadership in producing changes in response to this increasing diversity, the principal mused:

> it's not just . . . doing what we can to cater for the kids, it's giving our staff an awareness of who these kids are and where they come from and we've done over the last four or five years a number of sessions at staff meetings . . . Our staff need to understand . . . Africa is a huge continent, and even in the countries that we're getting refugees from there's a massive diversity. We had to avoid or discourage people from, in conversation or at meetings, from saying things like you know the African kids do this or the African kids think this way, because . . . you can't simply lump them all under the one group because they're certainly not . . . I mean their literacy background will depend very much on which way they got out of the country . . . But we had to get the staff to realise . . . what it was like in their country and what their experiences were. I guess their own relationship with . . . the colonial background of their country, so there's a whole range of issues.

In taking action to raise staff awareness of the diverse linguistic and ethnic diversity amongst refugee youth in his school and the differing histories of colonialism amongst various African nations, the principal demonstrates in response to the second question, "the productive and important role that members of privileged groups" such as school principals must play to support marginalised groups (Keddie, 2012, p. 275). In particular, the principal's insistence with staff that they engage in professional development in order to understand why, in terms of their language and actions, refugee students must not be "lumped together" in essentialising ways that reproduce gender and racial stereotypes is admirable. In one sense, the principal is seizing upon the staff use of essentialising language as a powerful teachable moment. His actions reveal a level of political awareness that, it has been argued, is crucial for educational leaders to develop as part of glocal literacies which "inform and enhance their pedagogy and practice" (Brooks & Normore, 2010, p. 52).

Whether the principal's level of awareness of the differing histories of colonialism extends to how Australia's history of colonialism may impact on staff, students' and leaders' own subject locations is less clear. Niesche and Keddie's

(2014) work employing Foucault's notion of ethical substance is helpful here in unpacking the gaps and silences that emerge in the principal's telos of social justice as it emerges in the preceding quotations. In their analysis of the subject locations of two white female principals who led Indigenous Australian schools, they argue that whilst "acknowledging the tensions and complexities in knowing and speaking on behalf of Indigenous people . . . this necessitates undermining and working against the privileging of white knowledges and cultural authority" (Niesche & Keddie, 2014, p. 511). As Brooks (2012) suggests, such "undermining" work is what teachers and educational administrators need to carry out in order to undermine the explicit and implicit workings of racism. That is, we need to "unlearn" our "miseducation" about race and racism including becoming critically aware of the privilege our skin colour and class affords us (Brooks, 2012, p. 2). Importantly, however, this telos of socially just leadership is an ongoing process, rather than being an end point. Through drawing staff attention to the impact of the history of colonialism in various African nations, there is a suggestion that the principal is taking important steps in the development of his telos as a leader for social justice in order to challenge "white knowledge and cultural authority" (Niesche & Keddie, 2014, p. 516). This is a crucial part of the "substantive ethical work" of principals (Niesche & Keddie, 2014, p. 516).

In the next set of data, I tease these issues out further, as another member of the school executive in charge of refugee students in the school describes an approach he had undertaken to secure what Nancy Fraser (2008) has termed recognitive justice for this new student demographic. In Fraser's terms, recognitive justice is not simply the reification of the politics of group identity. Rather it is allied with the concept of "political representation (i.e., being heard and accorded a voice)" with such representation being "crucial in any conception of justice" for refugee students (Olson, 2008, as cited in Keddie, 2012, p. 273).

"We're going to call our kids 'African Aussies'"

In attempting to secure recognitive justice for refugee students, an executive staff member revealed how and why his consciousness had been raised in relation to issues regarding refugee students and refugees more generally. In so doing, he noted two critical incidents. The first incident has been discussed in Wilkinson (2017) and will be examined only briefly. In sum, as a result of a series of ongoing incidents of racism against refugee students in the school, the executive staff member felt he had no choice but to address the whole school assembly and talk about

> the good old days . . . I needed them to know that I lived in Washington DC in the 1960s. Washington DC is 65% African American. There were no African American students at my school. There were no African American students that lived in my neighbourhood. The only African Americans I ever saw were the ones that were working for white families in our street. I just wanted them to know that was part of the good old days and that racism was

a way of life when some of their parents were just growing up and that's no longer acceptable and I don't think it was acceptable at this school.

In his address to the assembly, the staff member appears to use his power as a member of the executive as a "site of intentional ethical work" in which his own subject location as a member of the white middle class of Washington DC is deconstructed as a "form of ethical substance" (Niesche & Keddie, 2014, p. 516). The series of declarative statements he makes as he reflects on his address to the school assembly about the problematics of racism in the US in the 1960s contain an extensive repetition of "I" in concert with action verbs ("I needed them to know . . . I lived in Washington . . . I just wanted them to know"). Discursively, the repetition of declarative statements underscores the "intentional" nature of this "ethical work". The executive member's response is particularly critical given that a recent of study of racism in Australian schools found that:

> young people born outside Australia are almost twice as likely to experience intolerance and discrimination as those born in Australia, with around four out of five children born in non-English speaking countries experiencing racism at least once a month.
> (Priest, Ferdinand, Perry, Paradies & Kelaher, 2014, as cited in Casinader & Walsh, 2015)

In the second critical incident, examined in detail in this section, the executive staff member expanded on why he loathed the term "refugees" and had invented the alternative term "African Aussies" to use when talking about refugee students at their school:

> About five years ago . . . it was a sort of a . . . little epiphinal moment. I just thought this is ridiculous. I hate the word "refugee". I hate what it means; I hate what it stands for. I've got some kids here who have been here now for five years, when do they stop being refugees? I was looking at the politicisation of language doing some work and research on that . . . and I just decided that if African Americans felt that they needed to be distinguished from not being black . . . I talked to the principal and the English as an Additional Language/Dialect [EAL/D] teacher and I've made a decision that we're going to call our kids African Aussies. I didn't ask them.

When asked if the term had been employed by others since he coined it, the executive staff member responded:

> [The two EAL/D aides who are of diverse African origin[5] and former refugees] use the term. When we were at a meeting in this office and I announced that that's what I'd like to do – I think if somebody was going to say, no stop that . . . they would have told me, no that's not appropriate or no I have an issue with that but they were both happy with the term . . . The logic behind

it was just if we keep talking about our kids being refugees then there is a whole lot of expectations that follow on from that. If we want to change those expectations then we have to change the language that comes with those... [expectations].

Later in the interview, the executive staff member expanded on the logic of his thinking:

I wanted the students to recognise that these kids are not staying for a week or a month or a year and then moving; they're here for good. They're part of us now so you better start getting used to the idea... Refugee has a tenuous sort of feel to it... it sounds like you're escaping and that's the only reason why you're here. There's not loyalty. There's no expectation or dedication to the new nation. It's all about we are here because we need to take from you because we haven't got these things because they were taken from us. Whereas using the "Aussie African" tag what I was hoping to do was to give the kids a sense of ownership, belonging, a degree of acceptance on the school's part at the very least.

There are a number of points that arise from the executive staff member's attempts to re-present the refugee students in the school in a more positive light. In the first critical incident, his anti-racist speech to the assembly suggests the opposite to the "colour-blind" approach frequently employed by school administrators in which responsibility for dealing with racism and/or raising student and staff awareness is hived off to EAL/D teachers, school counsellors or individual teachers (Santamaria & Santamaria, 2015, p. 24). The executive staff member's responses and speech at the school assembly suggest Freire's notion of conscientizacão, a level of critical consciousness revealing a "heightened and critical awareness of oppression, exclusion, and marginalization" (Brooks, 2012, p. 23). His speech suggests he understands how the whiteness of the Washington suburb in which he lived as a child had resulted in a form of epistemic violence, "intrinsically linked to unfolding relations of domination" in which the "construction of others as different, to, and inferior to... constructions of other" allowed the "dominant centre" to constitute itself (Weis, Proweller, & Centrie, 2004, p. 131). Furthermore, his willingness to openly raise with students at assembly the difficult topic of racism emulates the opening up of difficult but "critical conversations" about "race, language, culture, difference, access, and/or educational equity" (Santamaria & Santamaria, 2015, p. 28) so necessary for applied critical leadership practices.

In the second critical incident, the executive staff member's decision to coin a term that draws on the symbolic power of the term "African American" is underlined by his acute awareness of the *constitutive* nature of representation. He states, "[I]f we keep talking about our kids being refugees then there is a whole lot of expectations that follow on from that. If we want to change those expectations then we have to change the language that comes with those [expectations]". To dismiss terms such as "Aussie" as harmless labels elides the reality that language is political and has constitutive effects in the real world. As Moreton-Robinson (2000, p. xxii) notes in her study of Indigenous women and feminism, "Representations are more than mere symbols. They are a means by which we come to know, embody and perform reality". Representations of individuals as "refugees" thus have material and symbolic effects as "expectations" about refugees as a group are produced via language. These representations thus are both productive and self-productive (Wilkinson, 2005). The political nature of language is a crucial point that Regional High School's executive staff member recognises and acts upon through a range of actions including, but not limited to, the coining of the term "African Aussie" (c.f., Wilkinson, 2017).

The executive staff member's assertions draw attention to the reality that the term "refugee" in Australian parlance draws on an inglorious history of media discourses and representations of asylum seekers commencing with the flow of Vietnamese refugees in the 1970s. These discourses represent asylum seekers as so-called "boat people" and "illegal immigrants". Thus in Australian media and popular culture the term has played a "significant role in constituting the symbolic markers" of what constitutes an "Australian national identity" (Gale, 2000, p. 266) in the past few decades. It has done so by feeding into populist and jingoist constructions of such identities. As such, the employment of the term "refugee" can operate as a form of symbolic violence, by maintaining Anglo-Australian privilege (Gale, 2000) through its reproduction of degrees of belonging/whiteness (white Anglo-Australian) versus unbelonging/non-whiteness (non-white 'other').

On the other hand, the term "refugee" and the category it constitutes are crucial for humanitarian applicants when it comes to achieving political justice. Legal recognition of refugee status in Australia, as in many other nations who are signatories to the United Nations *Convention relating to the Status of Refugees 1951* (Australian Human Rights Commission, 2008) brings with it crucial resources including legal status, as well as political and economic rights. As such, the "distinctiveness" that is conferred by the term "refugees" can at times be "useful for particular political strategies" (McConaghy, 2000, as cited in Keddie, 2012, p. 275). At other times it may "limit, exclude and contain . . . possibilities . . . for attaining institutional, disciplinary and political capacity" (McConaghy, 2000, as cited in Keddie, 2012, p. 275) through reinforcing particular attitudes and stereotypes. As the executive staff member observes, "Refugee has a tenuous sort of feel to it . . . it sounds like you're escaping and that's the only reason why you're here".

There are a number of issues raised by the executive staff member's laudable efforts to re-present this demographic of students. These issues in turn foreground the paradoxes and gaps in educational leadership scholarship and practice which often lead to a misrecognition (Bourdieu, 1986) that white, male domination is part of the 'natural order of things' when it comes to school leadership. Firstly, through his employment of the term "African Aussies" the executive staff member re-fuses the binaries of belonging/unbelonging that are connoted in media and popular culture's discourses of refugees. Instead he attempts to symbolically expand the possibilities for refugee student subjectivities. Yet, the selection of terms is highly problematic and may instead work to reproduce the very binaries he is attempting to re-fuse. In Australian parlance, "Aussie" is a phrase which is employed in the vernacular to symbolically mark the territory of Anglo-Australian whiteness. For instance, in the Olympics, the chorus of "Aussie, Aussie, Aussie, oi, oi, oi" is frequently used by crowds when Olympic Gold is achieved. The media will often reproduce this chorus as a headline, usually accompanied by photographs of blonde-haired Anglo-Australian swimmers achieving medals. As such, the term "Aussie" forms part of the mediascape, or imagined world that feeds into constructions of Anglo-Australian ethnicity (Apparadui, 1996). The coupling of "Aussie" with the highly essentialising phrase "African" is well intentioned, therefore, but nonetheless, problematic, for in some ways, the latter phrase essentialises the students. It does so by implicitly re-fusing the distinctiveness of the range of ethnicities in the continent of Africa (a point to which the principal has drawn staff attention) and connoting their non-whiteness as 'other' to Anglo-Australian "Aussies".

Secondly, in his attempts to re-fuse the construction of such binaries, the executive staff member rightly draws attention to the point that the ethnicity of refugee students is not a "biological category but a political one" (Ang, 1995, p. 69). His assembly speech powerfully draws attention to this point as he recounts the intersection between one's subject location as white and middle class in reproducing asymmetrical relations of power vis à vis Black minority working-class Americans in 1960s US. Later in the interview, he describes how he brought these political insights to his decision to re-present students of refugee origin: "I talked to the principal and the English as an Additional Language/Dialect [EAL/D] teacher and I made a decision that we're going to call our kids African Aussies. I didn't ask them". He describes the EAL/D aides' reactions to his decision, observing:

> When . . . I announced that that's what I'd like to do – I think if somebody was going to say, no stop that . . . they would have told me, no that's not appropriate or no I have an issue with that but they were both happy with the term.

There are a number of interpretations that can be placed on the executive staff member's preceding account. On the one hand, in a manner similar to the critical incident at the school assembly, he deploys his positional authority in the meeting with the EAL/D aides to advocate on behalf of the students, engaging in what Anderson (2009) has termed "advocacy leadership", that is, "a relation that leaders deploy in speaking out for their schools and communities" (Keddie & Niesche, see chapter in this volume). Such a relation is a crucial form of "political subjectivity that exemplifies a key part of the ethical self-formation of the individual" (Keddie & Niesche, see chapter in this volume). Both incidents require that he be prepared to take risks to advocate on students' behalf. Moreover, in so doing, he lays bare the inherently political nature of leadership as a social and political phenomenon rather than as it is more commonly portrayed in mainstream leadership literature, as a politically neutral state or set of behaviours.

On the other hand, one of the inherent dangers of advocacy leadership is that can unwittingly re-inscribe relations of domination and oppression (c.f., Ellesworth, 1989, as cited in Keddie & Niesche, see chapter in this volume). For instance, the executive staff member interprets the EAL/D aides' reactions as assent. This may have well been the case. However, the reality is that in a manner similar to the appellation of "African Aussie", how the EAL/D aides (and other staff) interpret the executive staff member's declaration is subject to multiple realities, depending on one's subject location within the ethnoscape of a globalised exchange of ideas and information in a globalising world (Apparadui, 1996). Furthermore, whether they be "happy with the term" or not, what is less clear in this account is whether the aides felt they were in a sufficiently powerful position to respond to the decision. In this sense, it is unclear if the executive staff member gave consideration to his own racialised and classed position in relation to the EAL/D staff, particularly given they are "not permanent staff . . . it's only really one day a week" when announcing his decision.

In terms of the staff member's appellation of the students as "African-Aussie", though such a move may be well-intentioned, it runs the risk of constituting a form of paternalistic advocacy which potentially may silence the very voices the executive staff is attempting to re-present (Keddie, 2012, p. 208). It suggests that with the best will in the world, the very binaries the executive staff member is attempting to disrupt may be in danger of being re-inscribed. Michael Apple's distinction between intentional and functional explanations is apposite here. Intentional explanations, he argues, are "those self-conscious aims that guide our policies and practices", whereas functional explanations are more "concerned with latent effect of policies and practices" and are "more powerful" (Apple, 2004, p. 75). It is the functional explanation that I have attempted to highlight in the latter part of this account in tracing the possible "latent effects" of the executive staff member's practices in relation to students of refugee origin.

Discussion and conclusion

In making the preceding points, I do not overlook the laudable attempts undertaken by the executive staff to work in socially just ways with their rapidly changing student demographic (c.f., Wilkinson, 2017; Wilkinson & Langat, 2012; Wilkinson, Forsman, & Langat, 2013). Nor do I underestimate the courage of their risky and challenging attempts to disrupt long-held socially unjust values amongst staff and Anglo-Australian students. They do so in regional locations where "Black bodies are highly visible and are discursively cast as 'out of place'" and in which "discourses of rural Whiteness" have historically produced "schooling exclusions that implicate schools in the spatial regulation of unbelonging" (Edgeworth, 2015, p. 351).

Rather, I use their accounts to draw out a number of broader points in regard to educational leadership scholarship and practice that are suggested by my initial discussion of the disconnections between and within mainstream and critical educational leadership research, and my subsequent analysis of the executive members' practices in relation to refugee students. Firstly, in the initial section of this chapter, I argued that the lack of connection within and between critical and mainstream school leadership scholarship has major implications for how school leadership for/of diversity continues to be researched, understood and practised. I would argue that this lack of connections also has major implications for how school leadership is *represented, embodied* and *enacted* in research, policy and practice. These bodies of research in themselves constitute forms of representation; that is, they are both constitutive (they have material effects on educational leadership policy and practice) and are political. Hence, mainstream educational leadership scholarship for diversity (and mainstream leadership research more generally) that marginalises, denies or overlooks the socially constitutive and political nature of their research engages in a form of (mis)scholarship, (mis)leadership and (mis)representation.

Secondly, the above point is critical for principal and school executive *practice*, for no school leader is an island. Principals and their executive staff do not work in isolation but instead their practices form part of the broader ecologies of practice that link up to and connect with policy, research, professional learning, teaching and student learning, educational systems and sectors (Wilkinson, 2017). Hence, connections between research (e.g., school effectiveness literature which takes whiteness and masculinity as the unexamined norm of school leadership) and policy (e.g., the production of a Principal Standard which overlooks the homogeneity of its Principal Class when exhorting principals to cater for diversity) has constitutive and material effects on principals' practices. Such research and policy impact on principals' ways of knowing, understanding and enacting leadership for diversity and on the systems and sectors which imbibe such research and produce these kinds of 'colour-blind' policies and standards. Hence, the responses of the principal and executive staff member to an increasing level of ethnic and linguistic diversity amongst its student demographic were largely left to chance, i.e., to their individual *telos* and praxis as leaders (Kemmis et al., 2014). Fortunately for the students of refugee origin in their care, their telos suggested a strong sense of socially just leadership. However, I argue, in line with other critical educational leadership scholars, that such responses should not be left to chance alone. Rather, they should form part of a collective educational praxis: a system-wide, morally and ethically informed set of supportive approaches that both are responsive to the "specific nature of the specific oppressions" (McConaghy, 2000, p. 8) in educational sites and are informed by critical scholarship and reflexive standards of practice. To state this is not to criticise or point the finger at the school executive who had done a sterling job over a number of years. Rather it is to point out that there is a larger ethical and moral responsibility that researchers, policy makers and educational systems bear to reflexively support and scaffold principals and executive staff in regard to the question of what they need to know and do in leading and managing schools. In so doing, this needs to go beyond political rhetoric to forms of social action. Knowledge and expertise in terms of social action would then form a crucial part of a principal's *pedagogical* remit for leading learning, as opposed to narrower forms of instructional leadership research that are silent about learning and teaching as socially critical forms of educational praxis (Wilkinson, 2017).

Thirdly, the 'blind spots' I noted in the literature in the first section of this chapter connect up with gaps in the Australian Professional Standard for School Principals, which exhorts school leaders to "embrace inclusion and take . . . account of the richness and diversity of the wider school community and the education systems and sectors" (AITSL, 2016). However, the Standard fails to address the homogeneity of the principal and teaching population that lead such communities, systems and sectors. Nor does it address the necessity for principals, systems and sectors to begin to seriously engage with issues of white privilege, diversity and equity and its collective complicity in reproducing dominant societal norms of leadership. Yet, such serious engagement is the kind of necessary *pedagogical leadership* practice that should be foregrounded in a Principal Standard and undertaken as part of ongoing professional development, both in terms of principal preparation (c.f., Young, Marshall, & Edwards in this volume) and throughout the career of educational leaders. As Boler and Zembylas (2003) contend, such pedagogical leadership is high-risk but necessary work, for it requires educators, systems and sectors to engage in "pedagogies of discomfort" which

> recognize . . . and problematize . . . the deeply embedded emotional dimensions that frame and shape daily habits, routines and unconscious complicity with hegemony . . . by closely examining emotional reactions and responses . . . one begins to identify unconscious privileges as well as invisible ways in which one complies with dominant ideology.
>
> (p. 111)

Fourthly, I would argue that the time is well overdue for educational leadership scholars in mainstream research similarly to engage in these "pedagogies of discomfort" in order to open up substantive conversations both within mainstream leadership scholarship and with critical leadership researchers more broadly. Such a call is nothing new. As noted earlier, critical leadership scholarship has been engaging in such conversations over a number of years and its reflections and conclusions have much to teach the broader educational leadership research sector and schools and systems more generally (c.f., Blackmore, 2010; Bristol, Esnard, & Brown, 2015; Brooks, 2010; Santamaria & Santamaria, 2015; Theoharis & Scanlan, 2015; Wilkinson, 2007; Wilkinson, 2008; Wilkinson & Eacott, 2013). Such pedagogical research leadership is a fundamental part of the "ethical substance" of our work as leadership scholars, rather than, as so often occurs in mainstream leadership literature, an afterthought expressed as a token chapter tacked at the end of a research handbook.

Finally, the continuing homogeneity of school executive staff who lead increasingly diverse communities in Australia is a major ethical and moral issue which contemporary school systems need to seriously engage with and address.[6]

Engaging with this issue is a question of both distributive and political justice, for increases of minority groups in educational leadership would help to create what Nancy Fraser (2008, as cited in Keddie, 2012, p. 274) has termed "conditions of moral standing" for these groups. However, such increases must be accompanied by serious and substantive conversations and policy actions in regard to issues of white privilege. Conversations and actions to tackle dominant societal paradigms of leadership are long overdue in our educational systems. In an Australian society where fears of radicalisation of Muslim youth and terrorism have led to increasing levels of racism, prejudice and mistrust (Scanlon Institute, 2015), such initiatives would assist us in re-framing and re-imagining educational leadership as a powerful tool for social cohesion, reaching beyond its current symbolic domination via conventional tropes of masculinity and whiteness.

Notes

1. A landmark study of Australian television which analysed all dramas aired between between 2011 and 2015 inclusive found that 18% of main characters in the period were from non-Anglo-Celtic backgrounds, compared to 32% of the population. A notable exception to this trend is Indigenous representation, making a dramatic turnaround in screen presence. Only 4% of main characters had an identified disability compared to an estimated 18% of Australians, whilst 5% of main characters were identified as LGBTQI, yet this group is estimated to be up to 11% of the population (Screen Australia, 2016).
2. I adopt the definition of a refugee as "someone who has been assessed by a national government or an international agency (such as the Office of the High Commissioner for Refugees (UNHCR)) and meets the criteria set out under the *Convention relating to the Status of Refugees 1951* (Refugee Convention)" (Australian Human Rights Commission, 2008).
3. I would like to acknowledge and thank my co-researcher, Dr. Kiprono Langat, for his role in conducting this research. I would also like to acknowledge and thank the Faculty of Education, Charles Sturt University, for providing us with the research funds to conduct this study.
4. A pseudonym for the school has been adopted in the paper.
5. I have deliberately used a more general term in order to maintain the anonymity of the participants in this study.
6. There have been some attempts at state and federal government levels to challenge this homogeneity, i.e., through an Indigenous teachers' initiative (Department of Education, Employment and Workplace Relations [DEEWR], 2011), as well as attempts to increase the numbers of women in educational leadership. However, these have tended to be piecemeal and sporadic. Moreover, such initiatives risk misframing these issues in reductionist or simplistic ways that unproblematically "denigrate" or "exalt" minority groups (Keddie, 2012, p. 274) and divert the gaze from questions of white masculinist privilege in educational leadership.

References

Allard, A., & Santoro, N. (2006). Troubling identities: Teacher education students' constructions of class and ethnicity. *Cambridge Journal of Education*, 36(1), 115–129. doi:10.1080/03057640500491021.

Anderson, G. (2009). *Advocacy leadership: Toward a post-reform agenda in education*. London: Routledge.

Ang, I. (1995). I'm a feminist but. . . 'other' women and postnational feminism. In B. Caine & R. Pringle (Eds.), *Transitions, new Australian feminisms* (pp. 57–73). New York: St Martin's Press.

Apparadui, A. (1996). *Modernity at large: Cultural dimensions of globalization*. Minneapolis, MN: University of Minnesota Press.

Apple, M. (2004). Making white right: Race and the politics of educational reform. In M. Fine, L. Weis, L. Powell Pruitt, & A. Burns (Eds.), *Off white: Readings on power, privilege, and resistance* (2nd ed., pp. 74–84). New York: Routledge.

Australian Bureau of Statistics [ABS]. (2011). *2011 Census tablebuilder: Remoteness areas and cultural and language diversity classifications*. Canberra: Commonwealth of Australia.

Australian Human Rights Commission. (2008). *Face the facts*. Retrieved from www.hreoc.gov.au/racial_discrimination/face_facts/chap3.html

Australian Human Rights Commission. (2016). *Leading for change: A blueprint for cultural diversity and inclusive leadership*. Retrieved from www.humanrights.gov.au/our-work/race-discrimination/publications/leading-change-blueprint-cultural-diversity-and-inclusive

Australian Institute for Teaching and School Leadership Limited. (2016). *Australian professional standard and the leadership profiles*. Retrieved from www.aitsl.edu.au/docs/default-source/school-leadership/australian-professional-standard-for-principals-and-the-leadership-profiles.pdf?sfvrsn=8

Blackmore, J. (2010). 'The other within': Race/gender disruptions to the professional learning of white educational leaders. *International Journal of Leadership in Education: Theory and Practice*, 13(1), 45–61. doi:10.1080/13603120903242931

Boler, M., & Zembylas, M. (2003). Discomforting truths: The emotional terrain of understanding difference. In P. Trifonas (Ed.), *Pedagogies of difference: Rethinking education for social justice* (pp. 110–136). New York: Routledge.

Bourdieu, P. (1986). The forms of capital. In J. Richardson (Ed.), *Handbook of theory and research for the sociology of education* (pp. 241–258). New York: Greenwood.

Bristol, L., Esnard, T., & Brown, L. (2015). In the shadow/from the shadow: The principal as a reflective practitioner in Trinidad and Tobago. *Journal of Cases in Educational Leadership*, 18(3), 215–227.

Brooks, J. S. (2009). The mis-education of an educational administrator: Culturally irrelevant educational leadership. In A. K. Tooms & C. Boske (Eds.), *Bridge leadership: Connecting educational leadership and social justice to improve schools* (pp. 153–170). Charlotte, NC: Information Age.

Brooks, J. S. (2012). *Black school, white school: Racism and educational (mis)leadership*. New York: Teachers' College Press.

Brooks, J. S., & Normore, A. (2010). Educational leadership and globalization: Literacy for a glocal perspective. *Educational Policy*, 24(52), 52–82. doi:10.1177/0895904809354070

Casinader, N., & Walsh, L. (2015). Teacher transculturalism and cultural difference: Addressing racism in Australian schools. *The International Education Journal: Comparative Perspectives*, 14(2), 51–62.

DEEWR. (2011). *7.5 million to help increase Indigenous teacher numbers*. Retrieved from http://ministers.deewr.gov.au/garrett/75-million-help-increase-indigenous-teacher-numbers

Edgeworth, K. (2015). Black bodies, White rural spaces: Disturbing practices of unbelonging for 'refugee' students. *Critical Studies in Education*, 56(3), 351–365. doi:10.1080/17508487.2014.956133

Ferfolja, T., & Naidoo, L. (2010). *Supporting refugee students through the Refugee Action Support [RAS] program: What works in schools.* Retrieved from www.researchgate.net/publication/272821130_Supporting_refugee_students_through_the_refugee_action_support_RAS_program_what_works_in_schools

Fraser, N. (2008). *Adding insult to injury: Nancy Fraser debates her critics* (K. Olson, Ed.). London: Verso.

Gale, P. (2000). Construction of whiteness in the Australian media. In J. Docker & G. Fischer (Eds.), *Race, colour and identity in Australia and New Zealand* (pp. 256–269). Sydney: University of New South Wales Press.

Hage, G. (1998). *White nation: Fantasies of white supremacy in a multicultural society.* Sydney: Pluto Press.

Ho, C. (2015, August). "People like us": School choice, multiculturalism and segregation in Sydney. *Australian Review of Public Affairs.* Retrieved from www.nswtf.org.au/files/people_like_us_-_school_choice_multiculturalism_segregation_in_sydney_-_christin_ho.pdf

Keddie, A. (2012). Schooling and social justice through the lenses of Nancy Fraser. *Critical Studies in Education, 53*(3), 263–279.

Keddie, A., & Niesche, R. (2017). The role of ethical practices in pursuing socially just leadership. In J. Wilkinson & L. Bristol (Eds.), *Educational leadership: Interrogating the culturally specific sites of leading practices* (pp. xx–xx). Singapore: Routledge.

Kemmis, S., Wilkinson, J., Edwards-Groves, C., Hardy, I., Grootenboer, P., & Bristol, L. (2014). *Changing practices, changing education.* Singapore: Springer.

Ladson-Billings, G. (2005). Is the team all right? Diversity and teacher education. *Journal of Teacher Education, 56*(3), 229–234.

Markus, A. (2015). *Mapping social cohesion: The Scanlon Foundation surveys 2015.* Retrieved from http://monash.edu/mapping-population/

Matthews, J. (2008). Schooling and settlement: Refugee education in Australia. *International Studies in Sociology of Education, 18*(1), 31–45.

McConaghy, C. (2000). *Rethinking indigenous education: Culturalism, colonialism and the politics of knowing.* Flaxton, Queensland: Post Pressed.

McKenzie, P., Weldon, P., Rowley, G., Murphy, M., & McMillan, J. (2014). *Staff in Australian Schools 2013: Main report on the survey.* Australian Council for Educational Research [ACER]. Retrieved from https://docs.education.gov.au/system/files/doc/other/sias_2013_main_report.pdf

Niesche, R., & Keddie, A. (2014). Issues of Indigenous representation: White advocacy and the complexities of ethical leadership. *International Journal of Qualitative Studies in Education, 27*(4), 509–526. doi:10.1080/09518398.2013.771223

Oliver, M. (2012). Standing up, reaching out and letting go: Experiences of resilience and school engagement for African high schoolers from refugee backgrounds. *The Australasian Review of African Studies, XXXIII*(1), 151–164.

Robinson, V., Andersson, R., & Musterd, S. (2003). *Spreading the 'burden': A review of policies to disperse asylum seekers and refugees.* Bristol: Policy Press.

Santamaria, L., & Santamaria, A. (2015). Counteracting educational injustice with applied critical leadership: Culturally responsive practices promoting sustainable change. *International Journal of Multicultural Education, 17*(1), 22–41.

Schaffer, K. (1988). *Women and the bush: Forces of desire in the Australian cultural tradition.* Cambridge: Cambridge University Press.

Screen Australia. (2016). *Seeing ourselves: Reflections on diversity in Australia TV drama.* Retrieved from http://apo.org.au/resource/seeing-ourselves-reflections-diversity-australian-tv-drama

Sinclair, A. (1994). *Trials at the top: Chief executives talk about men, women and the Australian executive culture*. Parkville, Melbourne: University of Melbourne.

Theoharis, G., & Scanlan, M. (Eds.). (2015). *Leadership for increasingly diverse schools*. New York: Routledge.

Vedoy, G., & Moller, J. (2007). Successful school leadership for diversity? Examining two contrasting examples of working for democracy in Norway. *International Studies in Educational Administration, 35*(3), 58–66.

Walker, K. (2004). From page to playground: Educational policy and solving educational problems. In J. Allen (Ed.), *Sociology of education: Possibilities and practices* (3rd ed., pp. 381–389). Southbank, Victoria: Social Science Press.

Weis, L., Proweller, A., & Centrie, C. (2004). Excavating a 'moment in history': Privilege and loss inside white working-class masculinity. In M. Fine, L. Weis, L. Powell Pruitt, & A. Burns (Eds.), *Off white: Readings on power, privilege, and resistance* (2nd ed., pp. 128–144). New York: Routledge.

Wilkinson, J. (2005). *Examining representations of women's leadership in the media and Australian universities*. Unpublished doctoral thesis, Deakin University, Australia.

Wilkinson, J. (2007). But what do we know about women? Feminist scholarship for/about women academic leaders. *New Zealand Journal of Educational Leadership, 22*(2), 13–21.

Wilkinson, J. (2008). Good intentions are not enough: A critical examination of diversity and educational leadership scholarship. *Journal of Educational Administration and History, 41*(2), 101–112.

Wilkinson, J. (2009). A tale of two women leaders: Diversity policies and practices in enterprise universities. *The Australian Educational Researcher, 36*(2), 39–54.

Wilkinson, J. (2017). Leading for social justice: Examining educational leading through a practice lens. In K. Mahon, S. Francisco, & S. Kemmis (Eds.), *Exploring practices through the lens of practice architectures*, pp. 165–182. Singapore: Springer International.

Wilkinson, J., & Eacott, S. (2013). Outsiders within? Deconstructing the educational administration scholar. *International Journal of Leadership in Education, 16*(2), 191–204.

Wilkinson, J., Forsman, L., & Langat, K. (2013). Multiplicity in the making: Towards a praxis-oriented approach to professional development. *Professional Development in Education, 39*(4), 488–512.

Wilkinson, J., & Kemmis, S. (2015). Practice theory: Viewing leadership as leading. *Educational Philosophy and Theory, 47*(4), 342–358. doi:www.tandfonline.com/doi/full/10.1080/00131857.2014.976928

Wilkinson, J., & Langat, K. (2012). Exploring educators' practices for African students from refugee backgrounds in an Australian regional high school. *The Australasian Review of African Studies, XXXIII*(II), 158–177.

Wilkinson, J., & Lloyd, A. (forthcoming). The role of everyday spaces for learning for refugee youth. In R. Elmeksy, C. Camp Yeakey, & O. Marcucci (Eds.), *The power of resistance: Culture, ideology and social reproduction in global contexts*. Bingley: Emerald Press.

Wilkinson, J., & Santoro, N. (2017). Sudanese refugee youth and educational success: The role of church and youth group in supporting cultural and academic adjustment and schooling achievement. *International Journal of Intercultural Relations*.doi: 10.1016/j.ijintrel.2017.04.003

Withers, G., & Powall, M. (2003). *Immigration and the regions: Taking regional Australia seriously. A Report on options for enhancing immigration's contribution* to regional Australia. Chifley Research Centre. Retrieved from file:///C:/Users/CrownUser/Downloads/rep03_immi.pdf

Young, M., Marshall, C., & Edwards, T. (2017). Left out: Gender and feminism in the educational leadership curriculum. In J. Wilkinson & L. Bristol (Eds.), *Educational leadership: Interrogating the culturally specific sites of leading practices* (pp. xx–xx). Singapore: Routledge.

5 Is she in the wrong place? Exploring the intersections of gender, religion, culture and leadership

Saeeda Shah

Introduction

Literature in the field of gender and leadership is increasingly emphasising the significance of gender for leadership theory and practice (Blackmore, 2009; Connell, 2009; Grogan & Shakeshaft, 2011; Morley, 2013; Shah, 2012, 2016). The debates further underline that the discourse of "female leadership" is formulated not just by the biological gender but more importantly by how biological gender is constructed in respective cultural, societal and organisational contexts (Blackmore, 1999; Oplatka, 2001; Reay & Ball, 2000). Evidence from research studies across many societies highlights that leadership is predominantly associated with male gender, not only in traditional and conservative cultures but also in developed societies (Griffin, 2006; Osler, 2012; Shah, 2016; Sobehart, 2009). The quote below from Osler (2012) is an interesting example of how even in a higher education institution in a developed country where women form about half of the student population and half of the workforce they are still not expected to be in leadership positions:

> Attending my first meeting of senate some weeks later, armed with what was clearly a bundle of senate papers, a well-meaning man pointed out that I was in the wrong place. He explained: "This, my dear, is senate".
>
> (2012, p. 297)

The message is clear: She is seen as being in the wrong place. Gender defines women's spheres of activity and emerges as an important factor impacting on their access to leadership roles as well as their practices and experiences of leadership (Blackmore, 2009; Connell, 2009; Grogan & Shakeshaft, 2011; Morley, 2013; Shah, 2012). Societies, developed or developing, Western or Eastern, are all still uncomfortably grappling with the phenomenon of female leadership. To understand women's leadership role and practices in any particular context it is essential to examine the range of factors that interact to define gender and leadership in that society. Gender is lived and experienced in a societal context and any discussion of women in educational leadership that "ignores important factors such as cultural differences, economic and social-political divisions, race and nationality, religion and identity would not only be unrealistic but may present a distorted picture" (Oplatka & Hertz-Lazarowitz, 2006, p. 3).

Literature provides evidence of increasing recognition of cultural and belief systems in shaping leadership conceptualisations and practices in educational settings (Shah, 2008, 2016). Hofstede's (2001) landmark study highlights the relationship between culture and leadership, citing examples from diverse societies to draw attention to the effect of societal culture on leadership concepts and practices, while literature on spiritual leadership (Burke, 2006; Fry, 2003; Keyes et al., 1999), servant leadership (Greenleaf, 1996), leadership in Catholic schools (Feheny, 1998) and religious leadership in faith schools (Shah, 2006) draws attention to the impact of faith and belief in shaping educational leadership. However, as Wilkinson and Bristol argue in Chapter 1, "considerations of the intersections between various categories . . . and their impact on leading practices" (p. 64) have largely remained under-explored. There is a scarcity of literature investigating the interplay between various factors, particularly religion, discourse formation, power, culture, gender and leadership and the resulting complex intersectionalities. It is this gap in literature which the current study seeks to address. This chapter draws upon a study of women vice chancellors in Pakistan, a South Asian Islamic state which claims to follow the religious practices as interpreted by those with power over discourse formations. How the participating women vice chancellors experienced and practised leadership at the intersection of these diverse factors would help us to understand how gender and leadership were shaped at the intersections of diverse factors in a specific societal context, pointing to the need to develop complex theoretical constructs to understand and theorise gender and leadership.

Educational leadership and its cultural embeddedness

Educational institutions are social organisations. Pugh and Hickson discuss education as a "deeply cultural institution" (2003, p. 11) where theory and practice are shaped by the values, beliefs and ideologies embedded in the respective worldviews that shape roles, practices and patterns of behaviour. 'Leaders' and the 'led' participate in related activities informed by their worldviews, learned through living and sharing within a group or community as its members. In religious communities, worldviews are explicitly or implicitly located in faith with implications for cultural practices. Cultural practices are not just rituals or actions but are embedded in values and worldviews that help to construct culture and the discourses that flow from culture.

Culture is broadly defined in anthropology as an integrated system of learned behaviour patterns which reflects shared characteristics of the members of a society (Hoebel, 1966). Indigenous scholars of leadership also emphasise "the specific Indigenous cultural contexts and local ways of knowing and understanding the world from which leadership derives" (Wilkinson, & Bristol, Chapter 1, p. 2). Geertz emphasises that "to discover who people think they are, what they think they are doing and to what end they think they are doing it, it is necessary to gain a working familiarity with the frames of meaning within which they enact their lives" (2000, p. 16). These "frames of meaning" are admittedly not fixed as culture itself is dynamic and evolving; nevertheless it remains embedded in the respective worldviews that inform practices in the public and the domestic and shape patterns of behaviour. In the case of religious societies and communities the shared worldview is embedded in shared belief and accepted religious teachings, which account for similarities of concepts and practices across many Muslim societies. As I argue elsewhere (2010), Muslim women leaders are caught between the given religious discourses around 'what it means to be a "good" Muslim' woman that advise to remain invisible, while aspiring for or functioning in very visible leadership roles, struggling to balance the two under huge physical and emotional stresses. Discussing female leaders in economically developing, often faith-based, nation states, Blackmore (2010) underlines "how women struggle with their own professional and personal aspirations within their own cultural and religious contexts" (p. 49).

Impact of belief systems on leadership conceptualisations and practices

Belief is interpreted as underpinning faith or religion in theology. A faith or religion is, broadly speaking, a set of beliefs and practices held by a human community that influences social practices and shapes the culture. Weber (1993) explains the concept of religion as a system of symbols and beliefs, which via its effects on the consciousness of the believer can decisively mould and direct the content of social action. Geertz (1973) explains religion as a meaning-making process which guides and helps its followers to give meaning to their existence. It guides perceptions and actions of its followers and in making sense of their life. Weber describes religion as a cultural system (1993) and explains the relationship between religious belief, individual attitudes and values and social action – thus linking belief to social practices. He highlights the role of religion in determining 'action' in social sites, arguing that 'social action' is conceptualised and enacted in different institutions of social life determined by ideational systems that are embedded in ideologies, values and beliefs, and reflect the way a community perceives reality. His analytical framework of formal rationality and substantive rationality is a useful tool to explain the impact of ideational systems (cultural, religious and political) on social institutions and the practices therein.

The extent to which a religion or a belief system influences social action is linked to the role it is accorded in a community. According to Day and Lynch (2013) religion can be, in certain contexts "an organising centre for the lives of individuals and groups" (p. 199). One such example is Islam. It demands from its followers that they conduct all activities of their life – social, economic, political and others – according to its religious teachings (Shah, 2006, 2016). For Muslims, even if/when they may not be practising Muslims, religion remains a guide to life in all matters and activities. In spite of variations in the interpretations of the religious texts and the subsequent implications for practice,

Muslims acknowledge the role of religion in guiding action. The ultimate leadership model in Islam is the prophet Mohammed and any leadership conceptualisations in Muslim societies are expected to be modelled on his characteristics and practices (Shah, 2006). Furthermore, the prophet Mohammed being a male also makes women non-leaders in many Muslim societies. Islam exercises a highly significant role in shaping discourses and practices in Muslim societies that define how gender is constructed and experienced in the professional and the domestic with implications for women in educational leadership positions.

The study

This chapter draws on a study of women vice chancellors in Pakistan, exploring how these women educational leaders perceived, experienced and practised leadership, drawing attention to the intersections of gender, culture, religion and leadership. At the time this study was conducted, there were eight women vice-chancellors in Pakistan – five in women-only public universities, two in co-educational public universities and one in an elite semi-autonomous women-only higher education (HE) institution which had satellite university status. In view of the exploratory nature of the study and the sensitivities linked to the focus of the research I planned one-to-one interviews for data collection. The access was ensured through personal relationships and networks as I had previously worked in higher education in Pakistan for about two decades and most of the women vice chancellors knew me or of me. All eight vice chancellors expressed willingness to participate. However, due to issues of their availability during my visit to Pakistan, interviews could be conducted with only five vice chancellors including three vice chancellors of women-only public universities, one vice chancellor of a co-ed public university and the vice chancellor of a women-only HE institution with satellite university status. The coding used for these interviews was VCF1–5. These women had extensive experience of senior leadership roles and were approaching retirement within the next five to seven years. The data generated was extremely rich, highlighting complex and sensitive issues facing senior women leaders in Pakistan. However, for the purposes of this chapter the focus will be on the intersections of culture and religion and its impact on these women leaders' professional roles, their experiences and practices. The discussion will draw on the research data and the relevant international literature to explore and debate the interplay between religious and cultural dynamics and their intersections with gender and leadership in the Muslim society of Pakistan.

Pakistan: A Muslim society

In the proclaimed Muslim society of Pakistan, education, educational concepts and practices are influenced by religion and its teachings. Pakistan is an Islamic state, demanded and created in the name of religion on the basis of a religious ideology (Jaffrelot, 2005; Shah, 2009a). Islam is "the state religion of Pakistan" (Constitution of Pakistan, 2004, p. 3) and around 97% of the population is

Muslim (The World Factbook, 2007). It is stated in the constitution of Pakistan that all the laws and policies will be formulated in conformity with the teachings of the Quran and the Sunnah (the Prophet's way), making it mandatory in the country to observe Islamic law (*sha'ria*), "wherein the Muslims shall be enabled to order their lives in the individual and collective spheres in accordance with the teachings and requirements of Islam as set out in the Holy Quran and Sunnah" (Constitution of Pakistan, 2004, p. 1). Therefore, educational institutions in Pakistan are not only required to provide teaching of Islamic studies up to pre-university stage to promote knowledge of Islam and its teachings among the students but also all Muslim applicants to public sector jobs, including education, are required to possess basic knowledge and understanding of Islam and therefore are asked questions about religion during job interviews. This emphasis on religion as part of the state ideology exercises a significant influence on how social institutions in general and educational institutions in particular and the practices therein are defined and enacted, with considerable implications for women's roles and their participation in the public domain.

In religious societies, religion determines those power structures and social controls that regulate and legitimise discourses and practices. Foucault argues that discourses are shaped and attain power and control in societies through those "who are charged with saying what counts as true" (1980, p. 131). In Muslim societies, these discourses are produced and manipulated by religious scholars through a self-acquired power of interpretation (Shah, 1999, 2006, 2016). These interpretations are accepted by the followers as religious teachings, mainly because of the high status of knowledge and knowledge-givers in Islam (Shah, 2016). Secondly, these interpretations are supported by powerful patriarchy because these reinforce male power. Esposito argues, "Patriarchy and its legacy, legitimated in the name of religion, remain alive in various Muslim countries" (2011, p. 101), and Pakistan is no exception. The patriarchal assumption that women cannot be leaders at the highest level, reinforced by religious discourse of male leadership, is implicit in the Constitution of Pakistan (Khan, 1973), which requires the head of the Islamic Republic of Pakistan to be male. The controversy in religious circles following the election of a woman (Benazir Bhutto) as the first female prime minister of Pakistan in 1988, and the efforts on the part of her party to conciliate the critical *Ulema* (religious scholars) by stressing the difference between the "head of the state" and the "head of the government" to legitimise Benazir Bhutto as head of government is an example of the oppressive force of patriarchal traditions, validated through given interpretations of religious texts, in forming discourses and setting agendas. Prior to that, the Ansari Commission recommended:

> requiring a women to be at least fifty years of age (a man need be only twenty-five) and to secure her husband's permission before becoming a member of the *Majlis-e-Shura*, prohibiting women from leaving the country without a male escort, and refusing to allow an unmarried, unaccompanied woman to serve abroad in the foreign service.
>
> (Weiss, 1986, p. 103)

Although these recommendations did not exactly become the law they have often served as guidelines in practice. This power of religious ideology over policy making and discourse formation has historically reinforced the gendered cultural practices encouraging segregation and female confinement to the domestic. The participating women educational leaders directly and indirectly referred to the impact of the interplay between the religious discourses and cultural practices that marginalised and disempowered women even when in leadership positions, as discussed in the next section.

Leading at the intersections of gender, culture and religion

The data highlighted how the combined power of cultural and belief systems functioned to control and discipline (Foucault, 1980) what Afshar (1987) called the disruptive potential of independent women. These participating women leaders, who had been successful in accessing senior leadership and had been functioning as vice chancellors for some time, still felt constrained by gendered religious discourses and the cultural practices that reinforced the given interpretations of religious texts and teachings. They acknowledged that being in a position of power as vice chancellors they felt empowered to exercise this positional power, affirming Acker's experience of being a chair in a university, that "As a chair, I was seen to have a formal authority position which appeared to carry power" (2012, p. 424). However, they also emphasised that "structural constraints and the power of discourses must still be acknowledged" (Acker, 2012, p. 423) and specifically pointed to female role constructions in the Muslim society of Pakistan, the segregated education system and spaces and the cultural concept of *izzat* (honour) as having serious impact on their leadership practices and experiences. In a segregated Muslim society where social structures determine gendered inscriptions and associated power/disempowering, the women vice chancellors positioned as senior educational leaders seemed to function at complex intersections of various elements. However, for the purposes of this paper, the discussion is structured around three main elements highlighted by the participants:

- Female role in a Muslim society
- Segregated systems and spaces
- Cultural concept of *izzat* (honour)

Female role in a Muslim society

Women in Islam have a nurturing responsibility towards the family, which has encouraged prioritizing of women's domestic role through given interpretations of the notions of motherhood and family. Deep-rooted patriarchal traditions in the Muslim society of Pakistan, reinforced by the emphasis on the significance of family in Islam and the male role as "maintainers" (the Quran, 4:34) have contributed to gendered constructions of male/female roles and practices. The male as head of family is by default entitled to all leadership positions. In addition, certain aspects of the teaching of Islam such as family obligations, primacy of the domestic role of women and motherhood are interpreted and generalised in ways that deprive women of equal rights, effectively restricting their participation in the public and the professional spheres.

Family, as an institution, generally reflects the relationships among people in a society. Mies emphasises that women are discriminated against "in the family and by the institution of the family" (1986, p. 21) because of the gendered power relations where authority rests with male members of the family. In Islam, family is the basic unit of its social fabric and serves as a primary reference for rights and duties. The relationships through marriage determine social as well as legal rights and obligations. Although marriage in Islam is defined as a contract between a consenting male and female with equal rights to set the conditions (Ahmed, 1992, p. 77; Badawi, 1994, p. 90), cultural constructions of the female role and its association with the domestic (Brock, Dada, & Jatta, 2006) deprive them of equality in practice. The Quran is explicit that "women have rights over men similar to those of men over women" (2:228), stating that men and women have been created "from a single soul and created its mate of the same" (4:1). However, it also mentions women's nurturing role towards the family, which is then availed in Muslim societies to emphasise women's domestic responsibilities and to constrain their participation in the public sphere, thus creating a "discourse of motherhood and wifely duty to household for honorable, implying otherwise who extend the sphere of activities" (Afshar, 1987, p. 73).

Role socialisation and the discourses of the good Muslim woman impact on women leaders' practices, which become marginalised because of given interpretations of the role of women within family (Afshar, 1987; Ahmed, 1992; Mernissi, 1991). A 'good Muslim woman' is constructed as the subordinate, silent and serving member of the family – traits which are generally perceived as contrary to the accepted leadership characteristics. *Ayahs*, i.e., verses from the Quran are interpreted out of context to emphasise male superiority and authority, requiring women to submit to them and thus perpetuating gendered social roles and cultural practices. Such interpretations of religious texts and teachings ignore the essential principles of equality underpinning the religious ideology and reinforce the cultural traditions of female subordination in all spheres of activity. This results in discourses and practices where the "scriptures about women's and men's spiritual equality are neglected" (Redfern & Aune, 2010, p. 155). These cultural practices, validated by given interpretations of religious texts, emerge as "the social, cultural, psychological and political realities that oppress them [women]" (Kassam, 2010, p. xxiii–iv).

According to the Quran, Muslim women share in all social, economic, political and religious rights including the right to property and earnings:

> Unto the men [of a family] belongeth a share of that which parents and near kindred leave, and unto the women a share of that which parents and near kindred leave, whether it be little or much – a legal share;
>
> (4:7)

and

> Unto men a fortune from that which they have earned, and unto women a fortune from that which they have earned.
>
> (4:32)

These references to earnings and ownership suggest participation in the public domain, announcing women as "masters of their own possessions and earnings" (Afshar, 1994, p. 131). Muslim women scholars who offer interpretations of Islamic religious texts and teachings from a female perspective (Barlas, 2006; Wadud, 1999) challenge male interpretations, emphasising the moral and spiritual equality of men and women as espoused by Islam (Lovat, Samarayi, & Green, 2013). However, powerful cultural traditions and patterns of behaviour determine the practices, resulting in submission to the discourses of male authority and gendered roles. The seductive power of the 'good Muslim woman' discourse entices even women in leadership positions to identify with the domestic role. El-Saadawi mentions a Muslim woman professor who in spite of being a feminist argued on national television that in Islam women were for family and children and men were for work outside the home (El-Saadawi, 2010). This discourse of female role in the family emerged powerfully in Pakistan as well. For the participating women leaders, family obligations required attending to family first even if that meant stress and inconvenience in home/work balance:

> When my husband is home then it is challenging. I have to keep him happy, give him time. The moment I am home, I am a mother and wife. My husband would never like me to act other than as a mother.
>
> (VC2)

Being a good wife or good mother is synonymous to being a good Muslim woman, and no Muslim women, vice chancellor or no vice chancellor, would like to be constructed as "not honourable" or "not a good Muslim woman", so they willingly went the extra mile or even miles:

> I would not work at home, no files or nothing till the children go to bed. Then I do my work like after 10 o'clock to late night or till early morning. This is how I balanced – you can say women have to do extra effort than men.
>
> (VC5)

Cherryholmes (1988) discusses this willing acceptance of dominant discourses as "desire":

> Power operates visibly and invisibly through expectations and desires. It operates visibly through formal, public criteria that must be satisfied. It operates invisibly through the way individuals think of themselves and

operate . . . Often power is most effective and efficient when it operates as desire, because desire often makes the effects of power invisible.

(p. 35)

The participating women leaders were happy, willing and even proud to "look after homes, support them (husbands) or at least never trouble them about home responsibilities and never give any problem so as not to annoy them" (VC2). It was evidence of being a 'good Muslim woman', which was the priority. The discourse of mother/wife, validated through interpretations of religious texts, appeared to command uncomplaining submission. The professional role was secondary to the family role, and there was no attempt to reject, resist or challenge these constructions and perceptions. Female leadership even in the professional space was exercised in the shadow of male leadership in all spheres. At workplace, they practised and experienced leadership in full awareness of the power of patriarchy and when back from work, in the domestic sphere, they left their professional role and position outside the door, as emphasised by another vice chancellor innocently saying, as quoted above, that when back home, "my husband would never like me to act other than as a mother/wife" (VC2). This was not a complaint but a statement of fact. This learning of male superiority in the family was transferred to other spheres of activity, reducing women's confidence and pressuring them to keep low profiles. Aptheker (1989) discusses this as a classical colonisation "technology":

> At the heart of the colonisation of women is a belief in the superiority of men, in the infallibility of male judgement and authority and in the absolute priority given to achieving male approval and validation.
>
> (p. 8; also see hooks, 1981)

Cultural norms validated by religious discourses command submission. The participating women leaders affirmed this seductive power not only by their actions (to which they submitted willingly) but their explicit allegiance to religion. They emphasised that it was their duty as 'Muslim women' to follow Islamic teachings and traditions:

> Being a Muslim it is mandatory for me to live my life according to these ideas. I will dress carefully . . . I am grounded in my own culture. I am not doing things to imitate the West. It is important that I establish those protocols of behaviour which are in consonant with who I am and that is being Pakistani and Muslim.
>
> (VC1)

This compliance to the discourse of Muslim woman, as emphasised by the participants, also points to an obvious blurring of boundaries between the religious and the cultural, leading to an uncritical acceptance of dominant practices and discourses. Apple (2013) explains religious women's submission to such discourses as grounded in a call to act on their duty as religious women. The cultural becomes legitimised in the name of religion to justify submission. Whether women's identification with these constructions was a willing response to what they perceived as religious/cultural duty or under pressure is a different debate, but this identification had implications for their leadership role and practices in the professional domain.

Even in their professional capacity, the women leaders acted the role ascribed to them within the family with associated connotations of gendered positions and norms. Gross argues that the dilemma faced by educated religious women with growing awareness of their rights in today's world is "how to integrate into the new structure of economic, political and social opportunities that modernity provides, without losing the religious and cultural particularist uniqueness" (2013, p. 4). The challenge is enhanced in leadership roles which historically and culturally are associated with men, and as stated by a participating vice chancellor:

> Men do not want to see women in the administrative (leadership/management) positions. These are real biases of the society and you have to face it. People unwillingly accepted me – it was unwillingly and I have to face problems.
>
> (VC4)

Their work in the public and professional spheres was constructed as an extension of their domestic role and not as a serious professional contribution, as another vice chancellor explained:

> They think that she is a woman. So she is just unnecessarily – you know – being problematic about things . . . just shows that she has opinion, has a point of view.
>
> (VC1)

The roles remained gendered and the women's professional contributions were belittled, promoting a widespread discourse of degrading female work and their contributions:

> Men don't value our work even when we are in senior positions – they just think we are working with [a] few other women. If there is any problem or conflict, he [husband] just says "quit job".
>
> (VC2)

A woman in a powerful leadership position is perceived as being in the wrong place, a violation of accepted cultural norms, a reversal of roles, and therefore liable to retaliation. Women vice chancellors were careful to avoid such situations and adopted the strategy of not questioning male authority:

> That's why in mixed professional contexts I have always tried to minimize that kind of situation and have tried to put my point of view or my opinion

across as diplomatically as possible so that it is not that we are questioning their authority or that they feel that their authority is being undermined.

(VC1)

This practice is what Davis, Krieg, and Smith (2015) define as culturally sensitive leading which is embedded in cultural awareness and the particularities of the context. The participants admitted conducting themselves in mixed-sex settings in "an accommodating way rather than having a confrontational attitude" (VC1) so as not to disrupt culturally accepted gendered patterns of behaviour. They acknowledged that "When women lead they are disrupting the norm. . . [T]his meant they were vulnerable and exposed to retaliation" (Strachan, Akao, Kilavanwa, & Warsal, 2010, p. 74). Rausch (2012) mentions a Muslim woman in China who had opportunities for education and personal development as a Muslim woman but was subjected to punishment when she aspired to religious leadership. Her

> position in her religious community benefited from the established rights of women to Islamic education and professional training, but her career also demonstrates the severe punishment meted out to women who dared to think and act outside the social boundaries defined by a patriarchal society.
>
> (Rausch, 2012, p. 53)

Strachan et al. (2010) argue that "Women are brought up in cultures that emphasize male superiority and from an early age are taught how they should behave towards men. . . . This can also render women silent within the workplace" (p. 69). The participating women leaders often opted for keeping low profiles. They were very explicit in emphasising that they conducted themselves in ways fully conscious of cultural and religious expectations and observed the norms carefully. Gordon (2002) mentions historically constituted codes of behaviour that determine how people interact and behave, and "to do otherwise would be seen as behaving inappropriately" (2002, p. 152). This research evidences how codes of behaviour defined gender dynamics, roles and practices for the woman leaders in that society, who therefore adopted a deferential manner towards equally positioned men, submitting to the deeper patriarchal structures instituting male authority, which were often validated by given interpretations of religious texts.

Segregated systems and spaces

Sex segregation and veiling are common features of many Muslim societies and are often legitimised as Islamic injunctions. Segregation is perceived as a religiously approved phenomenon in traditional Muslim societies, considered in line with Islamic values, principles and moral codes (Shah, 2009b). The socio-religious discourses of sex, marriage, family and family honor (*izzat*) further promote segregation. In Pakistan also, in keeping with these traditions and teachings, there is a large sector of women/girls-only (*zanana*) institutions. Nevertheless, university education in Pakistan has been co-educational since the creation of the country in 1947. It was in 1998 that the first women-only public university was set up near the federal capital, which was soon followed by legislation in 2003 to establish further four women-only universities, one in each provincial capital, leading to a widening of the provision of segregated education at the university level. Currently, there are 12 women universities in Pakistan and the trend seems to be favouring women-only universities, promoting segregated education at the university level as well.

Segregation in Islam, as I argue elsewhere is not to constrain women, but to restrain men **and** women in accordance with the Quranic values and code of conduct (Shah, 2016). It aims at providing women with a non-threatening environment to ensure their participation in the public sphere. In the first Muslim society of Medina, during the Prophet's lifetime, two major sites of the public were the mosque and the battlefield. Muslim women participated in both, showing that the practice of excluding women from the public was not the intent of the Prophet (Ahmed, 1992; Fernea & Bezirgan, 1977; Mernissi, 1991). However, segregation in Muslim societies is often availed to confine and marginalise women and reinforced not only through religious discourses but by cultural practices, impacting on women's experiences in the domestic and professional spheres.

The sex-segregated educational and societal structure, generally perceived as "the confinement of women" (Mernissi, 1985) apparently created a space for women to access educational leadership. In all women universities in Pakistan, the vice chancellors had to be women. Out of more than 100 co-education public universities in Pakistan, there were only two women vice chancellors, while in all 12 women-only universities the vice chancellors and other senior leaders were all women. The participating women leaders emphasised the advantages of single-sex educational institutions as opening up spaces for women's leadership and creating opportunities for them.

Contending discourses of advantages/disadvantages of the segregated system make analysis complex. This paradox points to the power of cultural and belief systems that shape discourses and practices with implications for gender roles and practices. Segregation provided women leaders a space in which to manoeuvre without the threat of male interference and pressures. They felt advantaged by the comparative protection of the *zanana* in that cultural context. The cultural construction of zanana as women's space restricted male access to zanana, which according to Helms' (1995) argument keeps the intruders out. Although the women leaders generally were comfortable with the segregated system and spaces, nevertheless they also admitted that the constraints and barriers imposed by segregation caused many challenges for their leadership practices. For instance, it imposed constraints on their mobility, social and professional networking and visits to male spaces. It restricted their contributions in meetings dominated by men, where they culturally felt obliged to remain less vocal and less critical. In such situations they had to conduct themselves with cultural appropriateness because any violations of social norms could negatively affect their reputation as good Muslim women, possibly damaging their professional careers as well as their personal lives. The data highlighted that the women's access to leadership as well as the nature of the female leadership role and the women leaders' experiences and practices were influenced by the essential framework of that social structure and its religious basis, which shaped cultural practices and determined gender roles, organisational practices and gender power relations (Shah, 2008).

Izzat *or honour*

Izzat is a commonly used cultural concept in Pakistan embodying enormously powerful cultural judgements that transcend linguistic interpretation. Women are constructed as bearers of *izzat*, whether in the public or the domestic sphere (Shah, 2016). They are required to uphold *izzat* and the associated code of conduct, which has implications for their participation in the professional sphere. The concept is emphasised as having religious validation by interpreting it as consistent with Islamic moral code. One aspect of Islamic moral code relevant to this discussion applies to social conduct across the gender divide when non-*mehrum* men and women are sharing a space[1]. The Quran advises "believing men to lower their gaze" (24:30), and women to "cover their bodies when they go out" (24:31) to promote modesty and chastity, which are considered essential features of an Islamic society. However, in practice, this code is often relaxed for men and exaggerated for women in the name of *izzat*, constraining women who choose to move in positions of visibility (Afshar, 1987).

By associating disparate notions of *izzat* with women and men, and making women solely responsible for it (Weiss, 1994), the concept is given a gendered description that has serious implications for women leaders operating in the public. It promotes male control by subjecting women to "surveillance" and "discipline" (Foucault, 1980). Foucault (1977), while discussing the effect of constant surveillance in prison, argues that its aim is to instil anxiety so that the inmates come to scrutinise their own behaviour and eventually adopt the norms of conduct desired by the disciplinary institution, disciplining themselves into obedient subjects. In the case of women leaders, socio-religious discourses and norms disciplined their behaviour, practices, conversations and communication across the gender divide. The appropriate conduct demanded gender-specific culturally correct behavior and practices, and social surveillance ensured that they were disciplined into compliance. This promoted acceptance of prevailing social norms (Shah, 1999) and submission to the given code of conduct to be categorised as 'honourable' or 'good Muslim woman', often resulting in restricted/proscribed mobility and even withdrawal from the public.

Double moral standards for men and women (Afshar, 1994) and a politically constructed discourse of *izzat* forced women into silence and invisibility. When participating in the public, they performed under high pressure because of the given social norms and the associated threats to their careers, reputation and even family set-ups, thus often trying to underplay their leadership roles. They prefered to remain invisible and less mobile even when in leadership roles because a mobile and visible woman faced the threat of putting the family *izzat* at risk.

Participating women leaders as the subjects and objects of *izzat* were in a vulnerable position. They were culturally constructed as "site of familial honor" (Afshar, 1994, p. 129), and any violation of that code of *izzat* could not only affect the woman leader personally and professionally, but also would impact on the family. This often resulted in self-policing and submission to constraints. Foucault (1977), discussing the effect of constant surveillance on prisoners, argues that it instils anxiety so that the inmates come to scrutinise their own behaviour and eventually adopt the norms of conduct desired by the disciplinary institution, disciplining them into obedient subjects. Constructed as the bearers of *izzat*, the women leaders willingly submitted to the social norms. The power of cultural norms and religious discourses was very real, as pointed out by the participants – a capable woman leader could be eliminated from the public and the professional spaces through character assassination. These norms and discourses reinforced "expectations that men will be powerful and women subordinate, duplicating in the work setting the domestic division of labour" (Acker, 2012, p. 417). A woman in a leadership position was undertaking a gender-transgressive performance, subject to surveillance and demanding self-regulatory constraints. The quotes cited in the first section where women leaders explicitly admitted making efforts not to annoy or inconvenience husbands at home, and not to argue with male colleagues in meetings, point to these self-regulatory constraints. They highlight the level of compliance to socio-cultural norms in anticipation of the possible social and professional risks.

Discussion

Many scholars argue that in the teachings of the Quran, women are equal and different (Wadud, 1999) and share in all the rights, duties and activities of religious, social, economic and political life. The Quran maintains that "if any do deeds of righteousness, be they men or women, and have faith, they will enter paradise" (4:124). The stance frequently adopted by female Muslim scholars (Ahmed, 1992; El-Saadawi, 1982; Kassam, 2010; Mernissi, 1993), and often supported by non-Muslim women writers (Schimmel, 1982; Waddy, 1980; Stowasser, 1994), is that Islam and the Quran do not establish any inherent spiritual, intellectual or physical inferiority of women, although "there is no doubt that Islamic tradition and culture is patriarchal" (Al-Hibri, 1982, p. viii). In male-dominated Muslim societies, accepting women in leadership roles over and above men is not acceptable, as reflected in an interesting quote from Al-Khalifa (1992) about a Muslim male teacher in Saudi Arabia saying that, "It grates me to have a woman in position of authority over me" (p. 101).

Gender roles, constructed at the intersection of cultural and religious discourses invest men with a natural right to leadership, and a woman in a leadership position is seen as being in the wrong place. These cultural and religious scripts are immersed in and learned across the gender divide, reproducing social codes and behaviour. Therefore, even when women access leadership positions, their exercise of the leadership role is determined by the given social codes and patterns of behaviour. The challenge is not just ascendancy to leadership positions, but also "balancing socially constructed and normalized roles and responsibilities, and the issue of marginality both in their professions and in the public mind" (Curry, 2000, p. 4).

Historically, leadership has been associated with males, and a convenient transference of patriarchal structures from social to professional is evident from different theories of leadership associating male charisma, characteristics, abilities and styles with leadership. A dominant tradition of male leadership across religions is an added factor used as a tool wielded for male domination and control. Muslim societies are no exceptions, and in addition to the discourses of male authority and female subordination generally validated through interpretations of religious texts, multiple other factors intersect to enhance female marginalisation, impacting on almost all aspects of their lives and activities in the domestic and the professional spheres:

> Men and women in Muslim societies grapple with many gender issues ranging from the extent of the women's education and employment to their role in the family and the nature of their religious leadership and authority in Islam.
>
> (Esposito, 2011, p. 102)

In Muslim societies, as in most religious societies, interpretations of religious texts are often used as a tool of political legitimisation (Talbani, 1996) aimed at social control over the propagation, selective dissemination and social appropriation of discourses (Ball, 1990). The power of religion and by default of those who occupy places of interpretation and discourse formation in religion, and who always happen to be men, is pervasive in Muslim societies. Male power over religious interpretations has promoted patriarchal culture by providing it legitimacy through religious validation. People generally and women in particular submit to these interpretations because of the seductive power of the discourses or the fear of the consequences of challenging the discourses. In the Muslim society of Pakistan, discourses produced by those controlling religious interpretations tended to marginalise women. The power of these discourses was so strong that women were often seduced into submission.

Religion is a powerful phenomenon in the lives of its followers. In the case of Muslims, even those who do not practise religion would not admit not following religious teachings. To what extent is the submission to religion an expression of desire or submission to its seductive power, or fear of social exclusion and further marginalisation is debatable. However, its power over shaping and influencing social roles and practices is undeniable. Roles are socially constructed, and in this research context, social was enmeshed with religious to the extent that to disentangle and identify the discourses was problematic.

The complexities of women's leadership practices across cultures demand to examine the range of factors that interact to define gender and leadership. In this research context, cultural and belief systems emerged as defining factors underpinning those deeper structures or cultural forms that determined female role and positioning. The effects were quite constraining even when unobtrusive in nature, as affirmed by the responses from the participating women vice chancellors. The participating woman leaders appreciated the positional power but also underlined the gendered restrictions and traditions that confined women leaders to gendered spaces and positions even in professional contexts and roles.

Despite there being no legal bars to women accessing top leadership positions in Pakistan, there is only an occasional woman vice chancellor in co-educational universities. Studies from different countries and contexts affirm that gendered roles are deeply embedded in culture (Blackmore, 2008; Shah, 2009b; Strachan et al., 2010). Subordinate roles are the norm for women and "Women's leadership is viewed as deviant" (Strachan et al., 2010, p. 73); therefore not only may women themselves be reluctant to aspire for or to exercise such roles, men also do not wish to see them in senior leadership positions.

Gender inequities are deeply embedded in organisational and social structures. As Acker observes:

> This embedding takes place through a myriad of routine and taken-for-granted practices that reinforce expectations that men will be powerful and women subordinate, often duplicating in a work setting the domestic division of labour.
>
> (Acker, 2012, p. 417)

Therefore, even when in leadership positions, women's leadership can be seen as a gender-transgressive performance. Cultural perceptions and practices are reinforced by religious discourses in religious societies and women become relegated to subordinate positions. Any meaningful changes in the professional and social position of women are unlikely to occur without changing the values promoted by structures embedded in specific cultural and belief systems.

Multiple intersectionalities impacted on how women participants exercised leadership in this research context. For the women vice chancellors, the positional power, in spite of diverse barriers, emerged as an enabling factor for resisting gender discrimination in the professional domain. However, the exercise of power was mediated and negotiated rather than challenging and aggressive. Drawing on Foucault's analysis of power and its paradoxical aspects (1980), the state of domination existed at the interstices of gender, faith and culture, which prevented power from circulating freely. The segregated structure, social disapproval of women visiting male spaces, cultural traditions of male supremacy and the discourses of *izzat* (honour) and sex segregation emerged as imposing constraints on leadership practices. However, the positional power at the top of a structured hierarchical system in the case of vice chancellors, underpinned by teacher power within religious discourse, enabled power to operate. Their leading was reflective of what Bristol (2014) explains as site-based, culturally appropriate leading practices, informed by the knowledge of the context and embedded in cultural and belief systems.

Note

1 In Islamic sharia legal terminology, any male whom a Muslim woman is permitted by sharia to marry is non-mehrum or not mehrum. If they happen to share a space at any time it has to be in accordance with the Islamic moral code.

References

Acker, S. (2012). Chairing and caring: Gendered dimensions of leadership in academe. *Gender and Education, 24*(4), 411–428.
Afshar, H. (1987). Women, marriage and the state in Iran. In H. Afshar (Ed.), *Women, state and ideology* (pp. 70–86). London: Macmillan Press.
Afshar, H. (1994). Muslim women in West Yorkshire. In H. Afshar & M. Maynard (Eds.), *The dynamics of race and gender: Some feminist interventions* (pp. 127–147). London: Taylor and Francis.
Ahmed, L. (1992). *Women and gender in Islam: Historical roots of a modern debate*. London: Yale University Press.
Al-Hibri, A. (Ed.). 1982. *Women and Islam*. Oxford: Pergamon Press. Published as a special issue of *Women's Studies International Forum*, 5(2).
Al-Khalifa, E. (1992). Management by Halves: Women teachers and school management. In N. Bennett, M. Crawford, & C. Riches (Eds.), *Managing change in education* (pp. 95–106). London: Paul Chapman and Oxford University Press.
Apple, M. (2013). Gender, religion and the work of home-schooling. In Z. Gross, L. Davies, & K. Diab (Eds.), *Gender, religion and education in a post-modern Chaotic world* (pp. 21–39). New York: Springer Publishers.
Aptheker, B. (1989). How to do meaningful work in women's studies. In E. Abel & M. Pearson (Eds.), *The spectrum of women's lives* (pp. 5–16). New York: Gordon and Breach.
Badawi, L. (1994). Islam. In J. Holm with J. Bowker (Eds.), *Women in religion* (pp. 84–112). London: Pinter Publishers.
Ball, S. J. (1990). *Politics and policy making in education: Explorations in policy sociology*. London: Routledge.
Barlas, A. (2006). Women's and feminist readings of the Qur'an. In J. D. McAuliffe (Ed.), *Cambridge companion to the Qur'an* (pp. 255–272). New York: Cambridge University Press.
Blackmore, J. (1999). *Troubling women: Feminism, leadership and educational change*. Buckingham: Open University Press.
Blackmore, J. (2008). Re/positioning women in educational leadership. In H. C. Sobehart (Ed.), *Women leading education across the continents: Sharing the spirit, fanning the flame* (pp. 73–83). London: Rowman and Littlefield.
Blackmore, J. (2009). Re/positioning women in educational leadership: The changing social relations and politics of gender in Australia. In H. C. Sobehart (Ed.), *Women leading education across the continents: Sharing the spirit, fanning the flame* (pp. 73–83). London: Rowman and Littlefield.
Bourdieu, P., & Passeron, J. (1977). *Reproduction in education, society and culture*. London: Sage Publications.
Brock, C., Dada, J., & Jatta, T. (2006). Selected perspectives on education in West Africa, with special reference to gender and religion. In R. Griffin (Ed.), *Education in the Muslim world: Different perspectives* (pp. 211–238). Oxford: Symposium Books.

Cherryholmes, C. (1988). *Power and criticism: Poststructural investigations in education*. New York: Teachers College Press.
Connell, R. (2009). *Gender: In world perspective*. Cambridge: Polity Press.
Constitution of Pakistan. (2004). *Constitution of the Islamic Republic of Pakistan, Government of Pakistan*. Retrieved from www.embajada-pakistan.org/attach/Constitution%20of%20Pakistan.pdf
Curry, B. K. (2000). *Women in power: Pathways to leadership in education*. New York: Teachers College Press (Athene Series).
Davis, K., Krieg, S., & Smith, K. (2015). Leading otherwise: Using a feminist-poststructuralist and postcolonial lens to create alternative spaces for early childhood educational leaders. *International Journal of Leadership in Education*, 18(2), 131–148.
Day, A., & Lynch, G. (2013). Introduction: Belief as cultural performance. *Journal of Contemporary Religion*, 28(2), 199–206.
El-Saadawi, N. (1982). Women and Islam. In A. Al-Hibri (Ed.), *Women and Islam* (pp. 193–206). Oxford: Pergamon Press.
El-Saadawi, N. (2010). Muslim women in the market. In A. N. Horst (Ed.), *The essential Nawal El Saadawi: A reader (Essential feminists)* (pp. 114–124). London: Zed Books.
Esposito, J. (2011). Customs and culture. In J. Esposito (Ed.), *What everyone needs to know about Islam* (pp. 95–132). New York: Oxford University Press.
Feheny, J. (1998). *From ideal to action: The inner nature of a Catholic school today*. Dublin: Veritas.
Fernea, E. W., & Bezirgan, B. Q. (Eds.). (1977). *Middle Eastern Muslim women speak*. Austin, TX: University of Texas Press.
Foucault, M. (1977). *Discipline and punish: The birth of the prison* (A. Sheridan, Trans., from French). London: Allen Lane.
Foucault, M. (1980). *Power/knowledge: Selected interviews and other writings (1972–1977)*. Brighton: Harvester Press.
Geertz, C. (1973). *The interpretation of culture*. New York: Basic Books.
Geertz, C. (2000). *Available light: Anthropological reflections on philosophical topics*. Princeton, NJ: Princeton University.
Gordon, R. D. (2002). Conceptualizing leadership with respect to its historical contextual antecedents to power. *The Leadership Quarterly*, 13(2), 151–167.
Griffin, R. (2006). *Education in the Muslim world: Different perspectives*. Oxford: Symposium Books.
Grogan, M., & Shakeshaft, C. (2011). *Women and educational leadership*. San Francisco, CA: Jossey-Bass, Wiley and Sons.
Gross, Z. (2013). Introduction: Challenging patriarchy: New advances in researching religious feminism and religious education'. In Z. Gross, L. Davies, & K. Diab (Eds.), *Gender, religion and education in a post-modern chaotic world* (pp. 1–20). New York: Springer Publishers.
Helms, L. M. (1995). The haram as a sacred space for Muslim women. *The Muslim Education Quarterly*, 12(3), 62–72.
Hoebel, E. A. (1966). *Anthropology: The study of man*. Toronto, ON: McGraw Hill.
Hofstede, G. (2001). *Culture's consequences* (2nd ed.). Thousand Oaks, CA: Sage Publications.
hooks, b. (1981). *Ain't I a woman: Black women and feminism*. Boston, MA: South End Press.

Jaffrelot, C. (Ed.). (2005). *A history of Pakistan and its origins*. London: Anthem Press.
Kassam, Z. R. (2010). *Women and Islam*. Goleta, CA: ABC-Clio, Llc.
Lovat, T., Samarayi, I., & Green, B. (2013). Recovering the voice of women in Islam: Lessons for educators and others. In Z. Gross, L. Davies, & A. Diab (Eds.), *Gender, religion and education in a Chaotic postmodern world* (pp. 173–184). New York: Springer.
Mernissi, F. (1985). *Beyond the veil: Male-female dynamics in modern Muslim society*. London: Al Saqi.
Mernissi, F. (1991). *Women and Islam: A historical enquiry*. Oxford: Basil Blackwell.
Mernissi, F. (1993). *The forgotten queens of Islam*. Cambridge: Polity Press.
Mies, M. (1986). *Patriarchy and accumulation on a world scale: Women in the international division of labour*. London: Zed Books Ltd.
Morley, L. (2013). The rules of the game: Women and the leaderist turn in higher education. *Gender and Education, 25*(1), 116–131.
Oplatka, I. (2001). I changed my management style: The cross gender transition of women head teachers in mid-career. *School Leadership and Management, 21*(2), 219–233.
Oplatka, I., & Hertz-Lazarowitz, R. (Eds.). (2006). *Women principals in a multicultural society: New insights into feminist educational leadership*. Rotterdam, The Netherlands: Sense Publishers.
Osler, A. (2012). Higher education, human rights and inclusive citizenship. In T. N. Basit & S. Tomlinson (Eds.), *Social inclusion and higher education* (pp. 295–312). Bristol: Policy Press.
Pugh, D. S., & Hickson, D. J. (2003). On organisational convergence. In M. Warner & P. Joynt (Eds.), *Managing across cultures: Issues and perspectives* (pp. 45–60). London: Thomson Learning.
Rausch, M. (2012). Women Mosque preachers and spiritual guides: Publicizing and negotiating women's religious authority in Morocco. In M. Bano & H. Kalmbach (Eds.), *Women, leadership and mosques: Changes in contemporary Islamic authority* (pp. 37–58). Leiden: Brill.
Reay, D., & Ball, S. J. (2000). Essentials of female management women's ways of working in the education market place? *Educational Management & Administration, 28*(2), 145–159.
Redfern, C., & Aune, K. (2010). *Reclaiming the F word: The new feminist movement*. London: Zed Books.
Schimmel, A. (1982). Women in mystical Islam. In Al-Hibri (Ed.), *Women and Islam* (pp. 145–152). Oxford: Pergamon Press.
Shah, S. (1999). *Education management: Braving boundaries*. Islamabad: National Book Foundation.
Shah, S. (2006). Educational leadership: An Islamic perspective. *British Educational Research Journal, 32*(3), 363–385.
Shah, S. (2008). Leading multi-ethnic schools: Adjustments in concepts and practices for engaging with diversity. *British Journal of Sociology of Education, 29*(5), 523–536.
Shah, S. (2009a). Impact of societal culture on practice: People management in colleges in Pakistan. *Journal of Leadership, Policy, and Practice, 24*(2), 4–18.
Shah, S. (2009b). Women and educational leadership in a Muslim society: A study of women college heads in Pakistan. In H. Sobehart (Ed.), *Women leading education*

across the continents: Sharing the spirit, fanning the flame (pp. 344–381). London: Rowman and Littlefield with AASA.

Shah, S. (2012). Contested power! College heads in a Muslim society and leadership challenges. In C. Gerstl-Pepin & J. A. Aiken (Eds.), *Social justice leadership for a global world* (Chapter 4, pp. 59–76). Leadership for Social Justice Book Series. Charlotte, NC: Information Age Publishing, Inc.

Shah, S. (2016). *Education, leadership and Islam: Theories, discourses and practices from an Islamic perspective*. London: Routledge.

Sobehart, H. (Ed.). (2009). *Women leading education across the continents: Sharing the spirit, fanning the flame*. Lanham, MD: Rowman and Littlefield, with AASA.

Stowasser, B. F. (1994). *Women in the Quran: Tradition and interpretation*. New York: Oxford University Press.

Strachan, J., Akao, S., Kilavanwa, B., & Warsal, D. (2010). You have to be a servant for all: Melanesian women's educational leadership experiences. *School Leadership and Management, 30*(1), 65–76.

Talbani, A. (1996). Pedagogy, power, and discourse: Transformation of Islamic education. *Comparative Education Review, 40*(1), 66–82.

Waddy, C. (1980). *Women in Muslim history*. London: Longman.

Wadud, A. (1999). *Qur'an and woman: Re-reading the sacred text from a woman's perspective*. Oxford: Oxford University Press.

Wadud, A. (2006). *Inside the gender Jihad: Women's reform in Islam*. Oxford: Oneworld Publications.

Weber, M. (1993). Religion as a cultural system. In G. Clifford (Ed.), *The interpretation of cultures: Selected essays* (pp. 87–125). New York: Basic Books, Inc.

Weiss, A. M. (1994). Challenges for a Muslim woman in a postmodern world. In A. S. Ahmed & D. Hastings (Eds.), *Islam, globalisation and postmodernity* (pp. 127–140). New York: Routledge.

Weiss, A. M. (Ed.). (1986). *Islamic reassertion in Pakistan: The application of Islamic laws in a modern state* (Foreword by J. L. Esposito). Syracuse, NY: Syracuse University Press.

The World Factbook. (2007). Online. Retrieved from www.cia.gov/library/publications/the-world-factbook/print/pk.html

Zein-Ed-Din, N. (1982). Removing the veil and veiling. *Women's Studies International Forum, 5*(2), 221–226.

6 Exploring the successful school leadership literature in China

Qian Haiyan, Allan Walker and Li Jiacheng

Introduction

A rich body of literature attests to the importance of school principalship to successful school improvement and student learning (e.g., Gurr, Drysdale, & Mulford, 2006; Leithwood, Day, Sammons, Harris, & Hopkins, 2006; Sanzo et al., 2011). This has stimulated further interest over the past decade in determining what successful school principals usually do (and avoid doing) (e.g., Jacobson & Day, 2007; Garza, Drysdale, Gurr, Jacobson, & Merchant, 2014; Gurr et al., 2010; Notman & Henry, 2011; Winton & Pollock, 2016). The International Successful School Principalship Project (ISSPP) alone has contributed over 100 multiple-perspective case studies of successful principals across more than 20 countries (Garza et al., 2014).

A common understanding derived from these studies is that successful school principals, no matter where they are located, tend to use the same basic leadership practices. These core practices include: (1) setting directions, (2) developing people, (3) redesigning the organisation and (4) managing the instructional program (Leithwood et al., 2006). However, successful principalship studies also suggest that there is no single model for achieving success (Day et al., 2010; Leithwood et al., 2006). Rather, there are variable pathways by which principals become successful in their leadership practices (Notman & Henry, 2011). Thus, it is somewhat meaningless to study successful principal practices without referring to the wider social and school contexts in which they operate. As Wilkinson and Bristol state, the "meaning of leadership varies depending on the societal culture in which it resides" (Chapter 1 in this book, p. 6), thus it is necessary to adopt a social-cultural lens to examine school leadership.

This review attempts to explore the landscape of successful school principalship in China. Using "successful/famous principal/principalship" as key words, we searched relevant literature published between 2000 and 2014 in core journals in China. Our comprehensive review of the literature shed light on four questions: First, how is successful school principalship defined in China? Second, how is it practised in China? Third, how are successful school principals developed in China? Fourth, how is successful school principalship shaped by the cultural and societal context in China?

This review contributes to the leadership and culture scholarship in the following ways. First, it enriches the knowledge base of international school leadership by interrogating the definition and practice of culturally situated leadership. China participated in the ISSPP project as a research site. However, the research findings were drawn from two single case studies of two principals in Shanghai (Wong, 2005, 2006). Overall there is thin knowledge base of school principalship as presented in the English literature. For example, a comprehensive literature review identifies altogether 39 journal papers and 17 book chapters published in the English language between 1998 and 2013 (Walker & Qian, 2015). Among them, the successful English-language Chinese principalship studies published in recent years usually take the form of individual case studies (e.g., Gu, 2011; Qian & Walker, 2014a; Walker & Qian, 2011). As such, there is little general understanding of who can be classified as successful principals in China, what they do and how they are developed. This review provides a broader overview of successful school principalship in China according to the literature to date.

Second, the review helps to identify whether successful Chinese principals enact any culture-specific leadership practices. China is attracting increasing international attention for its outstanding student performance in international competitions (OECD, 2011, 2013). In the new trend of looking east, China is being constituted as a new reference society in education for Western nations (Schriewer & Martinez, 2004; Sellar & Lingard, 2013). However, there is much about educational performance in China that has not been well documented. This review can help to develop a greater depth of understanding of one of the most important yet underdeveloped aspects of regional educational development – successful school principalship. This review provides a better means for helping non-Chinese administrators and scholars learn about Chinese perspectives on the topic of successful principalship and may help foster greater dialogue about how Chinese and non-Chinese perspectives can inform each other (Walker, Hu, & Qian, 2012; Militello & Berger, 2010).

Third, this review depicts the complexity of the context that shapes successful principalship. China has experienced massive social and economic transition, moving from a largely closed system to one more open to external influence. As a result, schools are no longer dominated by a unitary culture (Bush & Qiang, 2002; Yin, Lee, & Wang, 2013). Instead, different values, beliefs and symbols are represented in schools. For example, Bush and Qiang (2002) believed that a hybridity of traditional, socialist, enterprise and patriarchal aspects of culture influenced and would continue to influence the Chinese education system. This review helps to explore how the mixture of cultural components affects the definition, practice and development of successful principalship in China.

The review is organised into six sections. Following this introduction, the next section briefly reviews the international successful school principalship literature. The third section explores the traditional and contemporary contexts that frame school principalship in China. The fourth section briefly introduces the review process and the fifth presents the major review findings under the categories of the definition, practices and development of successful principalship. The final section synthesises the review findings and discusses the relationships between societal cultural contexts, Chinese principalship and international understandings of successful principalship. It also draws a number of conclusions and highlights the research that is currently missing in China.

Successful school leadership research

A major body of international successful principalship research has arisen from the ISSPP project. Launched in 2002, the project has included over 20 participating societies and produced a series of project books and a number of journal publications (Garza et al., 2014; Notman & Henry, 2011). The ISSPP project provides strong evidence of successful principalship in at least three ways. First, an abundance of research has demonstrated that successful principalship matters (e.g., Gurr et al., 2006; Jacobson & Day, 2007; Leithwood et al., 2004). School principals can make a difference to student learning; within schools their influence is second only to classroom teaching (Leithwood et al., 2004, 2006). Second, many case studies conducted under the ISSPP project have provided evidence of the now common view that successful school leadership comprises at least four core dimensions: setting direction, developing people, redesigning the organisation and managing the instructional program (Leithwood et al., 2006; Leithwood & Day, 2007). In other words, successful principals tend to have a clear sense of the direction and purpose of their schools. They are people-focused and able to understand, motivate and inspire people. They are good at designing journeys for school development, and they are instructional leaders (Garza et al., 2013). Third, successful principalship has been described as context-sensitive. Although successful principals perform similar core practices, the way they enact these practices varies (Leithwood et al., 2006; Ylimaki & Jacobson, 2011). There is a need to pay due attention to the influence of global, national and local contexts to fully understand the practices of successful principals (Garza et al., 2013; Ylimaki & Jacobson, 2011). For example, Winton and Pollock (2016) explored the meaning of success and successful leadership in Ontario, Canada in its current neoliberal times. They observed that school success under neoliberalism was becoming narrowly defined as high academic achievement in comparison with other countries on international tests. As a result, a successful school principal is one whose students demonstrate high achievement on standardised tests (Winton & Pollock, 2016).

The participation of China in the ISSPP project was reported in Wong's (2005) basic study of two principals in Shanghai that aimed to examine the unique features of the Chinese educational system and cultural context that both support and constrain principalship. His study found that the two principals were appointed as a result of meritocracy, which has a rich tradition in China. They had been in different positions and had proven records before being appointed as principals. Furthermore, both of the principals were 'top-down' managers. Although consultative processes were used to allow the participation of teachers in major decisions in their schools, they were followed more in response to the initiative of the principals. As Wong (2005) noted, this was consistent with an expectation of how schools should be managed in China.

A major implication of Wong's (2005) study is that it is necessary to establish an understanding of successful principalship in China within the broad sociopolitical and historical context in which schools operate and principals manage and lead. The next section outlines the effects of historical values and contemporary reforms on school principals.

Understanding the traditional and contemporary context in China

Through much of its long history until the late 1990s, China was a closed system largely impervious to external influences (Bush & Qiang, 2002). Since its opening-up in the last quarter of the 20th century, China has been in an ongoing process of transformation. School education in China, as a microcosm of Chinese society, has undergone massive change. There appears to be no defined path – everyone, including principals, is tentatively and even unsteadily navigating their way forward (Huang & Wiseman, 2011; Liu, Murphy, Tao, & An, 2009; Walker & Qian, 2011). Their navigation is influenced by both traditional values and new reform initiatives. A synthesis of the literature (e.g., Bush & Qiang, 2002; Fu & Tsui, 2003; Pye, 1991; Qian & Walker, 2014a, 2014b) suggests that Confucian values, Communist/socialist ideologies and Western leadership philosophies are the three major types of values affecting leadership attributes and behaviour in China.

Confucian values

The traditional aspects of Chinese culture are rooted in the pervasive influence of Confucius (Bush & Qiang, 2002). Confucian values have a lasting impact on leadership in general. For example, Chinese business leaders around the world are known to exhibit a high degree of authoritarianism, show care to subordinates and demonstrate a high level of moral character in their actions and decisions (Farh & Cheng, 2000; Pye, 1991).

Specifically, the effect of Confucian values on leadership is mainly represented by four major virtues: the class system, obedience, the doctrine of mean and *renqing* (Fu & Tsui, 2003). The class system refers to maintaining the proper ordering of positions in society. The Chinese culture reveres hierarchy and the observance of positioned ordering is made possible by obedience to authority (Child, 1994). When conflicts do occur, the doctrine of 'the mean' (avoiding extremes) is adopted as a principle to handle those (Fu & Tsui, 2003). This recognises the importance of harmony – it is important to avoid open conflicts and keep good relationships between members of the same group (Child, 1994). *Renqing* refers to being kind, benevolent and righteous or respecting the feelings of other people (Fu & Tsui, 2003).

Under the influence of Confucian values, leaders such as school principals have positional authority within a hierarchical system, but they are also expected to be responsive to the dependency needs of the followers. There is a very high moral expectation of leaders; they need to lead with empathy to win genuine obedience and submission (Qian & Walker, 2014a).

Communist/socialist ideologies

China has remained a socialist society since the establishment of the People's Republic in 1949. Schools and principals are also under the influence of socialist ideologies. Before China's opening up in the late 1970s, almost everything of significance was under state control (Bush & Qiang, 2002; Pepper, 1996). Each school had a branch party secretary who had considerable power in all aspects of school governance and ideology (Bush & Qiang, 2002).

Overt state control has loosened since the 1980s, when competitive mechanisms were introduced to China to spark innovation and growth (Harvey, 2005). Issued in 1985, the education policy known as *Reform of China's Educational Structure: Decision of the Communist Party of China Central Committee* signified the beginning of an education reform process and the gradual alignment of the education system with the newly emerging marketisation of the economy (Hawkins, 2000). This policy also stipulated that schools should gradually start to adopt a "principal responsibility system". The principal responsibility system repositioned the school principal rather than the party secretary as the key leader in the school. Today, principals are the ultimate decision-makers at schools, but the post of party secretary remains "to make sure that educational policy follows the party's direction and provides political education to faculty and students" (Si, 1993, p. 29). In spite of their different role responsibilities, both principals and party secretaries are state employees and they are first and foremost accountable to the state (Qian & Walker, 2016).

Furthermore, most principals are also Communist Party members who must abide by Party policies. For example, they must be loyal and honest to the Party, resist against corruption, promote Communist moral codes and put the collectivist interests in front of their own (Fu & Tsui, 2003). In this way, there is a strong link between Confucianism and socialism; socialism also serves to reinforce the collectivist norms of traditional Chinese culture (Bush & Qiang, 2002; Cleverley, 1991). In other words, the systemic power steered by the state exerts a strong influence on schools (Habermas, 1987; Sergiovanni, 2000).

Western leadership philosophies

A central aim of the education reforms since the mid-1980s has been the transformation of traditional examination-oriented education into quality-oriented and student-centred education to cultivate a greater number of talented, innovative personnel in Chinese society (Dooley, 2001; Pepper, 1996).

Education reforms in China have adopted Western models as references. They share "similar roots and mirror global, often neo-liberalist trends" (Walker, 2003, p. 974). The Western vocabulary of reform, such as decentralisation, school-based management, competition, performance and accountability are now commonly used in Chinese policy documents (Qian & Walker, 2013, 2016). Various leadership models, such as transformational, distributed and curriculum leadership, have been introduced into China and can be found in different studies and principals' own writings (Qian & Walker, 2013; Walker & Qian, 2011). A challenge facing Chinese educators including principals is how to translate the imported policies and concepts into school realities (Wang & Wiseman, 2012; Yin, Lee, & Wang, 2013).

For example, the major reform initiative over the past two decades has been the curriculum reform launched in 2001 (Ministry of Education, 2001). The reform aims to transform teaching and learning to foster such capacities as creativity, innovation, collaboration, self-expression, engagement, enjoyment of learning, inquiry skills, problem-solving abilities and the ability to apply knowledge in practice (Guan & Meng, 2007; Sargent, Chen, Wu, & Chen, 2011). It demands that teachers and principals shift their norms of practice to facilitate student learning. Schools today are required to develop a school-based curriculum that caters to the specific needs of the students (Guan & Meng, 2007). Consequently, school principalship has become the key to successful curriculum reform. Principals are expected to display instructional and curriculum leadership capacities.

This brief sketch of the historical and contemporary context shows that the work environment of Chinese principals is complex. Principals face a multitude of expectations and challenges in successfully leading their schools. The next section outlines the review process.

Review process

We conducted the review according to the following process:

- We reviewed the literature published in core Chinese journals between 2000 and 2014. We decided to set our starting year as 2000 because two documents issued in 1999 – *Cross-Century Quality Education Project* (The State Council, 1999) and *Decisions on Deepening Education Reform and Promoting Quality Education in an All-round Way* (CCP, 1999) – marked the beginning of the full-scale promotion of quality education in China. Major reform initiatives such as national curriculum reform were launched after 2000. Thus, studies published after 2000 might have better revealed the complexities of the work environments of contemporary principals. We restricted our search to core journals, as they were widely recognised as being of higher quality and thus enjoyed wider circulation and influence.
- We searched the core journals in the *China Academic Journal Full-Text Database (Education and Social Sciences)*. We then used the key word "successful principalship" (*chenggong xiaozhang lingdao*) to search for relevant

publications. In the Chinese context, "famous principal" (*ming xiaozhang*) is often used in the place of "successful principal" (*chenggong xiaozhang*) (as discussed below). So, we carried out another search using "famous principalship" (*ming xiaozhang lingdao*). We identified 114 potentially usable studies. We then read through the abstracts and excluded unusable materials such as news reports and papers related to university, vocational school and preschool leadership.

- This process allowed us to identify 75 usable journal articles, which we divided into two simple streams: non-empirical and empirical. The first stream included non-empirical studies whose research did not use rigorous methodologies, as defined by Western research conventions. The second comprised studies reporting empirical research that adopted qualitative, quantitative or mixed methods. Table 6.1 provides a basic breakdown of the studies reviewed in this article.
- We analysed the two research streams separately. Non-empirical publications were examined for form and focus. Empirical publications were reviewed to collect details related to the research focus, sample and major arguments of the study. Of the seven empirical studies, one focused on a famous principal development program. One was a survey study that collected teachers and principals' views about the current famous principal evaluation system. The other five studies were case studies about successful/famous principals and their qualities. For non-empirical studies, we used the following labels for further categorisation:

(1) *Prescriptions*. These studies focused mainly on telling principals what qualities they needed to have and/or what they needed to do to be successful.
(2) *Commentaries*. Drawing on observations about the commonalities of famous principals, these studies commented on what successful/famous principalship meant and what famous principals did.
(3) *Stories of famous principals*. These studies told the stories of some renowned school principals. Such stories usually included concrete examples of what these principals did. However, the data were not collected and analysed in a rigorous way.
(4) *Successful principal development*. These studies focused on the practices for developing successful/famous principals across the nation.

Table 6.1 Breakdown of studies identified and reviewed

Literature	Number
Non-empirical	68
Empirical	7
Total	75

Table 6.2 Basic breakdown of non-empirical studies

Non-empirical studies	68
Prescriptions	20
Commentaries	21
Stories of famous principals	11
Successful principal development	16

We extracted information relevant to the following question from the different categories: How is successful principalship defined, practised and developed? The next section reports the results of our review.

Successful school principalship in China

This section reports the meaning of successful school principalship in China as depicted in the Chinese literature published between 2000 and 2014. The three subsections synthesise the literature related to the definition, practices and development of successful school principalship.

Definition of successful school principalship

The literature on the meaning of successful school principalship in China fell into the category of *prescriptions* and *commentaries*. Some papers from the category of *stories of successful principals* and a couple of empirical studies also discussed the qualities that made principals successful. This section provides an overview of the relevant literature and then synthesises some of the major features of successful principalship.

Some authors tried to define successful principalship (e.g., Chen & Sun, 2011; Wang, 2000; Yang, 2004). Wang (2000) believed that a successful principal was one who made his or her school successful. More specifically, these principals made their schools more dynamic, competitive and influential. Yang (2004) recognised that in the context of China, successful principalship was often used interchangeably with famous principalship. However, although all of the famous principals could be labelled as successful, not all of the successful principals were recognised as famous principals (Yang, 2004). Chen and Sun (2011) also explored the concept of the famous principal. They found that the famous principal was a relational concept, as there were different ranks of famous principals, including famous principal titles at the national, provincial/municipal and county levels. These principals needed to demonstrate their leadership performance to achieve such titles, that is, they needed to show they could improve their schools. They also recognised that famous principals were not necessarily principals of famous schools. Principals of famous schools also needed to exhibit a recognisable performance to achieve the famous principal title.

Many of the studies discussed what qualities were needed to make a successful principal (e.g., Chen, 2013; Lan, 2009; Xiang, 2003; Zeng, 2011; Zhang,

2003). They raised very high expectations, some of them too lofty to achieve. For example, Zhang (2003) suggested that a successful principal needed to be as wise as a philosopher, as smart as an economist and as strategic as an army leader. Zeng (2011) listed necessary qualities including a strong educational ethos, a personal charisma and a capacity to improve schools.

The expectations of a successful principalship in relation to the concept of educators (*jiaoyu jia*) were explored in a number of studies (Gu, 2010; Ren, 2009). The focus on educators mainly derived from a talk delivered in 2009 by then-premier Wen Jiabao, who advocated that Chinese society needed to prepare some educators and let them run the schools (Ren, 2009). The oft-cited prototypes of educators were those who were active in the 1920s–1940s, when China was threatened by war and poverty. These famous educators such as Cai Yuanpei, Tao Xingzhi and Zhang Boling were known for their dedication to educating the next generation, sacrificing their personal lives for the public good and persistently integrating theories with practices (Gu, 2010).

Some literature, particularly those published in the 2000s, emphasised how these successful principals made school development a priority and made their families and health secondary concerns (e.g., Liu, 2006; Sun, 2005; Yan, 2003). These stories implied that it was the dedication of the principals that allowed the schools to make substantial improvements. One extreme case involved a nationally renowned successful principal from Jiangsu Province (Yan, 2003). Although her daughter was seriously sick, the principal went to work and gave a talk as scheduled. In the middle of her speech, her daughter was sent to the hospital and died. The principal did not go to the hospital until she finished her speech, and she came back to work the next day. The author cited this story to show the principal's high devotion to her job and school. This sad story reflected the impact of socialist values that emphasised selflessness, dedication to serve the ruling power and the individual's sacrifice for the collective benefits (Louie, 1984). Such reports have been rarely seen since mid-2000s with the wider societal recognition of market economy, competitive mechanisms and individual well-being (Harvey, 2005).

More practical expectations for successful principalship were raised in some literature, many of which were written by actual principals (e.g., Hu, 2011; Lv & Xia, 2010; Wu, 2004; Ying, Wang, & Hu, 2004; Zhang, 2014). Lv and Xia (2010) highlighted three major qualities of successful principals: They needed to be willing to listen to teachers' views, to spend time getting to know teachers better and to give more decision-making autonomy to middle leaders. One practical tip they suggested was that principals needed to pay personal visits to teachers' homes. In this way, they could come to understand the teachers' personal difficulties (e.g., family members' sicknesses) and provide the needed support. When teachers received care and support, they would be better motivated and committed. Wu (2004) shared similar views. He believed that four basic qualities made a successful principal. These included recognising that teachers were the most important assets of a school, helping teachers to become action researchers and being constantly reflexive and tolerant.

Empirical studies provided evidence that successful principals demonstrated the expected qualities (e.g., Wang, 2012; Xiang & Yao, 2010). For example, a study of 10 successful contemporary principals revealed some common personal and leadership qualities, such as being empathetic, persistent, just, democratic, tolerant and creative (Xiang & Yao, 2010). In this paper, many of the examples cited about these 10 successful principals were related to the ways in which principals treated teachers and students. An exemplary empathetic principal was one who used text messages and emails to maintain constant communication with each teacher and sought every opportunity to help teachers achieve professional development. These good qualities largely overlapped with the positive features of principals as perceived by teachers (Yu, 2011). Yu (2011) reflected on several principals he worked with and believed that a successful principal was one who could recognise teachers' strengths and feedback, approach teacher evaluations and promotions fairly and make personal gains secondary to the collective interest.

The synthesis of the literature suggests the following preliminary claims about defining successful principalship in China:

- The concepts of "successful principal" and "famous principal" are interwoven in China. A common belief is that famous principals are also successful. The "famous principal" designation is a form of government recognition and a hierarchical title.
- Successful Chinese principals are portrayed in the literature as masterful, almost omniscient leaders with comprehensive expertise who can deal with all of the issues essential to school development. The successful principal literature tends to depict them as heroic and charismatic leaders. They are subjected to high expectations.
- Due to the national call to prepare more educators (*jiaoyu jia*), successful principals are expected to be future educators. Successful principals thus need to learn from the late educators who devoted their lives to education.
- Successful principals are expected to demonstrate tangible and visible school improvements. The indicators of principal performances can be in the form of student academic results, number and quality of school-based curriculum or the number of teachers achieving higher ranks.
- The way in which principals approach their relationships with teachers seems to be a key criterion of successful principalship. Successful principals who respect teachers and provide them with learning opportunities are trustworthy leaders.

Successful principalship practices

Successful principalship practices were mainly drawn from *commentaries* and *stories*. Cheng (2000) commented that there were notable differences in the way Chinese and Western researchers conceptualised research (*yanjiu*). Most studies conducted in China were aimed to arrive at some definitive conclusions or findings that could inform policy recommendations. Thus, both *commentaries* and *stories* could not be classified as empirical studies. For our purposes, however, the authors of the studies often based their opinions on in-depth observation and analysis, and therefore we could not deny the wisdom embedded in these non-empirical pieces (Walker, Hu, & Qian, 2012). This section discusses some of the common practices of successful principals as depicted in the literature.

Many successful principals designed and planned the direction of their school's development (e.g., Bai, 2014; Liu, 2006; Sun, 2005; Yan, 2003). In the context of China, many principals believed that a school needed to have some distinguishing features or uniqueness (*tese*). Part of the principal's job was to help identify and maximise this uniqueness. Successful principals were highly strategic in terms of identifying and selecting school uniqueness (*tese*); they could adjust their leadership focus at the different development stages of their schools (e.g., Bai, 2014; Liu, 2006; Sun, 2005; Xie, 2013; Yan, 2003). For example, Xie (2013) depicted the stories of a special-class (*teji*) principal, Principal Cai, in Shanghai. Principal Cai started his principalship at his school in 1992. At the time, the school was a poor rural school with a high turnover rate and low teacher morale. Principal Cai believed his primary job was to formalise school policies and let all of the teachers fully understand their job responsibilities. This stage took four years. In 1996, the principal believed that his teachers were better committed, although they lacked some confidence in the future of the school. At this stage, Principal Cai believed that the school would not be activated without its distinguishing uniqueness (*tese*). He then organised a school-wide discussion and encouraged teachers to share their views on the school's uniqueness. Different subject panels initiated their own plans. For example, the physical education panel proposed forming a boys' basketball team. The school then helped to invite famous basketball players to serve as coaches. Indicators of the school's uniqueness also extended to programs such as information technology, dancing and literature. In 2001, local governments recognised the school as exhibiting an artistic uniqueness. Principal Cai further recognised that only a small number of students could benefit from activities such as football and dancing. The school thus set up a new goal of promoting the all-round development of each student. Principal Cai adjusted his leadership strategy, applying a new focus on school-based research. The school formulated six action research project teams, and each teacher was encouraged to join one team. The purpose of the research was to improve the school curriculum to promote the all-round development of students.

Developing teachers was also a major leadership strategy adopted by many successful principals. Chinese principals engaged in providing various platforms for teacher development (e.g., Cao, 2003; Fan, 2014; Su, 2014). For example, Fan (2014) wrote that his school built a culture in which each teacher could make a difference. The school would send teachers to attend teaching competitions at different levels. Some schools adopted different strategies for motivating teachers. For example, Cao's (2003) school selected its "Ten Best Teachers" each year and the evaluation was based on the teachers' classroom teaching performance. The school also gave higher teacher rankings to those who excelled in school-based research. Developing teachers also involved caring for and supporting teachers.

Liu (2006) depicted a principal of Dulangkou School, a famous school in China. The principal adopted many strategies to turn the school around, such as showing concern for its teachers' personal lives. For example, the principal tried to find good doctors for sick teachers. When the teachers moved into new houses, the school principal and colleagues helped by moving furniture. When the teachers' children were admitted to university, the principal went to their homes to send personal congratulations. When the principal received awards for his excellent principalship, he donated all of the money to buy gifts for the teachers.

Successful Chinese principals prioritised pedagogy and curriculum. Many successful principals were promoted from successful teachers. One study (Ying, Hu, & Xia, 2005) provided some empirical data about the career tracks of successful principals. Of the 17 interviewed successful principals, 13 also had special-class teacher rankings and highly recognised expertise in their own subject areas. Most of the principals continued to closely monitor classroom teaching practices (e.g., Cao, 2003; Qian, 2014; Sun, 2005). Class observation was a routine job of most principals, who also discussed curriculum design with teachers. In recent years, more and more schools have emphasised school-based research (e.g., Fan, 2014; Su, 2014). It is common practice for a principal to lead a school-wide research project and different subject panels or year groups focused on a subtopic. As a result, many teachers have developed an awareness of the value in collecting data to inform curriculum decisions. For example, Su (2014) wrote about one research project conducted at her school. The project was designed to explore how to integrate Chinese textbooks with students' after-school reading. When teachers planned the research, they distributed questionnaires to students to gather an understanding of the reading habits of students.

Most successful principals advocated and practised distributing and sharing power with teachers. They continually experimented with new organisational structures and initiated new change strategies to improve their schools (e.g., Liu, 2014; Su, 2014; Zhang, 2014). For example, Liu (2014) discussed how her school, a famous primary school in Beijing, had piloted an executive principal policy. It was a big school with three campuses, and most of its middle leaders focused only on their own specific job responsibilities. To expand the middle leaders' horizon, the principal initiated this new policy and invited each middle leader to take a turn as executive principal at each campus. Each executive principal needed to write a reflective journal at the end of the day. Under this new policy, middle leaders acquired a stronger sense of ownership of the school. Zhang (2014) reported that one school changed its practice of running weekly teacher gatherings. The principal assigned five minutes at the meeting to invite one teacher to share his or her recent discoveries with his or her colleagues. Teachers could choose to report anything they considered meaningful. This small change boosted teachers' sense of belonging to the school.

These depictions of principalship practices suggest the following claims about what successful principals usually do in China:

- Successful principals in China have similar practices as depicted in the international successful principalship literature (Leithwood et al., 2006). These

practices include setting directions and planning school development, coordinating teaching practices and curricula, developing teachers and redesigning school organisations.
- Some principals become successful because they have turned around a high-need school. Successful principals can make use of the resources they have to make a difference even when they work at poorly resourced schools.
- Monitoring and improving teaching are priorities of a principal's job. Most successful principals are promoted from successful teachers and thus tend to spend a lot of time on instruction and curriculum. They share a lot of common qualities as those depicted in instructional leadership literature (e.g., Hallinger, 2003; Hallinger & Murphy, 1985). That is, successful Chinese principals are hands-on in teaching and instructional matters.
- Successful principals in China emphasise building good relationships with teachers. Chinese principals develop teachers by providing them with learning opportunities and taking care of their personal and family needs.

Successful principal development

This section reviews the 16 studies that focused on successful principal development. The dominant terms adopted in these studies were "developing famous principals" (*mingxiaozhang*) and "people's educators" (*renmin jiaoyujia*). We report the review results under these themes: who was developed, who provided development programs and the content covered in those development programs. We end this section with a few claims about successful principal development in China.

The general message flowing from the studies was that successful principal development was reserved for a few outstanding principals who had the potential to be future famous principals or educators (e.g., Hu & Ji, 2014; Lu, 2009; Ying & He, 2005; Zhang & Cheng, 2014). Thus, such development was elitist; attending such development programs meant receiving external recognition from the governments. For example, in Beijing it was made clear that the minimum eligibility requirements for famous principal development were achievements in the post of principalship along with the accrual of some fame in Beijing and other parts of China (Hu & Ji, 2014). Given such expectations, the number of participants was limited. For example, Jiangsu Province initiated its "People's Educator Development Project" in 2009 to prepare 200 people's educators by 2020 across the whole province (Shen, 2014). Some people (e.g., Wang, 2003) voiced the criticism that the highly selective procedures would favour principals from famous schools. No data served to indicate the ratio of principals from famous schools in the famous principal development programs. However, participation in such programs tended to bring principals better career opportunities. For example, of those who received the special-class (*teji*) principal title in Shanghai in 2008, 40% had attended the famous principalship development programs (Zhang & Cheng, 2014).

The studies showed a diversified combination of providers of successful principal development programs and suggested the presence of governments in one way or another in such programs. In other words, the governments initiated most of the programs, but commissioned different functional bodies to implement them. There were two main types of providers. One was organised by educational institutions and particularly the provincial-level Institute of Education. For example, Zhejiang Institute of Education was responsible for successful principal development in Zhejiang Province (Lu, 2009). Beijing Institute of Education organised famous principal development in Beijing during 2011–2013 (Hu & Ji, 2014). In the other type of development programs, renowned senior principals were invited to organise and supervise such programs. For example, Shanghai initiated its famous principal development plan in 2006. Eight development centres were established and eight senior principals were invited to be the hosts (*zhuchiren*) of the centres (Zhang & Cheng, 2014). Each hosting principal supervised no more than 20 principals selected from across the municipality. The participants and supervisor thus formed a community of practices and learned together.

The different development programs had certain common features. First, the programs recognised that the purpose of learning was to elicit change (*yixue cubian*) (Ying & He, 2005). Thus, most of the programs were practice-oriented. In Ying and He's (2005) words, famous principal development programs needed to prepare reflexive practitioners. Most of the programs included lectures, project learning and school visits. Second, most of the programs recognised that university researchers and experienced practitioners played equally important roles in developing successful principals (e.g., Lin, 2007; Wang, 2010; Zhao, 2013). Some of the programs (Wang, 2010) identified a double-supervisor system, in which each participant had one supervisor from an educational institution and one supervisor who was a well-known principal. The participants could visit and learn at their supervisor's school and the supervisor also visited their school and provided them with feedback (Zhang & Cheng, 2014; Zhao, 2013). Third, most of the programs required participants to complete an action research project (e.g., Hu & Ji, 2014; Lu, 2009). For example, Shao's (2008) program was designed to be task-oriented. Principals came with a particular school development problem that they needed to solve by the end of the learning process. In the famous principal development program organised in Beijing, the participants were grouped under three research themes: internationalisation of education, school structural change and the cultivation of student self-development competence (Hu & Ji, 2014). Principals needed to carry out relevant action research under the theme of their choice.

We make the following preliminary claims about successful principal development in China:

- Being included in successful principal development programs is a sign of high recognition from the governments. The famous principal development in China is elitist.
- Although there are more providers involved in principal development programs, such programs are organised and implemented in a top-down manner.
- There is a trend of involving senior principals in such programs. The wisdom of senior famous principals is widely recognised.

- Most programs are not purely lecture-based. Instead, concepts such as situated learning, action research and community of practices have been widely shared and embodied in successful principal development programs in China.

Understanding successful principalship in China: Implications

This review focuses on the literature related to successful school principalship published in Chinese core journals between 2000 and 2014. The review identifies 75 usable studies, only seven of which were empirical in nature. The small number of empirical studies we identified indicates that Chinese 'research' conventions remain dominant. The purpose of most studies in China was *prescriptive* rather than *descriptive* (Cheng, 2000). Although they did not conform to international research conventions, the majority of the non-empirical studies helped to sketch a picture of who successful principals are, what they do and how to prepare them. The results of this review have a number of important implications for our understanding of the effects of the three major types of values in China, including Confucian values, Communist/socialist ideologies and Western leadership theories.

We can delineate the effects of Confucian values in at least three ways. First, China as a society respects hierarchy, and any differentiation of rankings and titles is taken for granted (Child, 1994). Thus, it seems to be a common practice across China that principals are classified as famous and non-famous principals. Famous principals are further ranked into national-, provincial- and county-level title categories. Principals with different titles tend to have varied learning opportunities. With few exceptions (e.g., Wang, 2003), most of the researchers who write about successful principalship in China do not feel the need to review such a system. Second, aligned with traditional Confucian expectations of high leader morality, successful principals in China are expected to be role models in various ways. For example, they are expected to prioritise the collective interest of the whole school rather than their personal gains. They are also not expected to seek any personal benefits. Third, leaders in China are traditionally expected to manifest paternalistic concern for their followers (Pye, 1991). Successful principals also tend to adopt a paternalistic role and act with compassion for teachers. This care for teachers extends to both their professional and personal lives.

Communist/socialist ideologies are not overt present in the successful principalship literature. There is no explicit discussion about the political expectations of principals. However, the governments play an important role in successful principal selection, promotion and development. The central levels (national, provincial/municipal, district/county) are similarly strong and directive (Qian & Walker, 2014b). For example, the "famous principal" title must be formally accredited by the governments, and the selection criteria are formulated by local and national educational authorities. Without being formally recognised as famous principals, most of these principals are unlikely to participate in any successful principal development program. Thus, school principals are mainly held accountable to the authority of local governments.

Western leadership theories shape the way in which successful principals deal with contemporary reform initiatives. Successful Chinese principals display features of instructional leadership (Hallinger & Murphy, 1985; Hallinger & Heck, 1996). For example, many studies have shown that Chinese principals are hands-on and deeply involved in curriculum design and classroom teaching. Most successful principals are usually promoted from the ranks of excellent teachers, and this grants principals the expert role when they discuss instructional matters with teachers (Qian & Walker, 2013). Successful Chinese principals also seem to embrace and embody leadership concepts such as transformational and distributed leadership. They understand that it is important to share their decision-making ability with middle leaders and to provide individualised support and intellectual stimulation to teachers.

Thus, successful school principals in China are those who are externally selected and ranked by local governments, who are guided by traditional values and who emphasise improving schools by enhancing teaching and pedagogy and developing teachers. Successful school principals in China attach huge importance to their own professional expertise in pedagogy and/or subject knowledge. Principals believe that this professional expertise legitimises their authority in leading and guiding teachers. They also shoulder the responsibility of solving problems for teachers, regardless of whether those teachers encounter problems at school or at home.

Despite this preliminary understanding of successful principalship in China, there is a need for more empirical studies to build a more in-depth understanding. The following questions are worthy of further exploration:

- How has famous principalship policy been initiated, implemented and changed?
- How do Chinese principals manage changes modelled on Western education systems?
- What practices and beliefs have Chinese principals inherited from the traditional Chinese education system? How do traditional beliefs clash or cohere with the demands of modern reforms?
- How do successful principals allocate their time and prioritise their daily tasks?
- What are the relationships between principals who attend development programs and the senior principals who are assigned to be their supervisors?
- How do successful principals lead school-based research, and how do they carry out action research projects as part of the principalship development program requirements?

Note

The authors would like to acknowledge the support by the Research Grants Council of Hong Kong through an Early Career Scheme (ECS 28402814).

References

Bai, C. D. (2014). 从学校特色项目到学校文化特色项目的建设 [From building school uniqueness to developing a unique school culture]. *教育科学研究 (Education Science Research)*, 5, 18–19.

Bush, T., & Qiang, H. Y. (2002). Leadership and culture in the Chinese education. In A. A. Walker & C. Dimmock (Eds.), *School leadership and administration: Adopting a cultural perspective* (pp. 173–186). New York: Routledge.

Cao, P. (2003). 优秀校长的三重角色 [Three roles of the outstanding principals]. *人民教育 (People's Education)*, 18, 19–20.

Chen, S. B. (2011). 对话与融合：基础教育国际化的认识与实践 [Dialogue and integration: Thoughts on the internationalisation of the basic education]. *中小学管理 (Secondary and Elementary School Administration)*, 8, 28–30.

Chen, Y. K. (2006). 关于高层次人才培养的思考 [Thoughts on high-level talents cultivation]. *教育发展研究 (Research in Educational Development)*, 5, 10001.

Chen, Y. K. (2013). 新时期卓越校长的追求 [Pursues of the excellent principals in new era]. *人民教育 (People's Education)*, 17, 13–15.

Chen, Y. K., & Sun, H. J. (2011). 浅谈中小学'名校长'的角色内涵 [The role meanings of 'famous principals']. *教育探索 (Education Exploration)*, 9, 9–10.

Cheng, K. M. (2000). Understanding basic education policies in China: An ethnographic approach. In J. Liu, H. A. Ross, & D. P. Kelly (Eds.), *The ethnographic eye: An interpretive study of education in China* (pp. 29–50). New York: Falmer Press.

Child, J. (1994). *Management in China during the age of reform*. Cambridge: Cambridge University Press.

Chinese Communist Party (CCP). (1999). *Decisions on deepening education reform and promoting quality education in an all-round way*. Retrieved from http://old.moe.gov.cn/publicfiles/business/htmlfiles/moe/moe_177/200407/2478.html

Cleverley, J. (1991). *The schooling in China*. Sydney: Allen and Unwin.

Fan, S. H. (2014). 校长的教师领导力提升途径 [Channels for principals to improve their teacher development competence]. *中小学管理 (Secondary and Elementary School Administration)*, 8, 32–33.

Farh, J. L., & Cheng, B. S. (2000). A cultural analysis of paternalistic leadership in Chinese organisations. In L. A. P. Gosling & L. Y. C. Lim (Eds.), *The Chinese in Southeast Asia: Identify, culture and politics* (pp. 214–230). Singapore: Maruzen Asian.

Fei, Y. L. (2003). 好校长要有问题意识 [Good principals should have problem awareness]. *人民教育 (People's Education)*, 22, 22.

Fu, P. P., & Tsui, A. S. (2003). Utilizing printed media to understand desired leadership attributes in the People's Republic of China. *Asia Pacific Journal of Management*, 20, 423–446.

Garza, E., Drysdale, L., Gurr, D., Jacobson, S., & Merchant, B. (2014). Leadership for school success: Lessons from effective principals. *International Journal of Educational Management*, 28(7), 798–811.

Gu, M. Y. (2010). 希望更多的校长和教师成为教育家 [Hoping more principals and teachers to be the educationist]. *人民教育 (People's Education)*, Z2, 58–60.

Gu, Q. (2011). Leaders who build and sustain passion for learning: Capacity building in practice. In T. Townsend & J. MacBeath (Eds.), *International handbook of leadership for learning* (pp. 991–1010). The Netherlands: Springer.

Guan, Q., & Meng, W. (2007). China's new national curriculum reform: Innovation, challenges and strategies. *Frontiers of Education in China*, 2(4), 579–604.

Gurr, D., Drysdale, L., & Goode, H. (2010). Successful school leadership in Australia: A research agenda. *International Journal of Learning*, 17(4), 113–129.

Gurr, D., Drysdale, L., & Mulford, B. (2006). Models of successful principal leadership. *School Leadership and Management*, 26(4), 371–395.

Hallinger, P. (2003). Leading educational change: Reflections on the practice of instructional and transformational leadership. *Cambridge Journal of Education*, 33(3), 329–351.

Hallinger, P., & Heck, R. H. (1996). Reassessing the principal's role in school effectiveness: A review of empirical research, 1980–1995. *Educational Administration Quarterly*, 32(1), 5–44.

Hallinger, P., & Murphy, J. (1985). Assessing the instructional management behavior of principals. *The Elementary School Journal*, 86(2), 217–247.

Harvey, D. (2005). *A brief history of neoliberalism*. New York: Oxford University Press.

Hawkins, J. N. (2000). Centralisation, decentralisation, recentralisation: Educational reform in China. *Journal of Educational Administration*, 38(5), 442–455.

He, C. J., Li, Y. H., & Ji, W. L. (2005). 创新德育理念，增强德育实效 [Innovate the moral educational idea to inforce the effectiveness]. *中国职业技术教育 (Chinese Vocational and Technical Education)*, 1, 14–17.

Hu, B. H. (2011). 成功校长必备的几种素质 [Some qualities what successful principals must have]. *教学与管理：小学版 (Journal of Teaching and Management – Elementary School Edition)*, 3, 6–8.

Hu, R. K., & Ji, P. (2014). 名校长工作室：在研究'重要教育问题'中成就名校长 [Famous principals workshop: To be a famous principal by researching 'important educational issues']. *中小学管理 (Secondary and Elementary School Administration)*, 4, 35–36.

Huang, J. F. (2008). 现代校长的职业能力与专业智慧 [The occupational abilities and professional wisdom of principals in contemporary]. *中国教育学刊 (Journal of The Chinese Society of Education)*, 6, 27–30.

Huang, J. F. (2011). '好校长'：有情有能亦有识 ['Good principal': Full of love, abilities and sagacity]. *中小学管理 (Secondary and Elementary School Administration)*, 7, 40–41.

Jacobson, S., & Day, C. (2007). The International Successful School Principalship Project (ISSPP): An overview of the project, the case studies and their contexts. *International Studies in Educational Administration*, 35(3), 3–10.

Ji, P. (2009). 在'特别'处研究优秀校长的领导力 [To research the outstanding principals leadership from the 'specialties']. *中小学管理 (Secondary and Elementary School Administration)*, 7, 4–10.

Jiang, D. Q. (2008). 新时期校长的责任 [The responsibilities of principals in new era]. *教育理论与实践 (Theory and Practice of Education)*, 4, 22.

Jiang, M. Y. (2006). 在学校变革实践中实现校长的专业成长 [To develop principals' profession in school change]. *上海教育研究 (Shanghai Educational Research)*, 3, 76–77.

Jiang, X. L. (2010). 论中小学校长学习力的提升 [On the learning ability development of principals]. *教育与管理：理论版 (Journal of Teaching and Management-Theory Edition)*, 4, 17–19.

Jin, Y. C., & Li, G. S. (2014). 以合作实现资源整合，以联动促进文化互动 [On the value, mechanism and effect of cooperative training of principals in primary and middle schools in Yangtze Delta to achieve resource integration through cooperation and cultural interaction through collaboration]. 教育发展研究 (Research in Educational Development), 6, 40–44.

Lan, Z. J. (2009). 优秀校长应具备三种智慧 [Three kinds of wisdom for outstanding principals]. 中小学管理 (Secondary and Elementary School Administration), 2, 1.

Leithwood, K., Day, C., Sammons, P., Harris, A., & Hopkins, D. (2006). Successful school leadership: What it is and how it influences student learning (Research Report No. 800). United Kingdom: Department for Education.

Leithwood, K., Louis, K., Anderson, S., & Wahlstrom, K. (2004). How leadership influences student learning. New York: Wallace Foundation.

Li, C. S., & Zhong, Z. R. (2003). 中学优秀校长的培训策略 [The strategies of the outstanding principals training]. 中小学管理 (Secondary and Elementary School Administration), 7, 19–20.

Li, G. S. (2011). 让教育家讲述自己的故事 [Let the educationists narrate their stories: Field research on famous teachers and principals in Zhejiang China]. 中小学管理 (Secondary and Elementary School Administration), 5, 4–7.

Li, J. (2002). 发挥教育科研功能，大力推进素质教育. [To function the educational research to invigorate the quality-oriented education]. 现代教育科学 (Modern Education Science), 6(1–2), 11.

Li, Z. X. (2012). 对校长角色的思考与认识 [Thoughts on the roles of the principal]. 中国教育学刊 (Journal of The Chinese Society of Education), S2, 303–304.

Liang, G. L., & Ma, K. (2013). 也谈'道德领导' [Another thought on the 'Moral Leadership']. 教学与领导 (Journal of Teaching and Management), 1, 33–35.

Lin, P. (2007). 为名校长工作室的开放性叫好 [Applaud for the opening of the famous principals' workshop]. 中小学管理 (Secondary and Elementary School Administration), 8, 26.

Liu, C. (2014). 执行校长制度：中层干部成长的助推剂 [Executive principal system: Promoting the development of mid-level leaders]. 中小学管理 (Secondary and Elementary School Administration), 3, 9–10.

Liu, J. L. (2006). '三个一'：杜郎口中学良性发展的关键 ['Sangeyi': The key of the development of Dulangkou Middle School]. 当代教育科学 (Contemporary Educational Science), 1, 17–21.

Liu, Z. H., & Du, Y. C. (2011). 国际成功校长项目 [The international successful school principal project – the cross-national comparisons on successful school principals between China, the USA and Australia]. 外国教育研究 (Studies in Foreign Education), 38(6), 66–72.

Louie, K. (1984). Salvaging Confucian education (1949–1983). Comparative Education, 20(1), 27–38.

Lu, L. Y. (2009). 名师名校长培训体系的构想与实践 (The visualisation and practice of the training system for famous teachers and headmasters). 教育研究 (Education Research), 2, 103–107.

Lv, Y., & Xia, C. (2010). 怎样成为一个好校长？ [How to be a good principal?]. 教学与管理：小学版 (Journal of Teaching and Management – Elementary School Edition), 4, 8–9.

Militello, M., & Berger, J. B. (2010). Understanding educational leadership in Northwest China. International Journal of Leadership in Education: Theory and Practice, 13(2), 185–202.

Ministry of Education. (2001). *The curriculum reform guidelines for the nine-year compulsory education* (trial version). Beijing: Beijing Normal University Press.

Notman, R., & Henry, D. A. (2011). Building and sustaining successful school leadership in New Zealand. *Leadership and Policy in Schools*, *10*(4), 375–394.

OECD. (2011). *Lessons from PISA for the United States, strong performers and successful reformers in education*. OECD Publishing. Retrieved from http://dx.doi.org/10.1787/9789264096660-en

OECD. (2013). *PISA 2012 results in focus: What 15-year-olds know and what they can do with what they know*. Paris: OECD Publishing. Retrieved from www.oecd.org/pisa/keyfindings/pisa-2012-results-overview.pdf

Pepper, S. (1996). *Radicalism and education reform in 20th century China*. Cambridge: Cambridge University Press.

Pye, L. W. (1991). The new Asian capitalism: A political portrait. In P. L. Berger & H. H. Hsiao (Eds.), *In search of an East Asian development model*. New Brunswick, NJ: Transaction.

Qian, H. Y., & Walker, A. (2013). How principals promote and understand teacher development under curriculum reform in China. *Asia-Pacific Journal of Teacher Education*, *41*(3), 304–315.

Qian, H. Y., & Walker, A. (2014a). Leading with empathy. In C. M. Branson & S. J. Gross (Eds.), *Handbook of ethical educational leadership* (pp. 112–127). London: Routledge.

Qian, H. Y., & Walker, A. (2014b). Principalship in China: Emerging propositions. *Leading and Managing*, *20*(2), 60–74.

Qian, H. Y., & Walker, A. (2016). Leading as state agents: Narratives of Shanghai principals. In S. Clarke & T. O'Donoghue (Eds.), *School leadership in diverse contexts* (pp. 153–172). London: Routledge.

Qian, Y. H. (2014). 捍卫童年 [Defending childhood]. 人民教育 *(People's Education)*, *14*, 29–31.

Ren, Y. Y. (2009). 校长如何成长为教育家 [How principals develop into the educationist]. 人民教育 *(People's Education)*, *21*, 6–7.

Rui, P. N. (2008). 校长德育领导力和执行力初探 [Exploring principal moral leadership]. 上海教育科研 *(Shanghai Educational Research)*, *11*, 63–64.

Sanzo, K., Sherman, W. H., & Clayton, J. (2011). Leadership practices of successful middle school principals. *Journal of Educational Administration*, *49*(1), 31–45.

Sargent, T., Chen, M. Y., Wu, Y. J., & Chen, C. T. (2011). Wearing new shoes to walk the old road: The negotiation of opposing imperatives in high school new curriculum classes in China. In T. D. Huang & A. W. Wiseman (Eds.), *The impact and transformation of education policy in China* (pp. 79–98). Bingley: Emerald.

Schriewer, J., & Martinez, C. (2004). Constructions of internationality in education. In G. Steiner-Khamsi (Ed.), *The global politics of educational borrowing and lending* (pp. 29–53). New York: Teachers College.

Sellar, S., & Lingard, B. (2013). Looking East: Shanghai, PISA 2009 and the reconstitution of reference societies in the global policy field. *Comparative Education*, *49*(4), 464–485.

Shao, Y. F. (2008). '任务驱动式'名校长培训的实践探索 [The exploration of the 'task-oriented' training for famous principals]. 继续教育 *(Continuing Education)*, *10*, 50–52.

Shen, J. (2014). 开创教育家办学新时代 [To open up a new era of running school by educationist]. 人民教育 *(People's Education)*, *14*, 5–8.

The State Council. (1999). *Cross-century quality education project.* Retrieved from http://old.moe.gov.cn/publicfiles/business/htmlfiles/moe/moe_177/200407/2487.html

Su, L. P. (2014). 基于绿色指标的实证教研探析 [An exploration of empirical school-based research on green indicators]. 上海教育科研 *(Shanghai Educational Research), 8,* 63–66.

Sun, J. X. (2005). 办成功学校，做成功校长 [Run a successful school, be a successful principal: Five inspirations of running school by the principal Zhang Mingxia in Zhejiang China]. 中小学管理 *(Secondary and Elementary School Administration), 5,* 55–57.

Sun, J. X., & Wang, Y. P. (2010). 校长应该做价值引导的旗帜 [Principals should be the leader of educational values]. 教学与管理：小学版 *(Journal of Teaching and Management – Elementary School Edition), 6,* 6–8.

Tao, J. X., & Li, J. (2012). 用文化开启教师发展的生命之门 [To open the door of teacher development with culture]. 人民教育 *(People's Education), 17,* 56–60.

Tao, X. P. (2009). 普拉哈拉德公式 (C. K. Prahalad Formula). 中小学管理 *(Secondary and Elementary School Administration), 7,* 59.

Tian, A. L. (2012). 校长教育思想基本特征及形成路径分析 – 以几位苏浙沪名校长办学思想为例 [The essential features and formative path of the educational ideas of famous principals: The educational ideas of certain famous principals in Jiangsu, Zhejiang and Shanghai China]. 中国教育学刊 *(Journal of the Chinese Society of Education), 2,* 56–59.

Tian, H. Z. (2010). 基于资本积累的中学优秀校长成长 [The development of outstanding secondary school principals based on the Capital Accumulation]. 教育科学研究 *(Education Science Research), 12,* 37–40.

Tian, H. Z., & Meng, F. H. (2012). 中小学校长如何成为优秀管理者 [How the principals to be good administrators]. 首都师范大学学报 (社会科学版) *(Journal of Capital Normal University (Social Science Edition)), 6,* 126–131.

Tong, H. B., Wang, H., Zhao, S. X., & Fang, Y. (2013). 校长和教师眼中的名校长评价比较 [The comparative study on the famous principal appraisement models of principals and teachers]. 中小学管理 *(Secondary and Elementary School Administration), 10,* 37–39.

Walker, A. (2003). School leadership and management. In J. Keeves & R. Watanabe (Eds.), *The international handbook of educational research in Asia-Pacific region* (pp. 973–986). Dordrecht, The Netherlands: Kluwer Press.

Walker, A., Hu, R. K., & Qian, H. Y. (2012). Principal leadership in China: An initial review. *School Effectiveness and School Improvement: An International Journal of Research, Policy and Practice, 23*(4), 369–399.

Walker, A., & Qian, H. Y. (2011). Successful school leadership in China. In C. Day (Ed.), *The Routledge international handbook of teacher and school development* (pp. 446–457). London: Routledge.

Walker, A., & Qian, H. Y. (2015). Review of research on school principal leadership in mainland China, 1998–2013: Continuity and change. *Journal of Educational Administration, 53*(4), 467–491.

Wang, H. C. (2000). 论成功型校长的素质特征与要求 [The quality features and requirements for successful principals]. 现代教育论丛 *(The Modern Education Journal), 2,* 11–17.

Wang, H. X. (2012). 中小学名校长教育思想形成的影响因素分析 [Factors influencing the formation of educational thought of distinguished principals in primary and secondary Schools: An analysis based on grounded theory]. 教育发展研究 *(Research in Educational Development)*, *22*, 70–74.

Wang, P. (2010). 名师名校长培训中'双导师制'的探索与研究 [The exploration and research on the 'Dual Tutorial' in the training for famous teachers and principals]. 现代教育科学 （普教研究） *(Modern Education Science (General Education Research))*, *1*, 41–42.

Wang, Q. W. (2003). '名校长工程'实施中的误区及对策 [The misunderstandings and countermeasures in the 'Famous Principals Project' implementing]. 中小学管理 *(Secondary and Elementary School Administration)*, *11*, 25–26.

Wang, S. Y. (2007). 打造学校品牌 构建和谐教育 [Build school brand and construct harmonious education]. 中小学教师培训 *(The Inservice Education and Training of School Teachers)*, *5*, F0003.

Winton, S., & Pollock, K. (2016). Meanings of success and successful leadership in Ontario, Canada, in neo-liberal times. *Journal of Educational Administration and History*, *48*(1), 19–34.

Wong, K. C. (2005). Conditions and practices of successful principalship in Shanghai. *Journal of Educational Administration*, *43*(6), 552–562.

Wong, K. C. (2006). Contextual impact on educational management and leadership: A case of Chinese education. *Journal of Educational Change*, *7*(1), 77–89.

Wu, J. G. (2004). 成功校长必须做到'四要' [Four necessary requirements for being the successful principal]. 江西教育科研 *(Jiangxi Educational Research)*, *6*, 21–22.

Xia, Y. Z., & Zhao, Z. M. (2012). 名校长工作室：造就优秀校长的孵化器. [Famous principals workshop: An incubator for outstanding principals]. 当代教育科学 *(Modern Education Science)*, *22*, 49–51.

Xiang, H. Z. (2003). 现代校长的思维方式 [The principals' way of thinking in contemporary]. 全球教育展望 *(Global Education)*, *3*, 13–15, 29.

Xiang, H. Z., & Yao, X. H. (2010). 我国著名中小学校长人格特征的实证分析 [The empirical analysis of personal traits of the famous principals in China]. 中小学管理 *(Secondary and Elementary School Administration)*, *6*, 33–34.

Xie, F. (2013). 仁智勇：感悟一位农村特级教师校长的独特魅力 [Benevolence, wisdom and courage: The unique charm of a special-class principal in a rural school]. 中小学管理 *(Secondary and Elementary School Administration)*, *3*, 54–56.

Xie, M. D., & Li, J. (2010). 名校长与名书记共奏和谐乐章 – 武汉市钟家村小学校长危汉桥与书记陈昌华纪事 [The harmony between a famous principal and Party secretary: The cooperation between a principal Wei Hanqiao and a Party secretary Chen Changhua in a rural school]. 学校党建与思想教育 *(School Party Building and Ideological Education)*, *15*, 11–14.

Xu, J. Z. (2007). 校长要学会放权 [Principals should learn to decentralisation]. 基础教育 *(Journal of Schooling Studies)*, *3*, 22–23.

Xu, W. H. (2008). 办学思想在实践中生成 [Educational ideas formulate in the practice]. 教学与管理：小学版 *(Journal of Teaching and Management – Elementary School Edition)*, *8*, 8–10.

Yan, J. (2003). 缔造精神家园：江苏省名校长吴辰专访 [Create a spiritual home: The interview of Wu Chen who a famous principal in Jiangsu China]. 教育发展研究 *(Research in Educational Development)*, *9*, 61–63.

Yang, S. Z. (2004). 如何成为一名成功校长 [How to be a successful principal]. 教育理论与实践 *(Theory and Practice of Education)*, *24*(1), 56–59.

Ying, J. F., & He, J. (2005). 构建促进名校长成长的培训模式研究 [The construction of training models for famous principals' development]. 教育发展研究 *(Research in Educational Development)*, *3*, 77–80.

Ying, J. F., Hu, L., & Xia, J. F. (2005). 名校长成长过程与要素分析 [The analysis of the development process and factors of the famous principals]. 教育发展研究 *(Research in Educational Development), 1,* 22–25.

Ying, J. F., Wang, H. B., & Hu, L. (2004). 名校长素质特征的研究 [Research on the qualities of famous principals]. 教育发展研究 *(Research in Educational Development), 12,* 13–18.

Ylimaki, R. M., & Jacobson, S. L. (Eds.). (2011). *US and cross-national policies, practices, and preparation: Implications for successful instructional leadership, organisational learning, and culturally responsive practices.* New York: Springer.

Yu, Z. W. (2011). 教师心目中的好校长 [Traits of a good principal in teacher's mind]. 中小学管理 *(Secondary and Elementary School Administration), 1,* 52–53.

Zeng, J. F. (2011). 名校长成长的内在要素探析 [The internal qualities of famous principals]. 教育学术月刊 *(Education Research Monthly), 12,* 11–13.

Zhang, F. Q. (2008). 好校长应该做核心还是做服务 [Should good principals to be a core or server?]. 教育理论与实践 *(Theory and Practice of Education), 4,* 18.

Zhang, J. M. (2014). 试论现代优秀校长应具备的专业能力 [The professional abilities that contemporary outstanding principals should be equipped with]. 教育探索 *(Education Exploration), 4,* 8–10.

Zhang, J. M., & Cheng, F. C. (2014). 名校长基地培养模式探析. [Exploring on the patterns for famous principals training base]. 中国教育学刊 *(Journal of the Chinese Society of Education), 1,* 44–48.

Zhang, J. W. (2009). 也谈现代校长素质 [Another thought on the qualities of contemporary principals]. 中国教育学刊 *(Journal of the Chinese Society of Education), 10,* 89.

Zhang, W. (2003). 成功校长的素质 [On the qualities of successful principals]. 人民教育 *(People's Education), 7,* 11.

Zhang, X. M. (2008). 校长的道德使命与责任：学校发展的元动力 [The principals' moral mission and responsibilities: The motive power for school development]. 教育发展研究 *(Research in Educational Development), 15,* 112–114.

Zhao, C. F., Wang, X. J., Sun, W., Li, T. Y., Li, C. H., Zhang, S. L., Zhang, C. P., & Xin, H. X. (2007). 中小学校长成长规律的研究 [The patterns of the development of primary and secondary principals]. 当代教育科学 *(Contemporary Educational Science), 21,* 44–46.

Zhao, M. (2013). 专家与校长的互动互惠：柯中明校长工作室研究实践探索 [Interaction between experts and principals: Practices adopted by Kezhongming Principal Studio]. 教学与管理 *(Teaching and Managing), 10,* 6–8.

Zhou, H. T. (2007). 校长的'忽略'误区 [Principals' several 'neglects']. 教育发展研究 *(Research in Educational Development), 7B,* 107–108, 114.

7 Indigenist holistic educational leadership

Zane Ma Rhea

Introduction

The lens of Indigenist philosophy and practice can inform new forms of educational leadership, particularly holistic approaches, in postcolonial nation states. Its foundation is the *United Nations Declaration on the Rights of Indigenous Peoples* (UNDRIPs, 2008; see also, Australian Human Rights Commission, 2010). UNDRIPs recognises the human rights of Indigenous peoples as fundamental, and specifically their distinctive economic, linguistic and cultural rights within complex, globalised postcolonial education systems. From the outset of this discussion, I want you, the reader, to think about your relationship to Indigenous people in the place where you live and how you engage with the generic educational leadership narrative, in order to interrogate it and its requirements, and to develop a new type of leadership response that recognises the *sui generis* rights of Indigenous peoples. Drawing on the visionary work of Rigney (1999) and Wilson (2007), I employ the term Indigenist to convey the idea that a person supports Indigenous rights and perspectives without implying that the supporter is Indigenous. Wilson (2007, pp. 193–4) explains that "It is my belief that an Indigenist paradigm can be used by anyone who chooses to follow its tenets. It cannot and should not be claimed to belong only to people with 'Aboriginal' heritage'" (see also Wilson, 2008).

In addition to adopting an Indigenist perspective, I have also drawn on some generic change leadership approaches in developing the ideas discussed: double loop learning (Argyris, 1977), methods of achieving strategic change (Kotter, 2007, 2012, Cotter & Cohen, 2002), participatory action research (McTaggart, 1991) and complex adaptive systems theories (Bovaird, 2008). In the context of holistic education, Forbes (1996), Martin (2002), Miller (2000) and Forbes and Martin (2004) have attempted to describe a somewhat broad, diverse concept of relevance to the following discussion. In comparison, little has been written about holistic leadership, or indeed holistic leadership education although it is a relatively new field of research and practice (Elmuti, Minnis, & Abebe, 2005). In the case of cross-cultural leadership work on education, it provides a unique opportunity to bring together ideas about educational leadership, holistic education and Indigenous rights. As Martin (2002, p. 27) wrote of this emerging postcolonial, postmodern era:

> Once it is understood that the purpose and means for educating is interconnected with what is learned, then the significance for diverse approaches to learning becomes critical for supporting human development in a pluralistic society.
>
> (p. 27)

While this chapter draws on an Australian example, I have argued previously (Ma Rhea, 2015a) that there are three internationally relevant, fundamental elements that any educational leader needs to have in order to collaborate effectively across the cultural differences that exist between Indigenous and non-Indigenous peoples, in particular in public spheres such as education: first, the ability to develop meaningful partnerships; second, the understanding to proactively engage with the rights of Indigenous peoples in education afforded by UNDRIPs (2008) and third, the skills and knowledge to implement a concerted program of workforce development of education leaders in the Indigenous domain. We already know that partnerships *per se* between Indigenous and non-Indigenous people do not, of themselves, enable the breaking of the colonialist mindset. Such a shift requires a paradigmatic change towards an Indigenist, rights-based perspective (Rigney, 1999).

Moore (1995) makes a powerful argument about the work of public service professionals, highlighting the outcome of their work as being about the creation of 'public value'. In consideration of educational leadership, rarely have Australian Aboriginal and Torres Strait Islander peoples been involved in bringing forward their understandings about what such a creation of public value might involve. As this chapter will show, it is far more common for non-Indigenous leaders and administrators to identify the problem, design an approach to resolving it and assess its successes and failures without any consultation with knowledgeable Indigenous people. Such single loop thinking simply re-creates the same outcome *ad nauseam*. Drawing on strategic change management literature and using a rights-based approach, the chapter will explore the leadership of change through the creation of an approach underpinned by Indigenist perspectives and educational leadership principles.

Educational leadership and the colonialist mindset

More than 200 years ago in 1814 in Australia, under the leadership of Governor Lachlan Macquarie, the new colony implemented a 15-point plan for the provision of education services to Indigenous children. From its inception, the Native Institution established to implement this Plan was based on a premise that provision of education services to Indigenous people would be done by non-Indigenous people for Indigenous people. Aboriginal children and adults were counted, measured and classified, and given or denied access to goods and services depending on the political and policy drivers of the era. Unfortunately, the habits and practices of former times continue into contemporary provision of services to Indigenous Australians. Available statistics indicate that the various measures all point to the fact that the differences between Indigenous and non-Indigenous populations are still stark in comparison, particularly in education and health outcomes.

As I have previously argued (Ma Rhea, 2015a), my comparative analysis of past Australian education policies finds striking similarities of colonial thinking embedded in policy formulation and operationalisation up to the present time. The colonialist mindset reproduces itself particularly strongly during periods of instability and change and it is under such conditions that the change leader is likely to hold tightly to what has worked previously in order to deliver an acceptable outcome. But acceptable to whom? Anecdotally, Indigenous people report that non-Indigenous leaders commonly stymie Indigenous people in processes of change, are unwilling to share power and collaborate equally with Indigenous people and lack the willingness to bureaucratise such collaborative partnerships. Instead, leaders are often guilty of holding onto the legacy of 'executive power' enshrined from early colonial times. For example, in 1976, the Coombs Report (Australian Government, 1976, p. 337) identified that:

> . . . it seems that the administration is uncertain about the National Aboriginal Consultative Council's role, sceptical about its capacity for executive responsibility and suspicious of domination of tradition-oriented Aboriginals by more politically sophisticated and aggressive urban Aboriginals.

The concept of the "colonial mind" is a useful theoretical construct by which to examine educational leadership, and in particular how holistic educational leadership is impacted (Ma Rhea, 2015a). Heinlein (2002), in his examination of colonial administrators, defines the "official mind" as being the sum of ideas, perceptions and intentions of those policy makers who had a bearing on imperial policies. Similar to the experiences of Australian Aboriginal and Torres Strait Islander people, Robinson, Gallagher, and Denny (1963) observed that in India, "The white rulers became increasingly absorbed with the mechanics of administration and sought to solve their problems less in social and more in narrow administrative terms". The "colonial mindset" identified by Heinlein (2002), Robinson et al. (1963) and Nugget Coombs in the Coombs report (Australian Government, 1976) may be usefully employed when considering how change leaders envision, plan, enact and reflect on their work in education spaces in the contemporary era.

Into this seemingly "bland eternity of the same" à la Baudrillard (1990, p. 130), Australia endorsed the *United Nations Declaration on the Rights of Indigenous Peoples* (UNDRIPs) in 2008. Since Australia endorsed UNDRIPs in 2008, there has been opportunity to change the colonial narrative and begin thinking about how the Australian state can develop a postcolonial approach to its relationship with Indigenous citizens, particularly in the field of education and, the focus of this chapter, in educational leadership. A key requirement of such a change is to see Indigenous rights in education to be at the centre of such arrangements and for there to be a transfer of control of the education of Indigenous young people to Indigenous education experts, a recognition of the need for partnership between government-funded agencies and Indigenous people in the delivery of education services and that professionals are given opportunity to develop their skills, knowledge and understanding of the rights of Indigenous people so that they can begin the task of moving towards a postcolonial approach in their engagement with Indigenous people. This encapsulates the Indigenist perspective.

UNDRIPs represents a timely opportunity for educational leaders to reset their relationship with Indigenous populations whose *sui generis* rights were not extinguished by colonisation. The right for Indigenous populations to control the education of their children is a key focus of UNDRIPs and the Australian government has Indigenous education as one of its key policy areas under the policy called "Closing the Gap" (Council of Australian Governments, 2011). Even so, an approach that focuses predominantly on administratively measurable metrics, I would argue, derives directly from the colonialist mindset that seeks to contain and limit Indigenous presence in educational leadership (Ma Rhea, 2015b). This colonialist mindset has created a deficit approach that barely involves Indigenous parents or the wider Aboriginal and Torres Strait Islander communities in the education of their children. While such a strategy might protect the Education Minister, appeal to the majority and be administratively neat, it fails to recognise the urgent need for a new approach that does not re-inscribe the power relations that are so intrinsically embedded in the colonialist mindset that shapes educational leadership in Australia, and indeed across the globe.

Because of the influence of UNDRIPs, professionals in the public service in Australia are now expected to pay attention to the recognised rights of Aboriginal and Torres Strait Islander Peoples, but there has been scant focus on, or funding for, the development of the skills, knowledge and understanding of such professionals. It has been a slow road towards the development of the Indigenist, postcolonial mindset that would enable otherwise highly competent professionals to undertake their leadership roles effectively in the provision of education services to Indigenous Australians.

By way of example, research by Ma Rhea, Anderson, and Atkinson (2012) found that few educational leaders, such as policy makers, principals and government ministers, have any depth of knowledge about Indigenous matters, and fewer have come into public service with any specialist study at university level or in Indigenous studies or Indigenous education (Ma Rhea et al., 2012). In such circumstance, it is unsurprising that such professionals are prone to reproduce what is already familiar to them, not recognising that they are employing a colonialist mindset on a regular basis in the leadership roles they perform. The so-called recipients of their leadership, Indigenous people, can see clearly the way that systems designed to serve them are, in fact, reproducing colonial structures together with frustratingly predictable negative consequences.

In the case examined in this chapter, holistic educational leadership approaches of one part of the organisation are 'in tension' with the habituated colonialist mindset of the overall organisational philosophy. This can commonly occur when individuals holding holistic educational principles find themselves in a position to undertake transformational change. On the surface, there is nothing immediately incommensurable in the generally accepted definition of holistic education and the ways that many Indigenous communities speak about their aspirations for education, as Miller's (1999, p. 2) definition suggests:

> Holistic education is based on the premise that each person finds identity, meaning, and purpose in life through connections to the community, to the natural world, and to spiritual values such as compassion and peace. Holistic education aims to call forth from people an intrinsic reverence for life and a passionate love of learning. This is done, not through an academic "curriculum" that condenses the world into instructional packages, but through direct engagement with the environment. Holistic education nurtures a sense of wonder.

Even so, employing a concept such as holistic education can still betray a chasm of conceptual understanding. Mahood (2012, p. 1), for example, reflects on the lack of preparedness that most non-Indigenous people have when they become involved in the provision of services to remote Indigenous communities, noting that:

> . . . there don't appear to be any recognized training programs for people who aspire to work in a community, or screening criteria to weed out the mad, bad and incompetent who prowl the grey zone of Indigenous service delivery.

The next section argues for the need to develop a more sophisticated understanding of leadership in educational services provision in Australia.

Towards understanding of Indigenous holistic educational leadership: A case study of Green Trees

This section then leads into an analysis of a case study that demonstrates the adoption of an Indigenist, rights-based approach to holistic educational leadership. It falls outside the scope of this paper to undertake a full discussion of the residential education and well-being facility, Green Trees, that is the focus of this case study, and of its parent organisation, Bright Futures (pseudonyms), a rehabilitation and life education organisation for both Indigenous and non-Indigenous people. Even so, it is necessary to provide some context to the work and subsequent analyses that were undertaken. Bright Futures, the parent organisation, initiated their "Indigenizing Bright Futures" organisational change process because they recognised that their organisation had a fractured and poorly integrated approach to service delivery for Aboriginal and/or Torres Strait Islander clients. Outcomes were poor, Indigenous people did not like the service provision and expressed the strong view that the staff were ill-equipped to work with Indigenous people. Bright Futures implemented the first four steps of Kotter's *Eight Step Process for Leading Change* (2007, 2012; see also, Kotter & Cohen, 2002). Along with Kotter, the process was underpinned by a participatory action research approach drawing on some of the theoretical work being done in the field of complex adaptive systems as applied to the human services (see for example, Bovaird, 2008; Holland, 1995; Palmberg, 2009). At the outset, I was brought in as the external change management consultant to guide a key aspect of this work, the use of Indigenist holistic education techniques. This occured through my constant questioning of the 'normal' assumptions made by Bright Futures staff about Indigenous people during discussions, and presenting participants with alternative views based on the UNDRIPs, the rights of Indigenous Peoples and alternative views of their service given by local Aboriginal people. My investigations found that Aboriginal service users had been unhappy with the organisation for some time and had been giving negative evaluations to government funders, being mostly unaware of the organisational change strategy that had been implemented by Bright Futures leadership in order to "engage more effectively with Aboriginal communities" (internal policy document). During these initial discussions and opportunities to gather and begin to get a sense of the issues faced by Bright Futures, I was under the impression that there were few Indigenous clients involved as a proportion of the whole across the services at Bright Futures or its rural residential facility, Green Trees. Significantly, none of the leadership team mentioned there being any Aboriginal people employed.

With some surprise, a field trip to Green Trees revealed that there had been many years of involvement between local Aboriginal people and Green Trees, far beyond the wider organisational narrative of Bright Futures. Green Trees, located in a rural community, had a large proportion of Aboriginal people accessing its education and well-being services. High levels of government funding for the Aboriginal service users suggested that, at least in theory, Green Trees was financially viable. After analysis of data collected at Green Trees, the one 'standout' finding was that a leading partnership that had developed between Albert, an Indigenous worker, and John, the non-Indigenous 'leader', was innovative, unique and had developed 'off the radar' of the parent organisation so completely that none of the senior leaders of the "Indigenizing Bright Futures" process knew about the profoundly effective holistic educational leadership approach that they had developed at Green Trees. Ultimately, the power of the approach they developed together caused the parent organisation to rethink its approach to adult life education, rehabilitation and leadership under the guidance of Indigenous people.

In undertaking the evaluation of the implementation of the strategy for the organisation, it became apparent to me that there were important aspects of what had changed that needed to be further examined. Traditional, mainstream adult education settings, being very structured and bureaucratised, normally do not allow Indigenous people the trust and scope to control and guide the fundamental change in the approach to the education and rehabilitation of Indigenous people; it is even more rare that such approaches might be tried at a centre catering for the life education and rehabilitation of both Indigenous and non-Indigenous clients. Being a somewhat 'alternative' education setting, I concluded, had provided a rich context for a revolutionary change to occur that demonstrates important learnings for broader consideration in the field of educational leadership. Even so, it was the partnership between Albert and John that enabled me to gain an understanding of the conditions that will be needed to move beyond colonialist thinking in educational leadership.

After having a number of meetings with John and Albert as part of the "Indigenizing Bright Futures" implementation over the span of a year, it became apparent that a precious process had grown from their friendship that resulted in Albert being employed by the organisation. After some months of working together with them, they asked if it would be possible for me to share their story. After some discussion, we decided to employ a case study approach and I invited them to record a conversation together of what they did and what ideas had underpinned their approach. Their recordings of their conversations involved about four hours of recording in addition to many conversations between us all as my analysis progressed.

Tellis (1997) suggests that "Case studies are multi-perspectival analyses. This means that the researcher considers not just the voice and perspective of the actors, but also of the relevant groups of actors and the interaction between them". This proved a useful method by which to begin to understand the dynamics of change undertaken by the two leaders (see Yin, 1994, 2009; Stake, 1994, 1995 for more detail). They spoke together over a number of hours, weaving back and forth across their story of what they did, where it went wrong and where it had worked. I then thematically analysed the transcribed conversations using the techniques developed by Strauss and Corbin (1990). I undertook preliminary analysis of the data together with my observation notes, guided by Saldaña (2009) and Richards (2009), using three levels of analysis: first using techniques of open and axial coding, drawing out the main themes; second, undertaking a cluster analysis of key themes; and third, bringing the second-level analysis to understanding the processes and ideas underpinning their leadership approach.

Emergent themes

White administrators having some humility and acknowledging their ignorance

At the time of the change management facilitation, Albert was undertaking a Certificate IV at the local Technical and Further Education (TAFE) College and John, the new leader of Green Trees, was invited to speak to the students in Albert's class. In Australia, the purpose of the Certificate IV qualification type is:

> ... to qualify individuals who apply a broad range of specialized knowledge and skills in varied contexts to undertake skilled work and as a pathway for

further learning. Certificate IV qualifications are located at level 4 of the Australian Qualifications Framework.

(Australian Qualifications Framework, 2016)

The first thing to note here is that Indigenous people move in and out of TAFE and university systems depending on their knowledge needs. Albert's presence in this group belied his vast community experience and life commitment to ensuring that local Aboriginal people were being well served by local services that were supposed to be there for them. He recalls his first meeting with John, at the TAFE information session about Bright Futures and Green Trees. John brushed off a question put to him by Albert. Because of John's brush-off, Albert decided that John knew nothing about Aboriginal matters. This first encounter between Albert and John provides graphic insight into how quickly impressions can be formed. Unwittingly, John had communicated that his service did not have the professional skills at the leadership level to engage with Aboriginal people. Albert then spoke about what happened next, something that surprised him and disrupted his first, negative impressions. John rang him after a couple of days and invited him to Green Trees. John explained that being from England, he had afterwards reflected that he knew very little about what Aboriginal people might need or want from Green Trees. He recalled that his motivation to find Albert and talk more with him was that:

> . . . I wanted to know. I'm interested in – I'm genuinely interested in different culture, I'm genuinely interested in Aboriginal and Indigenous culture . . . and also interested in not sticking my size ten boots in it and getting it wrong, and doing it properly and coming from a position of – this is something we have talked about a lot – coming from a position of humility.

Interestingly, in my facilitator notes what stood out for me were their reflections about the need for humility on both sides.

Providing role modelling of trust in shared leadership

Both Albert and John were very aware of the influence they might have if they worked together and developed trust. Albert reflected on this:

> . . . you know the [Bright Futures] manager could have said, "No, we are not going to do that here . . . it's not part of Bright Futures program" and as I've said all the way along I didn't come here to try to turn Green Trees into an Indigenous set-up. . . .

Albert reflects a common tension between Indigenous and non-Indigenous people at this vulnerable stage of relationship-building where non-Indigenous people are concerned that Aboriginal people will only pursue, and indeed are only capable of pursuing, an Indigenous agenda, and Aboriginal people are extremely wary of enthusiastic non-Indigenous people who seem supportive but may harbor the colonialist mindset in their worldview.

Acknowledging that everyone has the right to be proud of their culture and helping everyone involved to re-connect with their culture and own their identity

Developing an Indigenist holistic educational leadership approach relies on everyone feeling that their cultural background is respected, but this is more difficult that it might first appear. Many non-Indigenous Australians know little about their ethic cultural background, how their family came to be in Australia, where they come from, and are encouraged instead to forget the past and make a new life in contemporary Australia. Most Aboriginal people have some understanding of who they are, where they come from, and have a strong connection to both ancient and contemporary Australia. The interface between the two views can often lead to frustration and misunderstanding with non-Indigenous people wondering why Indigenous people are always harking back to the past and Indigenous people feeling angry and frustrated that non-Indigenous people have so little respect for what Aboriginal people have suffered at the hands of the ancestors of non-Indigenous people. This is particularly so for Indigenous Australians who are part of the 'Stolen Generation', often overrepresented in prisons and rehabilitation centres such as *Green Trees*. These descendants of Aboriginal people were stolen from their families because of a brutal colonial Australian government policy that spanned the years 1910–1970 (National Inquiry into the Separation of Aboriginal and Torres Strait Islander Children from their Families et al., 1997). This policy approach taken by successive Australian governments was based on the conviction that Indigenous children would be better off being brought up by white families or in government institutions. This policy had, and continues to have, profound and painful impact on Indigenous Australians with no family escaping its legacy. Much of the healing work that is needed comes from people re-connecting with their families, providing a powerful context for holistic educational leadership that acknowledges Indigenous intergenerational trauma and post-traumatic stress.

Albert led the Green Trees staff and clients on an educational journey of recognition of their past and helped them to understand its importance in their holistic development. Herbert (2012) emphasises the need for non-Indigenous people to move away from speaking about a history of Indigenous education towards understanding the "context of 'Indigenous histories of education"' (Herbert, 2012, p. 91) in colonised nations such as Australia. Albert takes up a leadership role here and explains it this way:

> I'm proud to express the love of my culture and the love of being able to share my culture to Indigenous or non-Indigenous. I feel it's an honour for me to sit and talk to someone who knows nothing about Aboriginal culture but they want to learn something even if it is something simple; they really are genuinely wanting to listen and learn, through to re-introducing an Indigenous person back to their own culture. Peeling off some of the layers of all the hurt [John: Yeah, yeah] . . . hurt from addiction, hurt from being taken away, hurt from being abused, hurt from whatever it might be they forgot how to love and to use their culture to heal. . . .

John suggests this possibility when he goes into a long speech that could be interpreted as self-justificatory, but Albert reminds everyone that John needs to be proud of his culture too so that he can understand the pride that Aboriginal people feel. John begins:

> You know I'm . . . I'm not a nationalist, I'm not you know a raving nationalist but I'm proud of my culture. I tend to believe you know despite evidence that the English are good at sport, that we are the best in music and we do the right thing and we're nice people and you know the blitz and World War II and the Battle of Trafalgar and . . . they're all part of me. And those sporting heroes or those war heroes or those writers and the poets and scientists and the people that have made *my* people great, I think . . . clearly other cultures would have something to say about it but it's like you know what I mean that's part of me [Albert: Yeah] and it's part of what was brought up with me . . . and because I feel that way about my culture I can see it in you . . . in Indigenous culture there would have been the heroic Nelsons and the Winston Churchills and the poets and the great warriors and the sportsmen and they have all been taken away.

Creating cultural safety – with genuine intent, not to tick boxes, no cynicism

> You've got to feel safe. You've got to be safe here. You cannot be opening yourself up and talking about your race and making yourself vulnerable unless you feel safe. And you and I have been the two leaders in this respect and on this subject at Bright Futures. And somehow and in some ways we've made it safe to be a Black man or a proud Black woman [Albert: Or a Greek or an Italian] or a Pom [and they both laugh] . . .
>
> (John)

Developing the conversations about culture and its place in holistic education, the two leaders, Albert and John, then began to embed the concept of cultural safety into the day-to-day education and rehabilitation services at Green Trees. Until they began this process of organisational transformation, there had been no visible or symbolic recognition that there was an Aboriginal presence at Green Trees. Local Aboriginal Traditional Owners had not engaged with the organisation, and there were no flags or other symbolic artefacts that might speak to the cultural safety needs of Aboriginal people. It was a surprise to non-Indigenous staff that this might be an issue. As Albert explained, it came back to non-Indigenous people not recognising that they have symbols of their cultural identity all around them every day that they take for granted. Albert gives this example:

> . . . speaking of the flag, look at that map we've got in the lounge room. Look at the overwhelming change when one of them young Indigenous people, male or female, see that up on the wall and can't get over there quick enough to show us their country and talk about family . . . a resident took

me in there the other day and showed me his links to the Torres Strait island where he's from and amazing pride was just gushing out of him, just gushing out of him. How wonderful that sort of stuff that's come from here because we decided to put that map up on the wall.

Albert and John agreed that they needed a language to describe what they meant about making changes that were culturally safe. Albert says, "We developed an idea about having Green Trees circuit breakers that gave us permission to change things". In one example of a "circuit breaker", John and Albert recounted the story of having a fire pit dug in the grounds as a place of healing and quiet reflection. It slowly became a place where Aboriginal people would go to chat, to connect with one another, and to encourage each other on their journey. Many graduating clients spoke positively of this as a really important initiative. Equally powerful, Aboriginal people began to invite non-Indigenous friends to join them at the fire pit, something that let John and Albert know that their holistic leadership style was beginning to show evidence of the changes that they were hoping to achieve.

Such 'circuit breaking' events are only possible within a considered organisational change strategy. John and Albert had such a vision and a plan. They engaged properly with the local community, both Aboriginal and non-Indigenous, they made Green Trees a place where Indigenous clients felt culturally safe, and they were inclusive of the needs of all staff and all clients, both Indigenous and non-Indigenous in a way that such new measures improved the provision of services for everyone involved.

Getting multiple viewpoints

As leaders, John and Albert knew they had to create a culture that allowed people to ask questions in a safe environment. They agreed that they had to model this desired behavior with each other and amongst the staff and clients. John explains:

> . . . and not be not be embarrassed by our own ignorance . . . here I'm able to ask those questions and say I don't know and can you tell me and that I don't even know how to pronounce that word [laughs] . . . well I don't you know! . . . Can someone, can you, can you tell me, can you guide me through this?

After some months of working together to get their strategy right, they brought the staff together to discuss their vision. Albert remembers:

> I think one of the greatest things was the time we had that staff meeting; John, you called everyone together and we had a little chat here in the office . . . we actually had an Indigenous lady here that day . . . and the suggestion was made that we should approach her to come to the meeting as an Aboriginal woman, not as a client, because then the staff then could get

an answer to the question from a male and a female. I thought it was a great idea and I said to her, "When you are in this meeting you are an Auntie, a proud Indigenous woman. As soon as you come out that door again you are here as a client again, so do not get this mixed up". What a proud woman she was there!

Albert was teaching John about Indigenous protocol of being sure to gather views from both women and men and together they were bringing the staff along slowly. The staff began to learn to ask questions. Changes started to become more obvious to the clients because the staff started to use different language, model different behavior and show respect for both Indigenous and non-Indigenous cultures. John explains:

> How do we get the staff along with us? Its character and its honesty and its humility and all of those things. But it is being able to see you as an Indigenous leader – we'll call you that whether you like it or not – and me as a leader of this organisation.

Doing things the "proper way"

Aboriginal people are used to non-Indigenous people developing systems and structures that suit non-Indigenous people's view of the world. They comment often, in a somewhat sympathetic way, that it is understandable because they do not come from one of the oldest living cultures on the planet. Albert, in teaching John about Aboriginal culture, was teaching him what Aboriginal people call the "proper way". Albert was also modelling this "proper way" to staff and clients alike. He explains:

> The Indigenous stuff rolls out to the non-Indigenous and it's just proven just being a worker you can walk around and you can see Indigenous people showing non-Indigenous where they are on the map or showing them down at the fireplace . . . Who knows what they're talking about but you can see there's this whole lot of interest and the care that they take on looking after the fire pit and making sure that everything's OK and respectable . . . all that wasn't here before we started!

John is able to reflect on his change of understanding of Indigenous rights, of the terrible past history, of the concerns of Indigenous people in contemporary Australia and how he is starting to learn the "proper way" to do things so that things can improve for both Indigenous and non-Indigenous people in Australia. He reflects that:

> . . . we have the Elders coming over from [the local rural community] and the local Koorie Court and us saying, "How you going?" and they say, "We're slow", and we say, "What do you mean?" and they say, "We're slow

because of you blokes" and we say, "What do you mean?" and they say, "Because people we used to see every three months we don't see at all or we see once every eighteen months, and it's all because of you". And you know that's throwing a rock in the pond but, no, it's the opposite . . . I don't know what the analogy is for that but it is calming the waters [Albert: Yeah] and you know from this little space here in the hills we've been able to create a calming effect for to start off with a few then dozens and now hundreds of people. . . .

Making sure at least it does not die

Word spread to the local Aboriginal and non-Indigenous community about their successes and that there was a greater integration of the education and rehabilitation services being offered by Green Trees. Moving from a self-motivated opportunity to work together to lead a positive change at Green Trees, John and Albert recognised that it was necessary to embed the changes they had made into the organisational structures of both Green Tress and also the wider organisation, Bright Futures. John had moved from wanting to fix the problems himself into a collaboration with Albert where together they led a holistic educational program, first for Aboriginal service users, and eventually for all service users.

More importantly, I believe, John began to understand the shape of an Indigenist perspective towards the work and eventually in his understanding of his friendship with Albert. He began to 'see' his organisation as Albert and other Aboriginal people saw it and quite early in the process began to make the argument with the leadership team of Bright Futures that the first step would be to employ Albert properly at Green Trees. He argued that to ensure that firstly, the steps he and Albert took were taken together were recognised and sustained, and secondly, that the local community saw Green Trees as doing more than providing education and health services to Aboriginal clients, employment of Albert was a necessary step. Then the community would see that Bright Futures was prepared to employ Indigenous people in their organisation, something that is still rare in the provision of publicly funded services to the Indigenous community in Australia.

In organisational terms, this is a very difficult first step. Commonly, organisations are wary of making a financial commitment of salaries on 'soft' program money, so John employed Albert in a role that was advertised, rather than setting up an Indigenous-specific position. Again, in organisational terms, this approach can be very effective if the manager and other staff have trust in the Indigenous worker's generic skills. Part of the colonialist mindset commonly tries to push Aboriginal people into Aboriginal-specific jobs and blocks attempts for Indigenous people to contribute to an organisation beyond a limited brief. As an outcome of the developing trust between Albert and John, they had managed to circumvent such a mistake.

They also recognised that it was attention to detail that would made sure that all their hard work would survive, that the changes were respected and that things were being looked after properly. Albert explains:

> Just imagine how bad it would be if an Elder walked in here and went over and used the fire pit for instance and it was just full of rubbish [John: Yeah] or here's the plaque on the door and some screws have fallen out and the thing's hanging cock-eyed or something [John: Yep]. We can't drop our guard for those little things, which I don't think will happen here anyway, but as long as we're aware of it then I think it's working well.

Conclusion

> We're not silly . . . we realise we don't hold a magic wand or a magic pill but by golly gosh there's some sort of magic happening here. . . .
>
> (Albert)

I have argued in this chapter that through the adoption of an Indigenist, rights-based approach to leadership that has drawn on principles of holistic educational change, Albert, John and the staff and clients of Green Trees are manifesting the intentions of the United Nations *Declaration on the Rights of Indigenous Peoples*. Their example also provides insight into some of the characteristics of effective, respectful, collaborative Indigenous–non-Indigenous partnering in educational leadership that can begin to emerge. Albert reflects that:

> Leadership's a really important one because you can lead someone down the garden path so to say [John: Yep] or you can lead them up the hill to where they are supposed to be going. The leader, if he's not serious about what they're doing, well then it's a lost cause . . . it's a joke. . . .

By leading Bright Futures to a shift from a colonialist, deficit-based mindset to a postcolonial, rights-based mindset, the above case study provides some glimmers of possibility for what can emerge, given the right circumstances. There needed to be a strategic change management plan developed by all involved in the process to achieve buy-in; and there needed to be a willingness on the part of Indigenous and non-Indigenous people to step into a new type of arrangement that moved beyond replication of the colonialist mindset. As discussed above in more detail, the main lessons communicated by Albert and John in their holistic educational leadership strategy included:

- White administrators having some humility and acknowledging their ignorance;
- The importance of having positive role modelling of trust in shared leadership responsibilities between Indigenous and non-Indigenous leaders;

- Acknowledging that everyone has the right to be proud of their culture and helping everyone involved to re-connect with their culture and own their identity;
- Creating cultural safety – with genuine intent, not to tick boxes, and without cynicism;
- Getting multiple viewpoints;
- Doing things the "proper way"; and,
- Making sure that successful Indigenous-led initiatives are not undermined, discredited and allowed to die though reassertion of the colonialist mindset.

As my analysis demonstrates, the concept of a respectful collaborative partnership between Albert and John was supported by a postcolonial approach to strategic change management planning in a facility designed to meet the educational and well-being needs of Indigenous and non-Indigenous people. But even with the best strategy employed, partnership does not just happen. Both Albert and John needed the skills, knowledge and understanding to enable the first steps to be taken in the "proper way". They could then be effective in leading the creation of the environment that was conducive to the holistic education philosophy of Green Trees. Doing things the wrong way had meant that, before, Indigenous people had walked away in disgust. From the outset, if John had continued to ignore the attempts by Albert and other local Aboriginal people to become involved, then John would have failed to achieve the organisational goals set for him in the provision of his education services. The fact that John was able to find a way to involve Albert from the beginning of his planning set the tone for how next steps were taken. This aspect alone provides a pivotal piece of the jigsaw that brings all other pieces together – Indigenous people need to be in position to lead the development of effective education initiatives that draw on the ancient wisdom of their cultures. Colonisation has blinded mainstream education systems to the profound opportunities still to be experienced.

Leaders working from the colonialist mindset in the provision of education and other human services to Indigenous peoples mistakenly believe that it is better to develop the plan and then involve Indigenous people once everything is sorted out. Such an approach treats Aboriginal people like children and is bound to restrict the potential of any change process because the start is already shaped by colonialist thinking. An Indigenist, rights-based postcolonial approach recognises that organisations have the resources, structures and responsibility for the provision of education services, but Indigenous people have the recognised right to control such monies and education services in meaningful ways.

Acknowledgements

I would like to acknowledge the willingness of the senior leadership team from Bright Futures and Green Trees staff and residents to engage with this program of work with openness and willingness, and for their commitment to reconciliation between Indigenous and non-Indigenous Australians. I would particularly like to thank the two leaders of the Green Trees, who gave freely of their time so that others might learn about how to lead effective change that also recognises the rights of Indigenous people. Thanks also to Jeane Freer for her transcription assistance with the research that underpins this analysis.

References

Agar, M. H. (1996). *The professional stranger: An informal introduction to ethnography*. New York: Academic Press.
Argyris, C. (1977, September–October). Double loop learning in organisations. *Harvard Business Review*, 115–125.
Ashcroft, B., Griffiths, G., & Tiffen, H. (1998). *Key concepts in post-colonial studies*. London: Routledge.
Australian Government. (1976). *Royal commission on Australian government administration: Report* (Coombs, N. C., Bailey, P. H., Campbell, E., Isaac, J. E., & Munro, P. R.). Canberra: Commonwealth of Australia.
Australian Human Rights Commission. (2010). *The community guide to the UN declaration on the rights of Indigenous peoples*. Retrieved from www.humanrights.gov.au/sites/default/files/document/publication/declaration_community_guide.pdf
Australian Qualifications Framework. (2016). *Certificate IV*. Retrieved from www.aqf.edu.au/wp-content/uploads/2013/05/6AQF_Certificate-IV.pdf
Bovaird, T. (2008). Emergent strategic management and planning mechanisms in complex adaptive systems. *Public Management Review*, 10(3), 319–340.
Clifford, J., & Marcus, G. E. (1986). *Writing culture: The poetics and politics of ethnography*. School of American Research advanced seminar, University of California Press.
Council of Australian Governments. (2011). *Closing the gap on Indigenous disadvantage*. Retrieved from www.coag.gov.au/closing_the_gap_in_indigenous_disadvantage
Deleuze, G., & Guattari, F. (1987). *A thousand plateaus: Capitalism and schizophrenia*. Minneapolis, MN: University of Minnesota Press.
Elmuti, D., Minnis, W., & Abebe, M. (2005). Does education have a role in developing leadership skills? *Management Decision*, 43(7/8), 1018–1031.
Fletcher, J. (1989). *Clean, clad, and courteous: A history of aboriginal education in New South Wales*. Carlton: J. Fletcher.
Fletcher, L. (1994). Schooling an empire. *Education Research and Perspectives*, 21(1), 1–112.
Folds, R. (2001). *Crossed purposes: The Pintupi and Australia's indigenous policy*. Sydney: UNSW Press.
Forbes, S. H. (1996, June). Values in holistic education. *Third annual conference on education, spirituality and the whole child*, Roehampton Institute London. Retrieved from www.putnampit.com/holistic.html
Forbes, S. H., & Martin, R. A. (2004, April). An analysis of Holistic Schools' literature. *American Education Research Association annual conference*, San Diego, CA.
Hammersley, M., & Atkinson, P. (2007). *Ethnography: Principles in practice* (3rd ed.). London: Routledge.
Heinlein, F. (2002). *British government policy and decolonisation 1945–1963: Scrutinising the official mind*. London: Frank Cass.
Herbert, J. (2012). 'Ceaselessly circling the centre': Historical contextualization of Indigenous education within Australia. *History of Education Review*, 41(2), 91–103.

Holland, J. H. (1995). *Hidden order: How adaptations build complexity*. Reading, MA: Addison-Wesle.

Kaomea, J. (2005). Indigenous studies in the elementary curriculum: A cautionary Hawaiian example. *Anthropology and Education Quarterly, 36*(1), 24–42.

Kitchen, J., Hodson, J., & Raynor, M. (2013). Indigenous teacher education as cultural brokerage: A university/first nations partnership to prepare Nishnawbe Aski teachers. *International Education Journal: Comparative Perspectives, 12*(1), 119–134.

Kotter, J. (2007, January). Leading change, why transformations efforts fail. *Harvard Business Review*, 96–10.

Kotter, J. (2012). *The eight-step process for leading change*. Retrieved from www.kotterinternational.com/kotterprinciples/changesteps

Kotter, J., & Cohen, D. S. (2002). *The heart of change*. Boston, MA: Harvard Business Review Press.

Liska, G. (1978). *Career of empire: America and imperial expansion over land and sea*. Baltimore, MD: Johns Hopkins University Press.

Ma Rhea, Z. (2011). Partnership for improving outcomes in Indigenous education: Relationship or business? *Journal of Education Policy, 27*(1), 1–22. doi:10.1080/02680939.2011.621030.

Ma Rhea, Z. (2015a). *Leading and managing indigenous education in the postcolonial world*. London: Routledge.

Ma Rhea, Z. (2015b). Unthinking the 200-year-old colonial mind: Indigenist perspectives on leading and managing indigenous education. *International Education Journal: Comparative Perspectives, 14*(2), 90–100.

Ma Rhea, Z., Anderson, P. J., & Atkinson, B. (2012). *National professional standards for teachers standards 1.4 and 2.4: Improving teaching in aboriginal and Torres Strait Islander education*. Melbourne: Australian Institute for Teaching and School Leadership. Retrieved from www.aitsl.edu.au/verve/_resources/MONASH_STUDY_FINAL_REPORT_09092012.pdf

Ma Rhea, Z., & Russell, L. (2012). The invisible hand of pedagogy in Australian indigenous studies and indigenous education. *Australian Journal of Indigenous Education, 41*(1), 18–25.

Ma Rhea, Z., & Teasdale, G. R. (2000). A dialogue between the local and the global. In G. R. Teasdale & Z. Ma Rhea (Eds.), *Local knowledge and wisdom in higher education* (pp. 1–14). Oxford: IAU Elsevier.

Macquarie, L. (1814). *Establishment of the native institution 1814*. NRS 1046 [SZ759, pp. 11–14; Reel 6038]. Retrieved from www.records.nsw.gov.au/state-archives/digital-gallery/lachlan-macquarie-visionary-and-builder/public-notices/full-transcript-establishment-of-the-native-institution-1814

Mahood, K. (2012). Kartiya are like Toyotas: White workers on Australia's cultural frontier. *Griffith Review, 36*, 43–60.

Martin, R. A. (2002). An exploration of learner-centered, progressive, and holistic education. *Alternative Education Resource Organisation*, 1–27. Retrieved from http://sane.at.org/print-material/06%20An%20Exploration%20of%20Learner-Centered.pdf

McTaggart, R. (1991). Principles of participatory action research. *Adult Education Quarterly, 41*(3), 168–187.

Miller, R. (2000). *A brief introduction to holistic education*. Retrieved from http://infed.org/mobi/a-brief-introduction-to-holistic-education/

Ministerial Council on Education, Employment, Training, and Youth Affairs (MCEETYA). (2000). *Achieving educational equality for Australia's aboriginal and Torres Strait Islander peoples: A discussion paper*. Retrieved from www.mceecdya.edu.au/verve/_resources/reporta_file.pdf

Moore, M. H. (1995). *Creating public value: Strategic management in government*. Cambridge, MA: Harvard University Press.

National Inquiry into the Separation of Aboriginal and Torres Strait Islander Children from their Families (Australia)/Wilson, Ronald, Sir, 1922–2005 & Australia Human Rights and Equal Opportunity Commission. (1997). *Bringing them home: Report of the national inquiry into the separation of aboriginal and Torres Strait Islander children from their families*. Human Rights and Equal Opportunity Commission, Sydney.

O'Donoghue, L. (1997). In Indigenous affairs nothing is new, just forgotten. *Australian Journal of Public Administration, 56*(4), 5–10.

Palmberg, K. (2009). Complex adaptive systems as metaphors for organisational management. *Learning Organisation, 16*(6), 483–498.

Price, K. (2012). Aboriginal and Torres Strait Islander studies in the classroom. In K. Price (Ed.), *Aboriginal and Torres Strait Islander education: An introduction for the teaching profession* (pp. 151–163). Port Melbourne: Cambridge University Press.

Richards, L. (2009). *Handling qualitative data: A practical guide* (2nd ed.). London: Sage.

Richie, N. D., & Alperin, D. E. (2002). *Innovation and change in the human services*. Springfield: Charles C. Thomas.

Rigney, L. I. (1999). Internationalization of an Indigenous anticolonial cultural critique of research methodologies: A guide to Indigenist research methodology and its principles. *Wicazo Sa Review, 14*(2), 109–121.

Robinson, R., Gallagher, J., & Denny, A. (1963). *Africa and the victorians: The official mind of imperialism*. London: Macmillan and Co Ltd.

Saldaña, J. (2009). *The coding manual for qualitative researchers*. London: Sage.

Sarra, C. (2003). Young and black and deadly: Strategies for improving outcomes for Indigenous students. Paper No. 5 in the *Quality teaching series*. Retrieved from http://austcolled.com.au/

Sarra, C. (2011). *Strong and smart: Towards a pedagogy of emancipation*. London: Routledge.

Sefa Dei, G. (1999). *Interview with Mike Gismondi*. Retrieved from http://aurora.icaap.org/index.php/aurora/article/view/22/33

Senge, P. M. (1990). *The fifth discipline: The art and practice of the learning organisation*. New York: Doubleday.

Stake, R. E. (1994). Identification of the case. In N. K. Denzin & Y. S. Lincoln (Eds.), *Handbook of qualitative research* (pp. 236–247). Thousand Oaks, CA: Sage.

Stake, R. E. (1995). *The art of case study research*. Thousand Oaks, CA: Sage.

Strauss, A., & Corbin, J. (1990). *Basics of qualitative research: Grounded theory procedures and techniques*. Newbury Park, CA: Sage Publications.

Thaman, K. H. (2013). Quality teachers for Indigenous students: An imperative for the twenty first century. *International Education Journal: Comparative Perspectives, 12*(1), 98–118.

United Nations. (2008). *United Nations Declaration on the Rights of Indigenous Peoples* [UNDRIPs]. Retrieved from www.un.org/esa/socdev/unpfii/documents/DRIPS_en.pdf

Wilson, S. (2007). Guest editorial: What is an Indigenist research paradigm? *Canadian Journal of Native Education*, *30*(2), 193–195.

Wilson, S. (2008). *Research is ceremony: Indigenous research methods*. Winnipeg: Fernwood.

Yin, R. K. (2009). *Case study research: Design and methods* (4th ed.). Thousand Oaks, CA: Sage Publications.

8 Communicating research
A challenge of context

Launcelot Brown, Laurette Bristol and Talia Esnard

Introduction

Trinidad and Tobago is a multi-ethnic, multi-religious island republic with a population of approximately 1.3 million people. Public (free) and private (fee-paying) schools are either denominational or secular. In denominational schools, religion (faith) is actively taught and promoted. This practice is legitimised by the Concordat of 1960, which protects the rights of the church to maintain the religious integrity and identity of its schools and its teachers. Parents who are opposed to this view have the privilege of enrolling their children in a government (secular) school.

The country is divided into eight educational districts. Each district is under the supervision of the School Supervisor III (SSIII), supported by School Supervisors II (SSII) and School Supervisors I (SSI). Like all administrative systems, the system is hierarchical. However, the hierarchical order also extends to the type of school in that principals of primary schools report directly to the SSI for their cluster of schools in the district, whereas principals of secondary schools report to the SSII for their district. With regard to denominational school principals, they also report to a denominational board of managers. Principals are appointed predominantly via a Teaching Service Commission interview, but denominational school principals are also interviewed by the denominational board of the school to which they are applying. Principals are appointed primarily through processes of merit, but there are cases where, depending on the particular circumstances and needs of the school, a teacher (both in denominational and government secular schools) may gain the position of Principal 1 Primary (P1) through seniority (years of experience).

Similar to what exists in many international spaces, the principal holds the senior position within the hierarchical structure of the school (Chubb & Moe, 1990; Mintzberg, 1979). Based on that position, she or he is seen as the leader, and is conferred with centralised authority, autonomy and respect within the school (Bristol, 2010, 2012; Brown & Conrad, 2007; Silins, 1994). However, the school is itself within a larger centralised bureaucracy and functions within constricting bureaucratic constraints imposed by the central authority of the Ministry of Education (Brown & Conrad, 2007). In many ways, these imposed bureaucratic constraints are a reflection of a colonial history which is so culturally embedded that it has been able to resist the call for modernisation of the system (Brown & Lavia, 2013).

Nevertheless, recent trends in educational development in Trinidad and Tobago have paid less attention to the practices of the principal with regard to his or her exhibited and/or expected behaviours as leader and central authority within the school. Rather, more emphasis has been placed on the school as the personification of a living, agentic organisation of stakeholders (GORTT, 2007). This attempt at decentralising the authority of the principals and placing greater emphasis on a shared leadership practice that is inclusive of teachers and other stakeholders has implications for the leading practices of principals, reconfigurations of stakeholders and community and staff conceptualisations of leading. This is particularly important given entrenched colonialist understandings of authority and the ways in which novice principals are socialised into practices of school leadership. Against this empirical context, we draw attention to a practice of communicating research: a dilemma which occurred after the active fieldwork was completed, after the data were collected and while the researchers were making sense of the data.[1]

The study

In this section we examine the challenge of research design as it relates to communicating (representation and re-presentation) research findings. The analysis and reflection which follow operate on two levels, first on the level of *choice of design* and second on the level of *reading and writing from the data* (communicating the field). In so doing, we take the position that (1) learning to lead is a social challenge of context (Brown & Conrad, 2007) and (2) researching leadership is a political challenge of context, particularly in contexts where there has been a history of oppression and misrepresentation. In these spaces, Bristol (2008, 2010, 2012) argues for the need for a "culturally ethical" mode of research engagement. Through her own research practice, she outlines the ways in which existing forms of cultural engagement can be used as rich sources of data and the means through which participants, sites for practice and researchers can experience empowerment through encounter (Chesney, 2011). For the researchers, adopting a culturally ethical position (Allen et al., 2009; Bristol, 2012) was a form of decolonising research practice which allowed for a re-imagining of alternative ways of theorising and representing the complexity of sites across, time, space and cultures.

We employed an interpretive research design, making use of in-depth semi-structured interviews that lasted between 45 and 90 minutes. Specifically, we interviewed 11 early career primary school principals (using a snowball sampling approach) from schools along the east-west corridor and the southern region of Trinidad and Tobago. We characterised an early career principal (ECP) as a person who has held the position of Principal 1 Primary (P1) for no more than five years. Of the 11 schools sampled, two were government schools and nine were denominational schools. Also, we conducted interviews with an executive member of the Trinidad and Tobago Unified Teachers' Association (TTUTA) and a district school supervisor. These interviews were conducted so that we could cross-reference the principals' experiences of being socialised into leadership with executive understandings of practice in relation to established policies for practice.

This research design, while limited by its sample size and the related restriction towards the making of generalisations, provided us with the opportunity to excavate the tensions, traditions and power structures which shape and construct the ways in which novice principals re-tell their truth of leadership initiation (Brown & Roberts; 2000; Haug, 2008; Jansson, Wandt, & Åse, 2008). The stories of socialisation as told by the principals become the vehicle through which we were able to access established rituals of professional socialisation and habits of leadership performances (Biott, Moos, & Møller, 2001; Jones, 2004). The stories elicited helped to make explicit the connections between social sites (schools and communities), social projects (education and socialisation) and practices (leading and learning to lead). The data were mined using analytic categorisation and axial coding (Neuman, 2006), with similarities of experience and social learning dissonance being highlighted. The rationalisation of choices related to this data analysis will be explained in later sections of this chapter.

A challenge of context

As researchers, we entered the site having mutually agreed-upon ways of encountering the leaders in the site. This was particularly important given the blurry lines of our insider/outsider status with participants. Two of us were born and educated in Trinidad and Tobago; the third was born and educated in a similar Caribbean island context, St. Lucia. All three of us practised as tertiary-level educators in Trinidad and Tobago. However, two of us work outside of Trinidad and Tobago, one in the United States and the other in Jamaica (previously in Australia) but returned to Trinidad and Tobago annually (to lead professional learning activities). We were very conscious of our inscribed power and status; in particular, we were conscious of the ways in which our external positioning might work to re-inscribe memories and practices of the coloniser. We were keen to ensure that historically located "hegemonic forms of knowledge production" did not come to "undermine localised knowledge about education and school systems", particularly those associated with leading (Chilisa & Ntseane, 2010, p. 617). Thus, in designing the research tools and setting the focus of the conversations with the principals, we wanted to reduce the opportunity for misrepresentation. We did so by encouraging storytelling, having multiple encounters and establishing open researcher relationships, thus making evident the intersection between our lives as researchers and former classroom teachers and the lives of the novice principals assuming leadership of their schools.

As co-participants in a lived postcoloniality, we accepted, as taught through the stories of our ancestors and lived in the contrapuntal movements of the 21st century, that reality is a "complex and contradictory [collection of] movements and shifts" (Gaztambide-Fernandez, 2012, p. 42). What we took for granted was the interrelationship between our analytical tools and our conscious (and unconscious) assumptions for making sense of the encounter. We unwittingly assumed that the power relationships between researcher and researched were bounded by and to the field of encounter. It is in the analytical phase that we began to realise that researcher positioning is not only a concern for action and power, which emerges prior to and while in the field, but also in the writing-up space as well (Bozalek, 2011).

In the first instance, the design of the study drew attention to the ways in which the theory of practice architectures (the theoretical framework for the study) encouraged an understanding of practice orders and arrangements as existing in the present (Kemmis & Grootenboer, 2008; Kemmis et al., 2014). The theory of practice architectures articulates what practices are made of, how they are held together in sites and how they are enabled and constrained through cultural-discursive (sayings), material-economic (doings) and social-political (relatings) orders and arrangements (Kemmis et al., 2014). But making such a claim as to the understanding of practice orders and arrangements required that the researchers observe the *sayings, doings and relatings* of the experiencing of the practice. We accessed the stories around the practice of socialising into leading (Brown, Esnard, & Bristol, 2014) through the discursive memories of the participants (i.e., in the re-experiencing or reflecting upon the practice). The data suggested that the orders and arrangements of the practice of learning to lead existed in a twin dimension of interrelated temporality. This sense of a practice can be situated in a connection between the histories and stories told about the past *sayings, doings* and *relatings* of a practice of socialising into leadership (past-spoken), as well as, in the observable/experiencing moment, in the *sayings, doings* and *relatings* of a practice of socialising into leadership (present-seen). However, the employment of a narrative research design allowed us access only to the past-spoken. Thus, while the space was created for us to access the principals' stories of how they learned in the initial stages to be principals, we were not provided with the opportunity to 'witness in the present' the process of their socialisation into leadership.

In the second instance, in communicating the story of socialising into leadership, the story which emerged was choppy, made up of connected but un-bridged parts. It became apparent that we could not present the *sayings* without connections to the *doings* and *relatings*. Attempting to do so would have ensured that we lost the nuances of the cultural dynamics of the site. For instance, we found that while the theory of practice architectures provided the frame that allowed us to describe the event that we conceptualised as a practice of socialising into leadership, in the description it also served to distil and decouple the bonds between the *sayings, doings* and *relatings*, orders and arrangements which constituted a practice of socialising into leadership. This *in-analysis-research* experience was contrary to the theory itself, which relies on the intersubjectivity of each dimension to make the practice in question meaningful.

In trying to read the stories of the principals through the theory of practice architectures, we found that we were filtering out elements of the principals' experiences. In the presentation of the *sayings, doings* and *relatings* surrounding leadership socialising experiences we were losing hold of the ontological (social) substance of the practice. These were explicit, historically entrenched ways of constructing and relating to women, the young, and authority figures, ways which provided an explanation of the relationships evident between the principal and staff, principal and community and principal and state and/or church. This was further complicated when we realised that activities which were constructed as evidence of *sayings* could also function as evidence of *doings* and forms of *relatings*. These complexities were not being comprehensively captured in the re-presenting of the field and the experiences of the principals in the field. This became a source of contention in the act of communicating *with, for* and *on* a field characterised by a particular set of historical forms of interacting, leading and learning to lead. We had to ensure that their stories and the arguments we were building were being understood within the context of the histories of the community (Layne Hatch, 2003). We needed to privilege the historical distributions of power "as well as processes for communicating, making decisions, and enforcing decisions" (Layne Hatch, 2003, p. 5). The challenge was how to capture this aspect in the interaction between theory, method and cultural obligations.

We chose to resolve the communication challenge by reframing our conceptualisation of the field, seeing it as a mosaic of overlapping social processes and animated landscapes. Thinking in this way provided us with the opportunity to identify the commonalities and differences within the stories and shared experiences of the principals, the union representative and the School Supervisor I (SSI). Treating the data as a mosaic of landscapes demonstrated the "multi-functionality of landscapes" (Lapka & Cudlinova, 2003, p. 324). It illuminated the interaction between the worlds of the principals, the union representative and the SSI – worlds that were connected through histories. This landscape analysis made the practice of socialising into leadership less opaque. It highlighted the ways in which the principals, the union representative and the SSI, while interacting with others, were able to select from a range of possible activities and tasks which comprised the interconnected social projects of education, religion/faith teaching, enculturation and school management (i.e., the work of schools). A landscape analysis defined the practice of making sense of data as an integrated "communicative space through which people [including the researcher] develop identities and form relationships based on shared practices and ways of doing and saying things" (Lloyd, 2010, p. 9).

Acting in this way ensured that we (1) made "adequate space for local narratives", making explicit use of the voices of the participants (Uddin, 2011, p. 463); (2) avoided the seduction of the granular for explanatory power, but instead privileged contestation, messiness and complex particularities as powerful resources for sense making; and (3) worked to ensure that a general theory or method did not become an "othering ideology" which could have worked to constrain "how non-Western people are heard and written about" (Chilisa & Ntseane, 2010, p. 618). Yet, we recognise the need to move beyond the accepted dualist, oppressive practice of 'the Western' on 'the non-Western' and begin to speak of the ways in which 'the researched' can be 'othered', often by researchers who share similar histories with the researched. We need to look at the ways in which hegemony and simplification, as an ideology of colonialism can be re-inscribed through research practices *in* and *on* various sites, by researchers internal and external to the site. Sefa Dei (2012), speaking from an African scholar's position, suggests that (Black) academics are politically and culturally obligated to

> pioneer new analytical systems for understanding our local/indigenous communities ... This is an opportunity and a challenge in the struggle to save ... ourselves from becoming "intellectual imposters", simply good at mimicking dominant theories and knowledges in the [Western] academy.
>
> (p. 102)

This is an endorsement for constructing different types of encounters through research and in the communicating of research. The ethic of care implicit in decolonising research *practices* is that it is not only about creating opportunities for empowerment for learners and members of a site. It is also about encouraging researchers to own the responsibilities of the consequences of their research, as a form of representing and re-presenting others, even when they share the same history and cultural experiences as those who are the subjects of the research. This requires that we recognise the historical compromises which condition educational and research practice.

With particular reference to the practices of socialising into leadership (which is integral to the role of the principal), viewing the practice of *communicating research* in this way works to reduce the possibility of the hegemony of "settler perspectives" (Tuck & Yang, 2012), that is, the ideologies of the coloniser, where a practice originating from a more developed site shapes what could count as knowledges of practices in another settled and developing site. Thus, in reading the data through historically animated landscapes and centring the local narratives, we work against a rehearsal of coloniser images that are revived through tacit practices. They portray local school leaders and policy makers as incompetent and inept, lacking vision or failing to see what is obvious.

Instead, we promote images of sites of compromise (in acquiring resourcing, politics, relationships) and novice school leaders whose consciousness and practices are shaped by a particular history of encounter (see Bristol, Esnard, & Brown, 2015).

Resolving the challenge: Highlighting the practice landscape

As a practice of communicating research, we illustrate a *practice landscape* (Bristol, Brown, & Esnard, 2014) which highlights the ways in which historical understandings, cultural-discursive (sayings), material-economic (doings) and social-political (relatings) arrangements negotiate the connection between age/experience, gender, the exercise of authority and learning to lead. The story as it is re-presented represents a complex arena in which historically constructed notions of age influence ideas of seniority and authority. In contemporary practices of leadership appointment and socialisation, these historical ideas are creating *social noise*, which prefigures the leading-learning experience of novice leaders.

Although changing, in Trinidad and Tobago chronological age signals earning of respect and a position of authority in the home and the wider community. Given that age is also a marker of increased experience, knowledge and wisdom, younger members of society are expected to unquestionably defer to their elders. This relationship between chronological age and positions of leadership has traditionally influenced leadership appointments and opportunities for training for leadership. This relationship is reflected in the schools where seniority, which is determined by the number of years of experience in the teaching service (Willams & Harvey, 1985), is an indicator of positional status: the more senior the individual, the higher they are ranked within the organisational hierarchy.

However, the recent push for school-based management has signalled a redefinition of seniority (GORTT, 2007, 2008), and with it a challenge to culturally accepted ways of relating between senior and junior faculty. Specifically, members of staff who were traditionally defined as junior based on chronological age are now gaining positional authority and seniority based on their own merit or academic qualifications in the field of education. This shift poses a challenge to the culturally accepted path to positions of authority, and as a consequence, the culture of the organisation.

Adding to the complexity of the situation is the linking of age to gender. When this occurs, as is often the case, this creates a different level of cultural challenge for the novice principal. As such, the hegemony of the man (even the junior man in leadership) appears to be more culturally acceptable than the hegemony of the woman (particularly the junior woman in leadership). Additionally, young women in leadership are confronted with expectations of "sexual purity", such that failure to maintain these expectations can result in a challenge to their leadership (Esnard, Bristol, & Brown, 2013). Understanding how good classroom teachers are socialised into the principalship therefore demands a consideration of this cultural relationship and the ways in which it influences opportunities to learn to lead and the capacity to establish legitimacy or the *cultural authority to lead*.

The data also revealed a clash between cultural assumptions of age, gender and demands for qualifications, both as an aspect of socialising into the principalship and as a feature of encounter while in the principalship. We were not able to capture this cultural overlay through a granular explication of the *sayings, doings* and *relatings* of the principals. Instead, we allowed the voices of the participants to make transparent the ways in which the discourse of policy (sayings), the new promotional pathways and activities of the Ministry of Education (MOE) and the church (doings) and the established expectations of the leadership (relatings) were negotiated through and by cultural notions of who was best qualified to lead and when they were qualified to lead.

Presentation of the data

The collective narrative below allowed the intersubjective relationship between the *sayings*, *doings* and *relatings* to unfold against a backdrop of cultural assumptions of and for authority. Thus, this is not the story of one early career principal; it is a narrative constructed through and by the mosaic of the similar, yet different, overlapping lived experiences of the principals, the school supervisor and the union representative. In particular, we highlight the relationship between age, gender and cultural authority to lead.

Age and cultural authority

Sally (SS1),[2] in addressing the issue of principal appointments, pointed out that, "now potential principals are required to have a first degree . . . preferably in [administration] because that would be part of the criteria for selection for the principal". Given the introduction of the first degree (bachelor's in education) as a requirement for promotion to principalship, a new phenomenon has occurred and it would seem, according to Paul, the union representative, as if the Teaching Service Commission has been

> making a concerted effort to appoint younger persons . . . In the past it was very common to see an older person maybe in their 40s and upwards becoming an administrator in a school. That seems to be changing now. . . . So they seem to be breaking from that tradition. . . . a lot of young people in their mid or late 30s are . . . getting appointed as principals and vice principals.

This new requirement in Trinidad and Tobago of a first degree and the phenomenon of younger primary school principals also coincides with the changes being made to the promotional structure for primary school teachers, through the creation of middle management positions such as Senior Teacher and Heads of Departments (HOD).[3] However, the principals who have experienced the changes to the promotional structure within primary education have not experienced it with the clarity referred to by Sally. Whereas Sally suggested that a principal appointment was based solely upon meritocracy, Matthew (in his late 30s and a principal with over 15 years of teaching experience) argued that with respect to denominational schools, "the board has the power to veto" the suggestion of an appointment made by the Teaching Service Commission and say, "Look, we don't want this person but we want this person". This practice of church boards vetoing appointments is supported by the Concordat of 1960, which outlines that "a teacher shall not be appointed to a school if the denominational board objects to such an appointment on moral or religious grounds" (GORTT, 1960).

Emily (in her early 50s, with almost 30 years of teaching experience), however, suggested that the shadow between the confines of qualifications and seniority was not only to be seen within the discursive framework of administrative policy but could also be perceived within the doings of the Ministry of Education (MOE). As Emily stated:

> it is a bit of a controversy since . . . some schools of thought say you need to have a degree in educational administration but I have seen people who have gotten the post and they don't have the degree.

This tension between qualifications and seniority and the apparent shifting practices and positions of denominational boards and the MOE, that appointments be based on merit, is resulting in a challenge of ageism, which is experienced by some of the younger principals.

As of 2009 with 79% of primary school teachers and vice-principals being female in Trinidad and Tobago (World Bank, 2014; Esnard et al., 2013), the societal and culturally imposed position of the female can add to the challenge of the principalship. This context shapes the social-political dimensions of their early experiences of learning how to lead. In referring to the younger principal phenomenon, Chloe (a principal with approximately 30 years' classroom experience) pointed out that

> they are now promoting these young principals, however, that experience, that administrative experience is really missing . . . So that they go into the schools as young principals and they meet a lot of senior teachers there with their backs up . . . It's not working for them . . . it has to do with age more than anything else. . . . anytime they appoint you in that 30s bracket . . . people look at you like, "This little girl come to tell me what I could do . . . because she has done her B.Ed". . . . It's creating a little problem.

Julia (in her mid-30s, with approximately 15 years of service) also recognises this challenge. In recounting the early days of learning how to lead, Julia stated, "The majority of them (staff members), 95% are older than me. So you got that impression that this is a young girl".

Julia and Chloe's positions present the ageism dilemma, which feeds the ways in which some principals were socialised within their schools and into the practice of leadership. The ageism challenge also has implications for questions around legitimacy and cultural authority. These become evident in the encounter stage of being socialised into the principalship, particularly in moments of conflict as the principals manage the interactions between themselves and the community. The data hinted that conflict resolution according to the letter of the law (enforcing regulations) or the spirit of the law (interpreting regulations in context) was influenced by the collective and past/historical experiences of the principal, how the principal interpreted the law guiding the practice of teachers and the accepted cultural legitimacy of the principal.

John (in his early 40s, with just over 20 years in the teaching service) told of addressing a management situation with teachers who turned up late for work. His story recounted a balance between discretion and law. As he tells it:

> We have teachers that reach here basically 10 o'clock on a morning, whereas I have a teacher that reaches here 6:15 every morning. Now, tell me when the teacher who reaches 6:15 tells me, "John, I have to go to my son's parents' day, I should have that teacher apply [for the time]? No . . . go ahead Miss; I will make an entry into the log[4] book! I [am not going to] let you apply, why should I let you apply? You are here from 6:15". . . . but then if a teacher comes here [to school] 10 o'clock, I [am] sorry you know . . . I will write the time you arrived because it is [a] consistent thing . . . some of them they don't want to recognise that it is nothing personal, but how can I justify this? As administrator I have to justify that.

Teacher absence and presence in school are recorded daily in the logbook. This is a part of the material world of the principal. In this case, both teachers will be logged in a sense, but next to the name of the first teacher there will be a note, which will indicate that the principal used his discretionary powers to allow that teacher 'time off', given a practice of exemplary punctuality.

Salome is the principal of a historically prestigious denominational single-sex (girls) primary school in a medium-sized town. In our conversations, she hinted at, but never openly acknowledged, that she is potentially "challenged" because of her circumstances of being a "novice" and "young" school leader. Although responding to a different type of staff indiscipline, Salome (in her mid-30s) adhered to the letter of the law. She is a principal with just over 20 years in the teaching service. She too shared her perception of how age and experience affect her experiences of leadership:

> I have one incident, where, a teacher was called into the office. I called [the teacher] to discuss a matter, something was happening in the school at the time, and [the teacher] refused to respond to me . . . and that is indiscipline; you must respond to your senior [the person in charge]. . . . I had to . . . write, I had to log . . . it was a tough time in the school for me . . . but I did what I had to do. . . . Once you summoned a junior member to your office regardless of how many times you have called them, [no matter] what is the situation they must respond, so, [the teacher] not responding to me was a pure case of indiscipline. . . . You must respect my office. . . . I feel it was a time where I was being tried . . . I gave orders, I gave directives, it was not followed through. . . . I try to maintain a good relationship with the staff, but where those things are concerned there is no room for that.

From the data age does not appear to be the only challenge to cultural authority. There is some evidence that sex and gender is also a significant factor.

Sex and cultural authority

Julia was in her mid-30s, had less than 20 years in the teaching service and was in similar educational and leadership circumstances to Salome above, but in a large primary school. She recounted handling a comparable situation of insubordination by a staff member by appealing to the rules and regulations governing conduct in the school. Unlike Salome, however, she acknowledged the ways in which being "young", "new" and "female" became part of her leadership challenge. In recounting her first few days in the position she highlighted that the staff were almost all older than she was and as a result as a novice leader she had

> the rumours to put up with . . . It means that you have to be constantly . . . on your guard . . . Because they look at you, they look at how you dress, they look at what you say, they look at how you discipline, even the teachers as well . . . Parents look at you . . . All eyes are on you.

Unlike Salome and Julia, Hannah (in her mid-30s with less than 20 years' teaching experience) made an explicit connection between the challenge of being young and the ways in which particular social/religious expectations for young single women shaped her experience of being socialised into leading. Specifically, she spoke of the ways in which these social criteria created conflict in the initial stages of being socialised as a principal. It must be noted as a case in point that Hannah was applying to be principal of a denominational school. In the quotation below we see the positional power and practices of the denominational board appearing to distort the boundaries between the rising practice of appointment by qualifications and the decreasing practice of appointment through moral preference:

> I am not married but I am also not living with a man. Right! If I were [living with a man] and it came out I could have been removed . . . you know women who are in this position are expected to live like nuns and the men can do whatever they want. . . . There are men who are not living the Catholic lifestyle [but they] get promoted because they need more males as principal[s] especially in schools where there are many males and they try to facilitate the males but sometimes the women go through a piece of hell in that interview.

In the interview for the position of a principal in a rural denominational school, Hannah's appropriateness to lead was viewed through her gender and her age. She was challenged and asked:

> "Are you one of those young 30-somethings who is going to get pregnant out of wedlock?" That was my question. My response was it is not my plan to be a single parent and I left it at that. But I do know that should I get pregnant out of wedlock while holding this post I would come under some heavy artillery fire . . . With the men, people don't know, you understand?

A challenge to the positional authority of the principal can be interpreted as a challenge to person, particularly given the distinct cultural patterns of relating between elder and junior, authority and subordinate, male and female. In this space, principals with less than 20 years in the teaching service and female principals were held to a double standard, i.e., they were expected to justify their legitimacy as leaders through their practice to the school community. In their anxiety to ensure and secure their authority, some used the letter of the law as a tool around which they structured their *sayings*, *doings* and *relatings* when leading. This was especially true for principals with less than 20 years in the teaching service. This was so given their formalised training in the university as a part of their qualifications for the position. However, their appeal to the letter of the law in times of challenge re-inscribed the image of the overseer,[5] cracking the whip over the backs of staff members who challenged the positional authority of the principals. The emergence of this *practice landscape* is made comprehensible against expectations for cultural legitimacy in leading. In a clash of management expectations, the rule of law functions as both the tool of authority and the understanding of compromising relationships in school leadership. It constructs learning to be a principal as a challenge of context.

Discussion

This project draws attention to the school leadership research field in two ways. First, it positions learning to be a principal as a challenge of context. Second, it posits that research is an encounter *with* and challenge *of* context (re-presenting and representing of the field). In terms of the first point – learning to be a principal as a challenge of context – the data suggest that in the context of Trinidad and Tobago, qualifications were not enough to gain the cultural legitimacy to learn to lead and to lead. To expect this was to: (1) set up teachers with less than 20 years' experience in the field to fail at being a principal; and (2) construct unnecessary elements of tension around their practices of learning and leading. This is particularly so in contexts where age equates to legitimacy to lead. What is required in this context is a recognition of the ways in which historical-cultural assumptions of authority (seniority) drive and undermine contemporary and internationalised practices of authority (qualifications).

It can be argued that schools, teachers and community stakeholders in Trinidad and Tobago (i.e., the church, the Ministry of Education and parents) needed themselves to be socialised into practices where qualifications gained through university degrees were recognised and accepted as legitimate symbols for leadership in the presence of limited experiential or cultural credentials. However, it is just as important to recognise that as far as the denominational boards were concerned, qualifications were only one of the criteria for becoming a principal. Whereas the Ministry of Education relied heavily on qualifications as the main (sometimes only) criterion, the boards also took into consideration issues of morality and religious practices and beliefs as catechised by the specific denomination. This system, which is enshrined in law through the Concordat (1960), requires compromise and often works well. However, it must be recognised that the structure also ensures the inevitability of conflict between the Ministry of Education and denominational boards.

In terms of the second point – recognising research (its findings and practice) as an encounter *with* and challenge *of* context – demands that: (1) researchers bear the historical, cultural and political responsibilities *of* and *for* context and (2) re-position and re-interrogate notions of insider and outsider research. This is principally the case when an insider researcher can unwittingly become a research coloniser if issues of representation and re-presenting the field are not explicitly addressed. It is not that we are saying that these issues are not present for the outsider researcher; rather we recognise that in the field of the research practice, the outsider researcher is more easily seen as a potential coloniser researcher. Rather, we are saying that the same potential exists for an insider researcher – both at the point of entering and engaging with the field – and at the point of *speaking about, speaking for and proclaiming on the field*. Insider researchers assume 'more voice' to speak for and on the behalf of a community to which she or he belongs, acquired through the sharing of common experiences. However, if this *privilege to speak on behalf of* is not continuously interrogated, then the opportunity for *culturally unethical practices* can arise.

For us, this potential was realised in the application of theory to the field, to make sense of and provide recommendations for practices of socialising into the principalship in Trinidad and Tobago. It became critical that historical-cultural overlays share primacy of space with how participants speak of, do and relate with the field while learning to lead. We acknowledge that a theory of practice architectures provides us as researchers with some of the explanatory power needed to make sense of practices in the sites, but it does not provide us with the re-presenting and representation agency needed to share the complexity and contradictory nature of the field. To do this, we relied on historical understandings of and for practice and a recognition of the phenomenon as landscaped and animated. Together these positions demanded the privileging of participant voices and the narrative unity of community experiences.

Notes

1 In other publications we have detailed the results from the data, paying attention to issues of gender performances and the contestation of emerging *practice landscapes* as novice leaders are socialised into leading practices. See (1) Bristol, L., Brown, L., & Esnard, T. (2014). Socialising principals: Early career primary school principals in Trinidad and Tobago. *Journal of Educational Administration and History* and (2) Esnard, F., Bristol, L., & Brown, L. (2013). Women as educational leaders: Emotional neutrality and psychic duality. In D. J. Davis & C. Chaney (Eds.), *Black women in Leadership: Their historical and contemporary contribution*. New York: Peter Lang. ISBN: 978-1-4331-1682-7
2 Identifying the school district will reveal the identity of the school supervisor.
3 Traditionally the more experienced teachers on staff assumed these positions and their related tasks. They were positions of authority and responsibility without the necessary remuneration. These positions were engaged in as a part of one's social

responsibility as a senior teacher. They also influenced success rates for promotion to vice-principal or principal.
4 This is a practice of making daily entries into the Log Book, which provides a record of the happenings in the school. This is a legal document and can be used to support any investigation into a staff- or student-related event. There is a practice of using entries as a punitive measure to keep teachers in line.
5 During colonial rule the overseer was given responsibility for ensuring the compliance of the enslaved population on the plantation. This person (a male) often carried a whip that was used to ensure compliance and obedience and instill fear into the enslaved population.

References

Allen, A., Anderson, K., Bristol, L., Downs, Y., O'Neil, D., Watts, N., & Wu, Q. (2009). Resiting the unethical in formalised ethics: Perspectives and experiences. In J. Satterwaite, H. Piper, & P. Sikes (Eds.), *Power in the academy* (pp. 135–142). Stoke on Trent: Trentham Books.
Biott, C., Moos, L., & Møller, J. (2001). Studying headteachers' professional lives: Getting the life history. *Scandinavian Journal of Educational Research*, 45(4), 395–410.
Bozalek, V. (2011). Acknowledging privilege through encounters with difference: Participatory learning and action techniques for decolonising methodologies in Southern contexts. *International Journal of Social Research Methodology*, 14(6), 469–484.
Bristol, L. (2010). Practising in betwixt oppression and subversion: Plantation pedagogy as a legacy of plantation economy in Trinidad and Tobago. *Power and Education*, 2(2), 167–182.
Bristol, L. (2012). *Plantation pedagogy: A postcolonial and global perspective* (Vol. 16). New York: Peter Lang.
Bristol, L., Brown, L., & Esnard, T. (2014). Socialising principals: Early career primary school principals in Trinidad and Tobago. *Journal of Educational Administration and History*, 46(1), 17–37. doi:10.1080/00220620.2014.855178.
Bristol, L., Esnard, T., & Brown, L. (2015). In the shadow/ from the shadow: The principal as a reflective practitioner. *Journal of Cases in Educational Leadership (JCEL)*, 18(3), 215–227.
Brown, L., & Conrad, D. A. (2007). School leadership in Trinidad and Tobago: The challenge of context. *Comparative Education Review*, 51(2), 181–201.
Brown, L., Esnard, T., & Bristol, L. (2014). Relating professional in-school networks, school leadership and assessment data to academic performance in Trinidad and Tobago: An exploration. *Caribbean Curriculum*, 22, 1–34.
Brown, L., & Lavia, J. (2013). School leadership and inclusive education in Trinidad and Tobago: Dilemmas and opportunities for practice. In P. Miller (Ed.), *School leadership in the Caribbean: Perception, practices, paradigms* (pp. 45–62). Oxford: Symposium Books.
Brown, T., & Roberts, L. (2000). Memories are made of this: Temporality and practitioner research. *British Educational Research Journal*, 26(5), 649–659.
Chesney, W. E. (2011). *Detranslation: A postcolonial discourse of education policy making in Guyana*. PhD, University of Sheffield, Sheffield.
Chilisa, B., & Ntseane, B. (2010). Resisting dominant discourses: Implications of indigenous, African feminist theory and methods for gender and education research. *Gender and Education*, 22(6), 617–632.

Esnard, T., Bristol, M. S. L., & Brown, L. (2013). Women as educational leaders: Emotional neutrality and psychic duality. In D. J. Davis & C. Chaney (Eds.), *Black women in leadership: Their historical and contemporary contributions* (pp. 74–90). London: Peter Lang.

Gaztambide-Fernandez, R. A. (2012). Decolonization and the pedagogy of solidarity. *Decolonization: Indigeneity, Education and Society, 1*(1), 41–67.

Government of Trinidad and Tobago. (1960). *The concordat of 1960: Assurances for the preservation and character of denominational schools.* Port of Spain: Government of Trinidad and Tobago.

Government of Trinidad and Tobago. (2007). *The national model for education in Trinidad and Tobago-early childhood, primary and secondary.* Port of Spain: Government of Trinidad and Tobago.

Government of Trinidad and Tobago. (2008). *Forty-eight session of the International Conference on Education (ICE): National report on the development of education in Trinidad and Tobago.* Port of Spain: Government of Trinidad and Tobago.

Haug, F. (2008). Memory work. *Australian Feminist Studies, 23*(58), 537–541.

Jansson, M., Wendt, M., & Åse, C. (2008). Memory work reconsidered. *NORA – Nordic Journal of Feminist and Gender Research, 16*(4), 228–240.

Jones, M. (2004). Mining our collective memory. *Souls: A Critical Journal of Black Politics, Culture, and Society, 6*(3), 71–76.

Kemmis, S., Edwards-Groves, C., Hardy, I., Wilkinson, J., & Lloyd, A. (2010). On being 'stirred in' to practices: Observations of 'learning' how to go on. Paper presented at the Australian Association for Research in Education 2010, Melbourne, Australia.

Kemmis, S., & Grootenboer, P. (2008). Situating praxis in practice: Practice architectures and the cultural, social and material conditions for practice. In S. Kemmis & T. J. Smith (Eds.), *Enabling praxis: Challenges* (pp. 37–63). Rotterdam: SENSE.

Lapka, M., & Cudlinova, E. (2003). Changing landscapes, changing landscape's story. *Landscape Research, 28*(3), 323–328.

Layne Hatch, G. (2003). *Arguing in communities: Reading and writing arguments in context.* New York: McGraw-Hill.

Lloyd, A. (2010). *Information literacy landscapes: Information literacy in education, workplace and everyday contexts.* Woodhead: Chandos Publishing Cambridge.

Mintzberg, H. (1979). *The structuring of organizations.* Englewood Cliffs, NJ: Prentice Hall.

Neuman, W. L. (2006). *Social research methods: Qualitative and quantitative approaches* (6th ed.). Boston, MA: Pearson Education Inc.

Sefa Dei, G. (2012). Indigenous anti-colonial knowledge as 'heritage knowledge' for promoting Black/ African education in diaspora contexts. *Decolonization: Indigeneity, Education and Society, 1*(1), 102–119.

Silins, H. C. (1994). The relationship between transformational and transactional leadership and school improvement outcomes. *School Effectiveness and School Improvement, 5*(3), 272–298.

Tuck, E., & Wayne Yang, K. (2012). Decolonization is not a metaphor. *Decolonisation: Indigeneity, Education and Society, 1*(1), 1–40.

Uddin, N. (2011). Decolonising ethnography in the field: An anthropological account. *International Journal of Social Research Methodology, 14*(6), 455–467.

World Bank. (2014). *World Bank education statistics – Trinidad and Tobago.* Retrieved from http://knoema.com/WBEdStats2014Apr/education-statistics-world-bank-april-2014?country=1001330-trinidad-and-tobago

9 Practice traditions of researching educational leadership across national contexts

Jane Wilkinson, Karin Rönnerman, Laurette Bristol and Petri Salo

Introduction

In this chapter we challenge the homogenising and largely taken-for-granted assumptions which underpin methods adopted by much of the educational leadership research field when analysing leadership practices within and across differing national contexts. Specifically, we examine participatory methodologies on/for leadership practices and how these methodologies draw on particular traditions within differing national and site-specific contexts. Drawing on practice architectures as our shared theoretical lens (c.f., Kemmis & Grootenboer, 2008), we provide examples of the varying methodologies we employed as researchers to analyse educational leadership practices in our study sites of Swedish preschools (research circles), Finnish principal groups (study circles) and an Australian secondary school (feminist and postcolonial methodologies). Our research in each of the sites is informed by differing historical, political and cultural traditions and settings. It is also informed by varied subject locations and our epistemological stances as researchers (i.e., action research, feminism, postcolonialism). In this chapter, we render visible the practice traditions of our respective settings, as well as our theoretical stance as researchers. We argue that attention to our subject locations as researchers, the research tradition being applied and our epistemological stances are critical in transforming, rather than reproducing, scholarship about educational leading as a practice. In so doing we stress the fluid and contested nature of these practice traditions, rather than assuming them to be 'fixed' and stable within an imagined unitary national context. The chapter concludes with a discussion of the implications and significance of explicating differing methodologies and researcher stances for educational leadership scholarship.

Methodological critiques of educational leadership scholarship

Until recently there has been a dearth of research in educational leadership scholarship which takes into consideration the "culturally bound" nature of educational leadership (Dimmock & Walker, 2005, p. 1) and the nexus of leading practices that unfolds in site-specific locations in all their ontological 'happeningness'

(Schatzki, 2006). The knowledges, understandings and meanings attributed to 'good' educational leadership practice vary within and across national contexts. However, educational leadership scholarship has tended to be highly ethnocentric. This is despite belated recognition that leadership and management are culturally constructed and that how educational sites are organised and led varies depending on differing cultural values and traditions (Hallinger, 2005, p. ix). The dominant research traditions continue to assume a "false universalism" dictated by Western individualistic and egalitarian values that do not apply to the same degree in other cultures (Dimmock & Walker, 2005, p. 205). These prevailing tendencies continue despite the rise in "super diversity" amongst the populations of nation states such as Australia and Sweden (Vertovec, 2007). This is a diversity reflected not only in increased immigration, but rising levels of stratification in terms of wealth distribution (Beach, Dovemark, Schwartz, & Öhrn, 2013; Öhrn, 2012; Vinson, 2015).

In terms of methodologies, educational scholarship has been slow to respond to the implications of the preceding changes in and across societies. The field has been colonised by positivist and functionalist paradigms drawn from particular bodies of Anglo-American and Eurocentric knowledges to the exclusion of socially critical theories such as feminism and postcolonialism (Scheurich, 1995, as cited in Blackmore, 2005, p. 178). Yet the rise in levels of ethnic diversity and social stratification has clear implications for the study of leadership practices. It suggests the need for new models, methodologies and modes of analysis informed by a range of disciplines to provide innovative ways to understand, examine and inform how these factors are impacting on educational leadership practices in diverse sites (Dimmock & Walker, 2005, p. 205). It implies that scholars need to examine not only the content, i.e., the *what* is being studied, but *how* we go about studying it – in terms of our research design, implementation and writing (Stephens, 2012). It also suggests that scholars need to lay bare the differing epistemological and ontological positions that inform our subject locations and actions as researchers.

This chapter responds to these critiques by attempting to render explicit both how we went about our research, as well as the differing epistemological and ontological stances we brought to our research. In so doing, we aim to challenge the homogenising lenses critiqued above. The chapter illustrates that despite some commonalities as researchers, e.g., adopting the same theoretical lens, our methods of attending to leadership practice and our varying subject locations as researchers required us to be culturally nuanced and historically and politically sensitive to the highly diverse nature of our sites. This in turn necessitated us drawing on a range of methodological tools. For instance, the Swedish study of preschool teachers deliberately employed research circles in which participants actively drew from and interrogated their own site-specific experiences and practices as leaders. In turn, the participants then contributed to building new knowledge about leading relevant to their site by reflecting upon and developing more critical understandings of their own practices. The use of research circles draws on Swedish traditions of folk enlightenment combined with action research methodologies. The employment of such methods was a deliberate attempt by Karin to enact her reflexive stance as a Nordic action researcher who had a core commitment to undertaking more critical and emancipatory forms of research.

Attention to these aspects of our research practice is crucial. Educational leadership requires new knowledges about how to lead in increasingly diverse and complex educational settings. Gaining such new knowledge necessitates a range of alternative methodological tools. Such tools help us to interrogate how particular bodies of knowledge about leadership may be produced and reproduced through how we conduct our research. Hence, in this chapter we present three differing cases in which a range of different methodological tools were drawn on and in which the researchers' methodological, epistemological and ontological stances were laid bare. Before doing so however, we provide a background context to our studies, by explicating the theoretical lens that binds these cases together.

A shared theoretical lens: The theory of practice architectures

One of the major trends in education systems in Australia, Sweden and Finland – reflected in the sites of educational leadership practice which follow – is the increasing accountability demands placed upon principals for improving the quality of education. This is an aspect of what Finnish educator Pasi Sahlberg has labelled the Global Education Reform Movement or GERM (Sahlberg, 2012). However, how different forms of accountability are understood and enacted depends greatly upon the differing regional and national contexts in which principals and other educational leaders are located. For instance, in our Swedish case, educational improvement was taken up in the preschools as part of an overall drive for leading systematic development of teachers for quality. In our Finnish case, there were 'light touch' forms of accountability through quality assurance, profiling and marketisation (Uljens & Nyman, 2013, pp. 40, 41). In our Australian case, the emphasis was on enhancing learning outcomes for low socioeconomic status (SES) students through improving teaching quality. Although accountability writ large may have been a common factor across our cases, there were key differences also, such as how broader practice arrangements including school reform intersected with other arrangements in our very different national contexts and educational settings.

To explain the process of leadership transformation in our respective sites, we turned to the theory of practice architectures (Kemmis & Grootenboer, 2008). The latter theory adopts a site ontological view of practice, that is, an approach which posits that in order to understand "human co-existence" we need to examine in all its particularity the "context... [or site]... of which it is inherently a part" (Schatzki, 2005, pp. 465, 467). On this view, organisations such as schools and preschools are inherently social phenomena, unfolding through the "happening" of practices and activities (Schatzki, 2006). A site ontological approach foregrounds that researchers attend to the *practices* of leadership and how they unfold in the specificity of a particular site, rather than to the work of individual leadership practitioners (e.g., principals, teachers) or systems.

Practice architectures is a theory of what practices are composed (c.f., Kemmis & Grootenboer, 2008; Kemmis et al., 2014). It suggests that educational practices such as leading (teaching, professional learning, student learning, researching) do not take place in a vacuum. Instead they are always mediated "by a lifetime of inhabiting the social world" (Kemmis et al., 2014, p. 4). Participants in a practice encounter one another in intersubjective spaces that are shaped by previously existing arrangements or architectures and the material objects brought in to these spaces through the medium of language, "space-time in the material world" and social relationships (Kemmis et al., 2014, p. 4). The inherent sociality of practices draws attention to how practices are variously prefigured (enabled and/or constrained) by the broader practice conditions or arrangements which shape a practice and give it a practical intelligibility in which it can be recognised as a leadership practice of a particular kind.

Practice architectures include the *cultural-discursive arrangements* that enable and constrain how we express ourselves in the medium of language, through participants' *sayings*. They include the *material-economic arrangements* in the medium of activities and work that prefigure participants' *doings*. Finally, they include the *social-political arrangements* existing in the medium of social space, through participants' *relatings* (Kemmis et al., 2014).

The theory of practice architectures emanates from a reflexive dialogue within the Pedagogy Education and Praxis (PEP) network. The network is a cross-national and cross-institutional network consisting of members from Australia, the Netherlands, Sweden, Norway, Finland, Colombia and Trinidad and Tobago. The network shares a common interest in the nature, traditions and condition of pedagogy, education and praxis and how they may be developed in different national contexts and educational settings. From this perspective, educational practices such as leading are not viewed as instrumentalist techniques which can be reduced to a set of individualised competencies or capabilities as mandated by state or national policies. Rather, they are located in a broader humanistic understanding of educational practices as practices with social and history-making consequences for humanity (Kemmis & Smith, 2008). We now turn to a more specific examination of each of our cases of educational leadership practice to further this reflexive dialogue between educational practice traditions.

Leading practices in preschools in a district in Sweden

The Swedish case of leadership practice is based on a long-lasting partnership between the researcher and a preschool teacher using action research for improving quality in the preschools in a municipal district. In Sweden, systematic quality work is part of the statutory obligations for municipalities, principals and all teachers within the educational system in which preschools[1] are its first stage. Systematic quality development thereby constitutes a great deal of teachers' everyday work. It is described as a continuous and systematic process with the purpose of planning, following up and developing education towards national goals described in school laws (SFS, 2010, p. 800) and the curriculum for preschools (Lpfö 98, 2010).

The manner in which the preschools in the study organised the leading of systematic quality work originated in 2004 when three preschool teachers joined a one-year action research course facilitated by one of us – co-author Karin. After finishing the course, the teachers initiated setting up communicative spaces across the preschool sites for all personnel to meet and share experiences from their everyday practices using the same facilitating set-ups they had experienced in the course (Rönnerman, 2008a). Their actions and reflections were guided by Karin's epistemological stance, based as it was on collaboration, sharing experiences and co-producing knowledge all embedded in action research and the tradition of '*bildung*' (in Swedish *bildning*). As an action researcher Karin was interested in how leading practices evolved over time. When conducting a follow-up to the action research course, she was surprised that a majority of teachers had continued to carry out action research, with 68% of teachers taking on a leading role and facilitating their colleagues (Rönnerman, 2008b). The results suggested that action research was not solely about developing one's own practice but was also generating leading practices for professional learning (Edwards-Groves & Rönnerman, 2013).

Some years later a handful of teachers from the original course contacted Karin, wanting to learn and understand more about their role as leaders. Rather than lecturing them, Karin organised a research circle where equal amounts of time were used for discussing research on leadership and sharing experiences of being a leader. To investigate what leading could be about and especially leading one's colleagues, a number of methods were used to foster participation and collaboration, including creating a mind-map for grasping the experiences of being a leader. Based on the teachers' individual mind-maps, a collaborative mind-map was created (c.f., Rönnerman & Olin, 2014; Rönneman, 2015). In this way experiences and knowledge were shared and deepened amongst teachers. In one case the discussions led to enhanced collective actions (c.f., Rönnerman & Olin, 2014).

The way the research circle was organised can be traced back to the Nordic tradition of *folk enlightenment*, in which the study circle is a key form for adult learning. Hence, coming together to meet, share and discuss one's individual and collective learning had its roots in important cultural practices for the teachers. These teacher-learning practices can be connected to *bildung*, i.e., the growth as a human (c.f., Rönnerman & Salo, 2012, 2014). In the 1970s, the original *folk enlightenment* study circles were transformed into research circles. This shift signalled that relevant research should be taken up in a study circle led by a researcher. Hence, the practice of the preschool research circles allowed 12 preschool teacher-leaders (all of whom were facilitating their colleagues in their own preschools) to come together every second month to share experiences about their leading practices through examining their practices, i.e., their sayings, doings and relatings. In the research circle, there was a specific focus on teacher-leaders' dialogue, with an emphasis on listening to one another and providing responses to other participants' sayings. The shared aim of this focus was to develop understandings of what leading was about. Moreover, the methods used in the research circle in turn enabled the facilitation practices to take root and flourish in the teacher-leaders' own preschools (Rönnerman & Olin, 2014).

The research circle ran at the same time as these teachers were initiating, planning and leading action research in their preschools. The methods in the research circle permitted teachers to distance themselves from their leadership, allowing them to discuss their role with other leaders, share their experiences and explore research on leadership in order to deepen and widen their knowledge and understanding of their practices.

As one preschool teacher remarked:

> We as facilitators have had more time together and by that had the opportunity to ventilate much about our commitments as facilitators, i.e., how to go on, together with good feedback and concrete things to change. It feels like we are working to improve our facilitation and I have got more knowledge to take with me. When you discuss what you are doing and put it in your own words, it gives you a different meaning and significance.
> (adapted from Rönnerman & Olin, 2014, p. 106)

The teacher's quote connects to Carr and Kemmis' (1986, p. 165) definition of action research, which refers to action research as improving one's practice, one's understandings of practice and one's understanding of where the practice take place. Rather than only 'improving' their practice, however, the preschool teachers were deepening their understanding of the context of the practice itself and the context in which the practice took place. In other words, the research study methodology facilitated an understanding of the cultural-discursive, material-economic and socio-political arrangements holding particular preschool practices in place (Kemmis et al., 2014).

The *cultural-discursive arrangements* which enabled this deepening knowledge were the traditions of the research circle. These practice traditions were familiar to participants as they had been part of the previous action research program. In this previous program, they were facilitated in groups with dialogue at the forefront, based on the democratic traditions of education and action research in Nordic countries (Rönnerman & Salo, 2012). The national discourse in Sweden foregrounds professional learning as *collegial*, rather than imposed from top-down, with professional learning built on teachers facilitating their colleagues in regard to a specific subject (Skolverket, 2015). These forms are, however, not called study circles, but 'collegial learning', in order to fit global (and Anglo-American) discourses of professional learning (c.f., Hattie, 2008; Timperley, 2008).

The *material-economic arrangements* which enabled these practices to flourish included the Swedish municipalities. These municipalities, which are responsible for education delivery in Sweden, funded the release time and travel costs of teachers to participate in the research circle. Furthermore, the preschool principals gave permission for the teachers to take the lead back in their preschools. The principals reorganised the preschool calendar so that teacher-leaders could foster a similar kind of communicative space to the research circles in the action research program. These dialogue circles were led by the teachers throughout the school year. Moreover, the principal used time in staff meetings for teacher teams to present ongoing work. At the end of the school year the teachers organised a professional learning day where the teacher teams shared the results of their action research. The three teacher leaders have since documented their work in a book co-authored with Karin (Nylund, Sandback, Wilhelmsson, & Rönnerman, 2010).

The *social-political arrangements* which enabled these practices to flourish suggested that even though each district had a hierarchical organisation with directors at each level, more collegial leading practices were able to be developed through a sense of growing trust and solidarity between professionals in the organisation. For example, one of the principals permitted the teachers to lead a study day, signalling their trust in the teachers' leading practices. When three of the teacher-leaders requested further time to continue to facilitate their colleagues in dialogue circles (an unusual request emanating from teachers rather than preschool directors), the municipal board responsible for education supported this request (Rönnerman, 2008b). In this latter instance, the teachers demonstrated a sense of agency arising from the intersubjective spaces that had been nurtured by the research circle. This practice was a form of professional activism (Sachs, 2010), and fits Noffke's three dimensions of action research: the professional, the personal and the political (Noffke, 1997, 2009). In other words, the teachers developed professionally through their leading practices, grew personally by taking on a leading position and they acted politically through leading professional learning at their site.

The Swedish case shows how Nordic traditions of education shaped and informed the epistemological stance (democratic dialogue, active participation and collaboration embedded in action research) taken by Karin in her research with the preschool teachers. In turn this approach enabled the teachers to adopt an action research approach in their own practices and in so doing, generated capacities to lead professional learning (Edwards-Groves & Rönnerman, 2013). Importantly, however, not all municipalities were as supportive of the teachers, with some teachers not being allowed to leave their teaching in order to take part in the research circle. Interestingly, three teachers have sustained their action research stance over 11 years. The action research practices they have developed and facilitated are now part of a new organisation where one of these three teachers is acting coordinator of 15 middle leaders in a district (c.f., Grootenboer, Edwards-Groves, & Rönnerman, 2014; Rönnerman, Edwards-Groves, & Grootenboer, 2015).

Developing collaborative leadership practices in a rural municipality in Finland

In the Finnish case, study circles were combined with an action research methodology in order to: (1) bring together nine principals working in a rural municipality for collegial sharing and reflection of their professional experiences and (2) to establish communicative spaces as a platform for action research. Petri (the researcher and co-author) has employed participatory research traditions and collaborative meaning making in study circles (c.f., Salo & Rönnerman, 2014) as a platform and vehicle for improving professional practices (c.f., Rönnerman & Salo, 2012). Epistemologically, these traditions and practices have sprung from a common ground. Individual and subjective experiences and insights are to be reviewed and refined as part of deliberation amongst practitioners in specific contexts. Practical being and acting are interrelated with relational and reflective forms of knowledge (Salo & Rönnerman, 2014; Reason & Bradbury, 2006, pp. 8–9).

Similar to the Swedish case, Petri's ambition was to: (1) bring principals together to share their professional experiences; (2) refine these experiences in a deliberative manner among peers; and (3) mobilise these shared professional understandings in order to enhance collaborative school leadership practices. Along with the ideal of study circles (Larsson, 2001), this ambition was underpinned by recognition of diverse professional identities, equal participation, horizontal relations and democratic decision-making which would support knowledge-informed actions. The Finnish educational context, characterised as it is by decentralisation and deregulation, provides municipalities, schools and principals with the opportunity to act autonomously and organise their educational practices according to local needs and circumstances. As a result of this professional autonomy and trust, Finnish teachers' and principals' work is based on a strongly individualised professionalism (Johnson, 2006, pp. 98–100; Sahlberg, 2007). Teaching and leading practices are privatised; by tradition teachers and principals work alone and bear a great personal responsibility for their professional practices. Taajamo, Puhakka, and Välijärvi (2014, p. 49) have identified a pressing need for opening up the Finnish classrooms and investing in collaborative professional development, supportive feedback practices, peer group mentoring and shared leadership. In comparison with other Nordic countries, participatory methods for professional development and action research are rare in Finland. Therefore, Petri's ambition of challenging individualistic professional leadership practices and turning them into collaborative site-based leadership development is of special interest (Forsman, Karlberg-Granlund, Pörn, Salo, & Aspfors, 2014).

Petri began the study by presenting his research-based understanding of school leadership and culture and suggesting that the principals form heterogeneous groups (considering gender, experience and school size) for conducting action research. As Salo and Rönnerman (2014, p. 63) have concluded, the cultural-discursive arrangements in study circles are characterised by openness, diversity and pluralism. The principals' responses were the opposite, arguing that study circles ought to be put together on the basis of school size and character. This unanimous response revealed two premises often overlooked in school leadership literature: firstly, the great diversity of school leadership conditions and practices, and secondly, principals' varying orientation towards and diversified meaning-making of their professional role and task. In order to follow the ideal of participation and democratic decision-making, Petri let the principals self-organise into three more or less homogenous groups: "principals" working in secondary and senior high schools (with 20–40 teachers), "principal-teachers" working in primary schools (with 10–16 teachers) and "teacher-leaders" working in small village primary schools (with 3–4 teachers). The scope and character as well as the time allocation for school leadership tasks varied greatly between the groups. "Principals" were full-time managers with a few hours of teaching obligations, whereas "principal-teachers" and "teacher-leaders" were teachers with some hours appointed to administration and leadership tasks. Nonetheless, all expressed a need for sharing of professional experiences and expressing their professional identity in a trusting and informal manner, among peers with a common understanding of leadership practices.

Due to the variation of contexts for school leadership practices and subsequent differences considering meaning-making of principals' tasks and role, Petri's ambition of initiating and facilitating collaborative action research was realised in a highly varying manner in the three groups. A similar observation applies to his tasks and role as facilitator and critical professional friend. The "principals'" understanding of their everyday practices and professional development was distant and academic. Their engagement in collaborative practices was realised through recurrent discussions on the complexity and the challenges of acting as a principal. For them, sharing and action meant involvement in analytical reflections on leadership practices and concepts such as pedagogical leadership. "Principals" mobilised their professional knowledge and experiences, but not in a constructively reciprocal and challenging manner, as an interchange of knowledge of various kinds (Rönnerman & Salo, 2012, p. 2). "Principal-teachers" struggled with making sense of their double-edged identity as a leader and colleague, "standing constantly on the threshold to the classroom". Their discussions focused on the dynamics of and the varying professional roles within their teaching staff, as well as leadership practices through which they could establish collegial discussions and collaborative action. They focused on *relatings*, the *social-political arrangements* of their tasks and duties. Still, they managed to organise a small-scale action research project focusing on classroom practices via shadowing of other principals.

The collaborative and participatory development practices among "teacher-principals" represented a textbook example of action research. They organised themselves effectively as a professional, collaborative and reciprocal study circle, with an ongoing process of mapping, sharing and acting on experiences formulated within the group, tightly coupled to everyday teaching practices. This group drew on their experiences and knowledge of different kinds, along with the reciprocal *relatings* between the four principals and Petri as the basis for their action research. "Teacher-principals" organised several in-service training afternoons in their schools and conducted a joint action research project on developing reading practices. The project included, amongst other activities, developing and distributing a reading practice, *Books up to the Ceiling*, invented by one of the teacher-principals in her classroom.

Cultural-discursive arrangements: The aims of collaborative and participatory inquiry were realised in highly different ways in the three groups.

Full-time "principals" consisting of four males interpreted the action research initiative as disputing their professionalism. Discussions were about convincing the researcher in regard to the justifications of their actions as school leaders. Petri had to justify his aims and undertakings with reference to research methods and ethics. The discourse within this group was about "distanced professional consulting". In contrast, the group of "principals-teachers" (one female and two males) used the study circles and Petri for an ongoing, spontaneous and non-analytical inventory of the experiences of balancing on the threshold to the classroom and handling the challenging dynamics within their teaching staff. They acted as each other's sounding boards and empathetic listeners. The practice of partnership was on the agenda throughout the meetings, with the focus on establishing practices for collegial discussions and collaborative action. Petri labelled this discourse "an intuitive struggle for partnership". Within the group of "teacher-principals", Petri acted as an aggregator and a secretary, structuring ideas from meeting to meeting, characterised by respectful dialogue, professional and personal trust (Forsman, Karlberg-Granlund, Pörn, Salo, & Aspfors, 2014, pp. 124–126). The organic coherence and shared professional identity were reflected early on by the group, who named themselves "The Four Roses", referring to a beautiful bouquet of flowers. They also constantly named the pedagogical practices developed through action research cycles (e.g., *Reading Adventures, Books up to the Ceiling*). The aims of collaborative and participatory inquiry were fully realised within the discourse of "The Four Roses".

Material-economic arrangements: All principals shared the educational infrastructure within the municipality and were familiar with each other from monthly meetings with their superintendent. They were equally engaged in various professional development activities within the municipality. None of the principals previously knew Petri. All the principals were released from their professional tasks in order to join the study circles. Despite the common overall material-economic arrangements, the professional study circles came to be formed and function in a highly different manner. The Four Roses and the partnership-oriented "principal-teachers" acted more or less purposefully according to the project's aims. The practices of collaborative inquiry and action research were fully adopted and realised by the Four Roses, both in the group itself and the schools in which the principals worked. For the full-time "principals" both the form and contents of study circles were mainly about distant professional consulting.

Social-political arrangements: The differences between the groups – in terms of acting as a study circle, conducting action research and using Petri as a resource for developing leadership practices – seemed to be dependent on social-political arrangements. These included: (1) *the professional practice traditions* of each school site, formed by the participants' closeness to and engagement in teaching practices and (2) *their professional position within and in relation to the teaching staff,* as a basis of their professional self-understanding and identity. The Four Roses group, principals in small village schools, formed itself effectively into a well-functioning action research group, constantly ready and capable of reciprocal inventories, planning actions and acting on them. Petri's task was to act as secretary and aggregator, structuring thoughts and ideas from meeting to meeting. The gatherings were characterised by respectful dialogue, professional and personal trust as well as a fully developed agency, as in the ideal of the study circle (Larsson, 2001). At the other end of the scale, the full-time principals acted as individualistic professionals, oriented towards distant intellectual sharing of experiences rather than acting on them.

Leading practices in secondary education in an Australian rural secondary school

In contrast to the Finnish study of a group of diverse principals, the Australian case examines how secondary school staff in a case study school – principal, deputy principal, teachers and school support staff – worked together in cross-disciplinary learning teams with the aim of facilitating school transformation, enhancing staff capacity and improving student academic performance (c.f., Bristol & Wilkinson, 2015). The focus was on the leading practices of the four teachers appointed to lead these teams, who were trained through a locally developed regional professional development initiative, the Literacy Numeracy and Learning (LNL) program.[2]

In order for the leading and professional learning practices of these teacher leaders to be made intelligible as leadership practices of a specific kind, their practices needed to be "continuously filtered" through the adoption of "culturally appropriate" methodological and theoretical lenses which were sympathetic to the material and historical practice conditions which characterised this particular school as a site (Bristol & Wilkinson, 2015, p. 192). As postcolonial and feminist researchers, Laurette and Jane were mindful of the need to employ specific methods such as storytelling in order to engage with a school staff whose recent history was characterised by low student performance and disengagement and low levels of staff morale. This was in stark contrast to the school's previous history as a lighthouse school and community hub. It is these researcher practices which need to be laid bare as part of a methodological approach that is culturally nuanced and sensitive to the "happeningness" of diverse educational settings (Schatzki, 2006).

The theory of practice architectures was drawn on to attend to the "intersubjective relationships among the leading, mentoring and professional learning practices embedded as part of a process of rural secondary school transformation and capacity building" (Bristol & Wilkinson, 2015, p. 188). The project was a 12-month action research case study where data was collected in two phases. First, in collaboration with the participants, Laurette and Jane engaged in interrogative conversations aimed at: (1) making explicit existing assumptions for and of teaching and leading practices and (2) articulating the possibilities for new actions (Bristol & Wilkinson, 2015, p. 188). Furthermore, as researchers carrying out the role of critical friends, they observed the teachers and their team leaders working in interdisciplinary teaching teams and mentoring pairs as the teachers and team leaders designed, implemented and evaluated

> intervention and support strategies for: (1) new scheme teachers as they pursued state accreditation; (2) teacher leaders as they transformed teaching and leading practices; and (3) students, as teachers adjusted and adopted new learning strategies and skills.
>
> (Bristol & Wilkinson, 2015, p. 189)

At the point of research contact, the school was in the early stages of its recovery, becoming a more safe, confident and transformative educational site. Thus entry into the site to engage in research, while supported and welcomed by the principal, was viewed with concern by some of the teachers, with fears of being evaluated and judged. Before research could begin, Laurette and Jane had to build a relationship of camaraderie with the teachers and the school through a range of strategies, such as attending Friday Morning Teas. Acknowledging and respecting the vulnerability and strengths of the site and its teachers significantly prefigured the ways in which they collaborated with the teachers in the designing and implementation of the research project.

Laurette and Jane's interaction with the teachers in the site was prefigured by conditions already existing in the site and by conditions (teaching and research experiences as strong advocates for social justice and cultural relevancy) that both Jane and Laurette brought to the site as researchers with previous histories of working with vulnerable spaces: Jane as a critical feminist and Laurette as a postcolonial migrant academic. In the sections that follow they outline the sets of conditions that prefigured their research relationships with the teachers, teacher leaders and principals in the site.

Cultural-discursive arrangements. How Laurette and Jane spoke of and with the teachers in the site was critical to their entry and acceptance in the site. They invested significantly in the first phase of the inquiry, encouraging team leaders to talk. This moved beyond the descriptive level of giving an account of their experiences as cross-disciplinary team leaders; rather this talk was characterised as *interrogative conversations.* These conversations were aimed at supporting team leaders as they moved from tacit understandings towards more explicit and articulated understandings of: (1) how they understood the leading practices of their colleagues and themselves; (2) the purposes of these leading practices against a shared understanding of the agenda of school transformation and capacity building; (3) what activities and actions (including language) these leading practices were composed of; and (4) reflections on how teachers leaders may have led differently where appropriate.

In order to gain these understandings, Laurette and Jane engaged in extensive hours of observation. For the first six months they visited the school on Fridays, typically participating in morning teas in which the whole staff gathered. In addition, they observed cross-disciplinary meetings in which team leaders and their staff engaged in processes of dialogue and reflection on their LNL teaching and learning strategies, after which the researchers engaged in a short de-briefing session with the team leaders. These cross-disciplinary team meetings allowed Laurette and Jane to witness gradual shifts in the language of the teachers in the school and an adoption of a shared language of learning and teaching; for instance, teachers began to use terms such as "learning" rather than "homework".

Material-economic arrangements: Typically the teachers collaborated in cross-disciplinary teams and in the latter stage of the study, teachers voluntarily began to observe each other teaching and provide feedback on specific practices nominated before the observation. The cross-disciplinary team meetings were structured into the school's timetable. Teacher meetings were organised in which teachers could reflect upon their practice, facilitated by the team leaders, and provided mentorship for each other or less experienced teachers. Practices such as a process approach that emphasised explicit learning activities such as visualising, predicting, questioning, summarising, monitoring and making connections in teaching and learning became embedded in curriculum design. These learning activities were based on information-seeking skills, which were at the core of the LNL strategy. Collaboration *(doings)* held a language of action or practice *(sayings)* in place. As one of the team leaders noted:

> So we started off with us as teachers just learning what [the Literacy Skills] were, recognizing them in our programs, then we put them in our programs. Now what we're doing is looking at practical applications. How are we actually *doing it* in the classroom? Because it's one thing to write it in your program, and use the activity, it's another thing to be actually *using the words and doing it in practice*. And we're using this buddy system as a way to monitor and improve the way each of us is using it within the classroom.

These material-economic arrangements were also reflected in Laurette and Jane's *doings* as researchers. They collaborated with volunteer teachers to design an action research project that was relevant to the existing concerns of and demands on the teachers and in which engagement with the teachers was based on mutual trust and respect, as critical peers rather than as researcher/researched (Meerwald, 2013). The activity and disposition of critical mutuality was also evident in their own collaborative researcher relationship: They met regularly before and after visits to the site to discuss strategies and areas of interest to be further explored.

Social-political arrangements: Shared language and practices of collaboration prefigured the nature of the relationships (*relatings*) that emerged amongst teachers and team leaders. Over time the language of the educators shifted from a deficit discourse to a dialogue which emphasised agency, advocacy, confidence and trust. These sayings were used to characterise new sets of relationships that were emerging amongst the teachers, amongst the teachers and students and between the school and the surrounding community. As another team leader observed when asked about changes he had observed in his practices of teaching and leading:

> I guess learning some of the language . . . spending time with other staff from other schools, talking to them about it, is good. I'm probably changing my relationship with the other three people who are on the [teacher leaders'] team . . . I'm just trying to get my head about learning . . . but it is changing the way I teach and what I see in kids.

These emerging social-political arrangements were also evident in the *relatings* between Laurette and Jane as researchers and the teachers in the site. At the end of the project, the teachers spoke of the actions (*doings and sayings*) that they as teacher-researchers had engaged in. The teachers spoke of Laurette and Jane's continuous curiosity (questions) and the lack of judgement that they as teachers had experienced in working with the two researchers. These research practices encouraged them to feel safe enough to: (1) interrogate their practice and that of their peers and (2) take risks in their pedagogical encounters with students, leading to a concomitant shift in students' risk-taking behaviour in learning. These new *relatings* had a subsequent impact on the surrounding school community where student numbers increased as trust in the school slowly grew.

Discussion and conclusion

This chapter examined the methodological implications that occur when the same theory is applied to different cultural contexts. In each of our sites, we examined how practice architectures as a theoretical framework could help to make sense of diverse leadership practices and sites in our three cultural contexts of Sweden, Finland and Australia. Although these three countries are all 'white' spaces, how the theory is applied methodologically to leadership research in these three countries varies because of the differing historical, political and cultural traditions of these countries. For example, Karin and Petri implemented the theory of practice architectures drawing on Nordic practices and traditions for action research, dialogue, collaboration and study circles. Yet though the sites in Sweden and Finland are in some ways similar, they are also historically different welfare state contexts. In the Australian context, Laurette and Jane attended to the specific culture of the organisational site. They noted how they used storytelling methods as a way of safely bringing teachers and team leaders into the practices of research, having participants tell stories about the way they made sense of their practices. As postcolonial and feminist researchers, they drew on their social activist roots to approach the teachers and team leaders in this way.

Despite differences between the national and cultural contexts in our three sites, there are some significant similarities in our approaches when employing the theory of practice architectures. These commonalities and the rationale for the approach can be located in the ontological situatedness of the theoretical orientation of practice architectures. For example, across the three contexts this theoretical lens prefigured how we as researchers attended to the *practices of educators*, rather than individual participants. This is not say that the lived/felt experiences of the participants were summarily dismissed; rather these experiences were located and connected to the set of practice orders and arrangements located within the site, which in turn composed the practices of leading as preschool teacher leaders, principals or team leaders.

Similarities were also evident in the Swedish and Finnish sites in terms of common Nordic research traditions of educative relationships. Folk enlightenment and *bildung* prefigured the kinds of respectful dialogue and professional and personal trust engendered between the participants, and amongst the participants and Karin and Petri as researchers. In the Australian case, there was also a researcher focus on practices that built dialogue, collaboration and professional trust amongst participants and researchers. However, rather than being located in a national practice tradition, this latter impetus came from recognition of the needs of the research site, as well as our own methodological orientations as feminist and postcolonial researchers.

Despite the significant differences in the core groups of participants across the national contexts, we also see similarities in our positioning as researchers. These included the moral and cultural obligations we felt for the participants and the types of aspirational and agentic agendas that guided our interaction, the nature of the investigation and the point of the inquiry. These shared aspects of the research studies could also be related to the action research approaches that were deployed in the different cultural contexts. These approaches were nonetheless united by an agenda of teachers identifying and solving through doing and reflecting on their everyday educational challenges. There is something then to be said about: the alignment between a particular theoretical orientation; the design and aspirations for a study in a site; the creation of community-oriented spaces for dialectic action; the ontological positioning of the researcher/s; and the ways in which these various aspects, working in accord, may create the opportunity for leadership practices to appear to be alike across dissimilar cultural contexts. This is the benefit of cross-national comparative research as it creates opportunities for us to learn from a common set of experiences.

Educational leadership research, which is typically Anglocentric, has tended to assume a homogenising lens, coming from an Anglo-American space and knowledge position. The cases that we present in this chapter are an illustration of educational leadership research that is neither homogenous nor embedded in an Anglo-American knowledge position. In the Swedish case we see the importance of the system and the statutory obligations that the municipalities carry, combined with an action research program embedded in Nordic traditions of study and research circles. Continuous professional development was not left to chance but was a disposition that was cultivated through the action research program. It became key to the everyday work of at least some of the preschool teacher leaders and was explicitly connected to the national goals and educational laws of the society. We see here the preschool teachers initiating leadership in a manner that was characterised as generative, that is, developing their own professional practices while generating new leadership practices in preschool communities. This was an important part of the teachers' cultural practices and was connected to a folk tradition, *bildung*, that focused on educating and developing the whole person. Here, the systemic approach to leadership development was not located solely in a regulated relationship. Rather, it served to provide a support system for a practice that was given value through cultural traditions, expressed in municipality responsibility and fine-tuned through the allocation of time for teacher dialogue and reflection.

In the Finnish case, decisions on professional development were delegated to municipalities and schools and organised according to local needs and circumstances of particular schools. Here, too, education was built on a strong tradition of *bildung* and there were strong sensibilities of research-based teacher professionalism and trust. In Finland we see educators working in highly autonomous spaces, but with a strong social drive to convert private learning spaces and practices into collaborative spaces based on reciprocity and mutuality. The collaborative approach employed by Petri is thus one that is aligned with his own researcher dispositions and the wider educative aspirations of the society. Of significance in the Finnish case are the nuanced differences between the three groups of principals, despite them sharing a common cultural and national space. These differences were evident in the *relatings* between principals, between the principals and the researcher and in the focus of principals' concerns for research. Thus, commonality cannot be assumed within national and cultural contexts.

In the Australian case, the social and cultural circumstances surrounding the teachers in New South Wales (NSW), Australia are starkly different. This was a space characterised by high levels of competition, mistrust and systemic oversight. Such factors had had an impact on the practices of teachers and team leaders, as well as on the ability of the researchers to access public educational sites. Whereas educators in Finland are characterised as autonomous, the teachers in NSW, Australia were characterised as vulnerable after having experienced long periods of systemic and intensive evaluation. This served to influence the methodological approach employed by Laurette and Jane and the ways in which, as researchers, they worked to privilege the importance of being culturally sensitive to the organisational needs of the site through storytelling and long periods of participating in social, community-oriented activities to foster relationships of trust.

Looking across the cases, what is interesting here is that it appears that there is a cultural difference between Nordic and Australian countries when it comes to research approaches, particularly in education. It seems as if at least for some Nordic educational researchers, there is a strong social-democratic tradition of how they approach their research practices that prefigures their methods. These research practice traditions are more socially oriented, dialogic and collaborative. In contrast, Australia has a more individualistic and hierarchical society. Hence as researchers working in Australia, it was Laurette's and Jane's ontological subject locations as postcolonial and feminist researchers that prefigured their more democratic and collaborative approaches to data gathering in their study site, rather than any pre-existing national cultural tradition.

In this chapter we have attempted to challenge a more traditional Anglo-American approach to educational leadership practice by illustrating how, even in the white spaces of our three countries and utilising the same theoretical lens, methods of attending to leadership practice and ways of working as researchers need to be culturally nuanced and historically and politically sensitive. It is important to note that the intention here is not to present an ethnocentric view but to illustrate the ways in which the historical traditions of the site and ontological positioning of the researcher (and sometimes this may include issues of ethnicity) can prefigure the justifications for and the ways in which leadership research is engaged. These are the uncomfortable and hidden issues of leadership research that have not entered the normative leadership research arena. By showing alternative research approaches that foreground more collegial and collaborative methodologies, we gain other forms of knowledge about leading practices. The arguments of this chapter serves as a way of 'talking back' to the leadership space, not only in the knowledge that is being produced through these studies, but in understanding how research in/for educational leadership practices in diverse contexts can unfold in ways that foster discourses of agency and social advocacy.

Notes

1 Preschools in Sweden are attended by children aged between one and five years.
2 In order to protect the identity of the school involved, we use pseudonyms for all participants and for the professional and student learning initiative.

References

Australian Institute for Teaching and School Leadership (n.d.). *Australian professional standards for teachers*. Retrieved from www.aitsl.edu.au/australian-professional-standards-for-teachers/standards/list

Beach, D., Dovemark, M., Schwartz, A., & Öhrn, E. (2013). Complexities and contradictions of educational inclusion: A meta-ethnographic analysis. *Nordic Studies in Education, 4*, 254–268.

Blackmore, J. (2005). 'The emperor has no clothes': Professionalism, performativity and educational leadership in high-risk postmodern times. In J. Collard & C. Reynolds (Eds.), *Leadership, gender & culture in education: Male and female perspectives* (pp. 173–194). Maidenhead, Berkshire: Open University Press.

Bristol, L., & Wilkinson, J. (2015). 'Quality education as worthwhile': Practices as interconnected sites for and of transformation in a school setting. In H. Heikkinen, J. Moate, & M. K. Lerkkanen (Eds.), *Enabling education: Proceedings of the annual conference of Finnish educational research association* (pp. 187–204). Jyvaskyla, Finland: Finnish Educational Research Association.

Brookfield, S. D. (1983). *Adult learners, adult education and the community*. Milton Keynes: Open University Press.

Carr, W., & Kemmis, S. (1986). *Becoming critical: Education, knowledge and action research*. London: Falmer Press.

Dimmock, C., & Walker, A. (2005). *Educational leadership: Culture and diversity.* London: Sage.
Edwards-Groves, C., & Rönnerman, K. (2013). Generating leading practices through professional learning. *Professional Development in Education, 39*(1), 122–140.
Grootenboer, P., Edwards-Groves, C., & Rönnerman, K. (2015). Leading practice development: Voices from the middle. *Professional Development in Education, 41*(3), 508–526. doi:10.1080/19415257.2014.924985
Hallinger, P. (2005). Foreword. In C. Dimmock & A. Walker, A. (Eds.), *Educational leadership: Culture and diversity* (pp. vii–xii). London: Sage.
Hattie, J. (2008). *Visible learning: A synthesis of over 800 meta-analyses relating to achievement.* Milton Park, Oxon: Routledge.
Johnson, P. (2006). *Stuck in structures? The integration process of basic education as a change challenge for the municipal school organisation* [Rakenteissa kiinni? Perusopetuksen yhtenäistämisprosessi kunnan kouluorganisaation muutoshaasteena]. PhD Thesis, University of Jyväskylä, Faculty of Education, Chydenius Institute Kokkola University Consortium.
Kemmis, S., & Grootenboer, P. (2008). Situating praxis in practice: Practice architectures and the cultural, social and material conditions for practice. In S. Kemmis & T. J. Smith (Eds.), *Enabling praxis: Challenges for education* (pp. 37–64). Rotterdam: Sense Publishers.
Kemmis, S., & Smith, T. J. (Eds.). (2008). *Enabling praxis: Challenges for education.* Rotterdam: Sense Publishers.
Kemmis, S., Wilkinson, J., Edwards-Groves, C., Hardy, I., Grootenboer, P., & Bristol, L. (2014).*Changing practices, changing education.* Singapore: Springer.
Larsson, S. (2001). Sevens aspects of democracy as related to study circles. *International Journal of Lifelong Education, 20*(3), 199–217.
Lpfö 98. (2010, revised).*Curriculum for the preschool.* Retrieved from www.ibe.unesco.org/curricula/sweden/sw_ppfw_2010_eng.pdf
Mattsson, M., Johansson, I., & Sandström, B. (Eds.). (2008). *Examining praxis: Assessments and knowledge construction in teacher education.* Rotterdam: Sense Publishers.
Meerwald, A. M. L. (2013). Researcher/researched: Repositioning research paradigms. *Higher Education Research & Development, 32*(1), 43–55. doi:10.1080/07294360.2012.750279.
National Assessment Program (n.d.). *National assessment program – literacy and numeracy.* Retrieved from www.nap.edu.au/naplan/naplan.html
Noffke, S. E. (1997). Professional, personal, and political dimensions of action research. *Review of Research in Education, 22,* 305–343.
Noffke, S. E. (2009). Revisiting the professional, personal, and political dimensions of action research. In S. E. Noffke & B. Somekh (Eds.), *The SAGE handbook of educational action research* (pp. 5–18). Thousands Oaks, CA: Sage.
Nylund, M., Sandback, C., Wilhelmsson, B., & Rönnerman, K. (2010). *Aktionsforskning i förskolan – trots att schemat är fullt* [Action research in preschools – in spite of a full schedule]. Stockholm: Lärarförbundets förlag.
Öhrn, E. (2012, March). Urban education and segregation: The responses from young people. *European Educational Research Journal, 11,* 45–57. doi:10.2304/eerj.2012.11.1.45.
The Pedagogy, Education and Praxis International Collaboration (unpub.) *Action research and practice theory: A new cross-national empirical research program.*

Reason, P., & Bradbury, H. (2006). Introduction. In P. Reason & H. Bradbury (Eds.), *Handbook of action research* (pp. 1–14). London: Sage Publications.
Rönnerman, K. (2008a). *Medvetet kvalitetsarbete – en uppföljning av kursen aktionsforksning i förskolan och dess inverkan på förskollärares handlingar i praktiken* [Conscious quality work – a follow up of the course in action research and its effect on ECteachers activities in practice]. IPD-rapporter No 07. University of Gothenburg, Department of Education and Didactics.
Sachs, J. (2010). *The activist teaching profession* (First published in 2003, reprinted in 2004). Buckingham: Open University Press.
Sahlberg, P. (2007). Education policies for raising student learning: The Finnish approach. *Journal of Education Policy, 22*(2), 147–171.
Sahlberg, P. (2012). *Finnish lessons: What can the world learn from education in Finland?* New York: Teachers' College Press.
Schatzki, T. R. (2005). The sites of organizations. *Organization Studies, 26*(3), 465–484.
Schatzki, T. R. (2006). On organizations as they happen. *Organization Studies, 27*(12), 1863–1873.
Skolverket. (2015). *Läslyftet* [Lieteracylift]. Retrieved from www.skolverket.se/kompetens-och-fortbildning/larare/laslyftet
Stephens, D. (2012). The role of culture in interpreting and conducting research. In A. Briggs, M. Coleman, & M. Morrison (Eds.), *Research methods in educational leadership and management* (pp. 46–60). London: Sage.
Taajamo, M., Puhakka, E., & Välijärvi, J. (2014). *Opetuksen ja oppimisen kansainvälinen tutkimus TALIS 2013. Yläkoulun ensituloksia* [The international survey on Teaching and learning TALIS 2013. First results]. Opetus- ja kulttuuriministeriön julkaisuja 2014: 15. Helsinki: Opetus- ja kulttuuriministeriö.
Timperley, H. (2008). *Teacher professional learning and development.* Educational practices. Series 18. Brussels: International Academy of Education.
Uljens, M., & Nyman, C. (2013). Educational leadership in Finland or building a nation with Bildung. In L. Moos (Ed.), *Transnational influences on values and practices in Nordic educational leadership: Is there a Nordic model?* (pp. 31–48). Springer: Dordrecht.
Vertovec, S. (2007). Superdiversity and its implications. *Ethnic and Racial Studies, 30*(6), 1024–1054.
Vincent, T., Rawsthorne, M. with Beavis, A., & Ericson, M. (2015). *Dropping off the edge 2015: Persistent communal disadvantage in Australia.* Jesuit Social Services and Catholic Social Services Australia. Retrieved December 21, 2015, from http://apo.org.au/resource/dropping-the-edge-2015-persistent-communal-disadvantage-australia

10 Conduct un/becoming

Discipline in the context of educational leadership research

Vonzell Agosto and Zorka Karanxha

Introduction

In this chapter we engage in a critical, reflexive process focused on researching and leading assemblages of discipline. Our interest in discipline stems from concerns about disparities in the educational experiences of students related to social differences, which for girls of colour is seldom to their benefit. We confront leading and researching on two interrelated fronts: (1) participants'/students' interactions with school-based leadership and (2) research as authors/researchers who aimed to mentor graduate students as novice researchers while involving youth as co-participants. More specifically, we address methodological and theoretical issues that surfaced in the context of studying school discipline and educational leadership with girls and their mothers from a diverse range of racial and ethnic identities.

This reflexive praxeological approach attends to the un/foldings of events over time (Reckwitz, 2002). We focus on the actions and interactions involved in the research process and findings in order to denaturalise them. Such accounts of praxeology, the study of human action and conduct, are typically ignored and excluded from publications (Schmidt, 2010). In our approach, critical postmodern perspectives are engaged, including a critical qualitative approach as described by Norman Denzin and vital materialism as described by Jane Bennett. According to Heck and Hallinger (2005), holding alternative ways of situating leadership is advantageous in the field of leadership and management when it addresses blind spots in the field's knowledge and disciplinary practices. In this chapter, we first present Reflexive Stage One, which focuses on findings about school discipline, followed by Reflexive Stage Two on un/becoming findings. In discussing each phase, we incorporate literature pertinent to educational leadership practice, theory and research to illustrate the active forces we found resonating across assemblages of discipline. The theoretical framework supporting this inquiry is described next.

Theoretical framework

We consider what Bennett's (2010) recommendation for the field of political theory might do for educational leadership. She argued that political theory would be better off if it paid attention to non-human forces in events, such as how the vitality or capacity of things can impede the will and designs of humans – acting as quasi-agents with active forces that have their own trajectories, propensities or tendencies. According to Bennett, in an interview with Gratton (2010), attending to the political ecology of things and developing a heightened sensitivity to the agency of assemblages could shift national politics away from a juridical model of moral responsibility, blame and punishment. Similarly, attention and sensitivity to the capacity of non-human forces to discipline and conduct events in schools could undermine the limited focus on judging students' morality, blaming them for behaving as they do and punishing them through belittling, bullying or exclusionary practices.

Bennett's hope is that the desire for scapegoats will lessen as public recognition of the distributed nature of agency increases, resulting in a less moralistic and a more pragmatic (à la Dewey) leaning in national politics. Our hope is that attention to the entanglements helps elucidate the complexity of how leading a discipline (i.e., educational leadership) study, or school culture (administrative disciplining) influences what becomes of girls and women. Along that stream of reasoning, we mean to provoke discussion of the power, people and 'things' (discipline policies, codes of conduct) that became possible to re-imagine when we explored discipline as contiguous and continually moving, active forces – an assemblage (Deleuze & Guattari, 2004).

Assemblage

Assemblages can be understood as constellations constituting cultures (discipline, girls and education), and in art (i.e., surrealism) as three-dimensional structures composed of various forms, objects or artefacts. Often assemblages are made of everyday objects – what some might refer to as junk and others have called a mosaic (i.e., Spinoza; Bennett, 2010). Nevertheless "assemblages of such material come at the spectator as bits of life, bits of the environment" (Alloway, 1961, p. 122). From an aesthetic and material culture perspective, we are interested in the imagery of the experiences that come to us through listening, watching and reflecting on how through the study we learned about discipline and what assemblages of discipline can do.

From a psychoanalytic and organisational culture perspective we are interested in the "incorporeal transformation of bodies" (Deleuze & Guattari, 2004 p. 80), or the attributes of events that occur when desires make certain statements possible, and some bodies possible (i.e., institutional, legal, student, machinic). According to Wise (2005), an assemblage is not a random collection of things but rather "the process of arranging, organizing, fitting together" (p. 77). We engage the concept of assemblage to "show how institutions, organizations, bodies", along with desiring and leading practices intersect and transform (Wise, 2005, p. 86). We argue that through combined energies and continual movement (i.e., gears turning, desiring) within entanglements of matter with varying vitality across contexts – there is flow between becoming~un/becoming. Such vitality, we acknowledge, is not solely the purview of Euro-Western scholars but also has roots in Indigenous philosophies with onto-epistemological perspectives (i.e., Aztec culture) (Maffie, 2014).

To explore un/becoming through the lens of research and leading practices associated with discipline in schools, we engage the following terms, most of which have multiple meanings:

- *Conducting*: Directing who one is (or is becoming), what one does (or is doing) or how one is (or is becoming).
- *Leading*: Influencing, for instance, through provocation or inspiration. Additionally, leading in inquiry contexts (i.e., questioning, guiding the witness) can also mean that the inquirer is influencing a predetermined answer to question or response. While these meanings of leading can overlap, leading in inquiry contexts such as research studies and courtrooms is often unwelcome.
- *Becoming*: The development of plans, products or people.
- By *un/becoming* we mean the devolvement (going to a less advanced state) of plans, products or people and/or unappealing or unattractive acts, events or qualities.

These working definitions are applied in subsequent sections.

Reflexive Stage One: The findings

We approach research studies and schools as sites of tension for researchers and students attempting to negotiate discipline. Guiding the overall multi-year, multi-site study was the question: How are girls of colour entangled in the dynamics of discipline in schools? Our inquiry into educational leadership and discipline has led us to ponder questions such as what/whose knowledge about girls of colour is elicited and disseminated, and what is the role of research and researchers in shaping the knowledge base that informs leadership theory, practice and preparation.

Leading discipline in schools

The majority of research on discipline in schools focuses on relational dynamics between teachers and students. While those relationships were predominant for the girls in our study, we were also interested in what they had to say about school administrators, how they came in contact with them and what they observed about their leadership with regard to discipline for racial or ethnic groups. While it is not uncommon for youth to be concerned with their social lives, it came as a surprise to us that much of their description of administrators also concerned sociality. In other words, the girls considered the social and behavioral conduct of administrators in their relationships with teachers, students, groups, activities and objects.

Boundaries between teachers and administrators

Gorgeous described the line she saw between teachers and administrators, whereby teachers were not privy to information held by administrators on the topic of discipline. She speculated that administrators might have been making up the (unwritten) rules. Following are her responses to the question of whether or not she believed the high school had unwritten rules:

> It's either that or the administrators are just making things up. But I feel like there is a line between teachers and administrators who just patrol and have their office and stuff. I feel like some teachers don't know what's going on. I feel like there's a boundary between certain administrators and teachers. They don't always tell them everything. It's not necessarily their fault or our fault.
>
> (Gorgeous, Interview 1, District 1)

We sensed her empathy for teachers who were not informed by administrators, yet recognised that this communication divide could be problematic for her, such as when some rules were being enforced by administrators while teachers remained unaware, due to the teachers being outside the circle of communication. Gorgeous further described how students might be affected by the boundary between administrators and substitute teachers in particular:

> We don't know what we're learning and the (substitute) teacher doesn't know. So that means students are more lost. And when you go and ask administrators, they know all about everything. But they're not the ones in the classroom. They are just walking around trying to find people to bust or whatever they're looking for.
>
> (Gorgeous, Interview 1, District 1)

In addition to administrators who "walk around" and "patrol", the question on Gorgeous' understanding of power prompted her to say more about administrators and other "people that work in that office" (who may be administrators but not principals or assistant principals). Nevertheless those other "people" figured into the assemblage she was describing. To the question, *How does the power in your school function – what is the makeup of that?*, she responded as such:

> Well there is an assistant principal and a principal. I don't know their names. I don't necessarily know what they look like. I don't see them a lot. I just see there are people in the office (not teachers), people that work in the office. They always have walkie-talkies and patrol. They walk around at lunch making sure students don't leave the area because you can sit outside or inside the area and make sure that they don't do certain things.
>
> (Gorgeous, Interview 1, District 1)

Conduct un/becoming 175

Image 10.1 Walk, Talk, Patrol

Implicated in Gorgeous' account of power was "that office" or as described by other girls, the "administrative office" (Madonna, Interview 1, District 1) and the "front office" (Elvira, Interview 1, District 1). They described the office as a nebulous space from which discipline emerged. In addition to "their office" there was "stuff" – like walkie-talkies – that "people that work in that office" used to patrol areas. From these accounts the objects, bodies, expressions, qualities and territories are vital, and the assemblage of desire provides a way of understanding how the girls are making sense of the question of power and leading practices.

Walkie-talkies support the incorporeal transformation of bodies into gears of the machine of discipline. The static that emanates from them is a reminder to communicate (as one patrols) with another gear in the machine. The walkie-talkies are part of the operation. They allow people ("that work in that office") to walk and talk to one another until the office draws them back in. As one researcher wrote about her impression of the (three) students' descriptions of school administration, "The principal's office was viewed as a place to avoid and [was] associated with fear" (Researcher B, District 1, Journal Entry).

Students and administrators: Deference or defiance?

The following descriptions of contact between the girls, or other students, and administrators speak to the subjective nature of discerning social behavior and the importance of communicating deference to as opposed to defiance toward figures of authority:

> So I was one day in school I was really tired and there was this administrator and she was like asking me something and I was just like okay. I just kind of waved her off. And she just like, "What?" I was like, "NO, I didn't, I didn't really mean it!" So she just talked to me about it. "If you have a bad attitude don't take it on anybody else, OK". Then I was like sorry and she was like "it's okay". So she let me go. So you can't really, you can't disrespect them – and cursing is not allowed.
>
> (Elvira, Interview 1, District 1)

The tension in her contact with the administrator pivoted on the extent to which the administrator understood Elvira's wave of dismissal to be an indicator of defiance or an indicator of reluctant conformity. As Elvira, added, "So you can't really, you can't disrespect them. . .". Her comment depicted sensitivity to the importance of subjectivity (i.e., what the administrators view as disrespect), which is a constant theme in the literature on the disproportional punishment directed at girls of colour in comparison to white students, who are punished for more objective infractions (Skiba, Michael, Nardo, & Peterson, 2002).

Unlike the descriptions of Black girls in particular as being loud (e.g., Evans, 1988; Koonce, 2012), or of those who are academically high-achieving as being silent (e.g., Fordham, 1993; Morris, 2007), this scenario involved motion (a wave) perceived by sight more so than by sound. However, the following account Elvira provided concerned sound (waves) and the question of what conduct is appropriate for students and administrators (in what context):

> I mean it, Mr. X [the assistant principal], nobody likes him. He can be way too much sometimes. I don't know. At a pep rally we were screaming and stuff and he was, "Guys quiet down or there's not going to be another pep rally". And we were like what do you mean, it's a pep rally we're supposed to be all pepped up. Yeah. I feel like that was just too much. I mean if you have a headache walk outside, but you can't tell us to calm down – it's a pep rally!
>
> (Elvira, Interview 1, District 1)

Her comment on how the assistant principal should have behaved echoed the sentiment of the principal: If you are having a bad day (or a headache), do not take it out on us (or walk outside).

Elvira's comments about her interactions with two administrators helped to illuminate for us as researchers an understanding of how vitality (life force) mattered. For instance, the wave of the hand and the sound waves at the "pep rally" allowed us to consider how one's life force – whether feeling tired or feeling "pepped up" is subjected to the desires in the discipline assemblage: desires for calm, desires for (school) spirit. In both scenarios how a wave mattered was not automatically defined by the context. As such, a wave (of the hand, of cheers and chants at a pep rally) was a gear, a conjoining of body/spirit in the discipline assemblage Elvira described. These "gears" involved disciplining by school administrators, correcting her perceived "bad attitude" and threatening punishment (the pep rally could be their last one).

Inconsistency in rules and rulings

As the topic of fairness arose during interviews, the girls spoke of how it varied among teachers and administrators by the race of students and administrators'/teachers' desire to exercise their brand of leadership. Gorgeous expressed her sense that administrators and teachers can be unfair: "I just feel like there's a couple of those teachers and administrators that just aren't fair – or they don't give it [punishment] out fairly" (Gorgeous, Interview 1, District 1).

A common view of the administrators held by the girls was that they were all-powerful when it came to disciplining students, leaving no room for deliberation. Elvira thought teachers were inconsistent in how they ruled. She characterised the administrators as unwavering in their enforcement of discipline. Elvira (Interview 1, District 1) wrote, "I would say that the punishment from the front office and the administrators, their ruling, is their ruling – and that's it. But for the teachers it definitely varies".

In addition to commenting on the inconsistency in their rules and ruling, the girls talked about unfairness of discipline among students from different racial groups. "Coloured students [Ashlee's terminology] get more suspensions" (Ashlee, Interview 1, District 2). More specifically, they spoke of unfairness in how administrators dealt with infractions:

> It depends on how much a kid does. Some of Black kids I know do get in trouble and it's like they know the administrators at this point. I think those kids get in trouble a lot more. The white kids, they don't – they get in trouble, they just don't get as many referrals or many things don't happen to them as often.
>
> (Elvira, Interview 1, District 1)

While the girls described few experiences of direct contact with administrators, those which they did describe pointed to leadership-enacted discipline across various aspects of the schooling experience, including the most personal such as determining how often students were allowed to use the bathroom and what they could put in and on their bodies. Here are a few of the quotes that support this interpretation:

> I think it's our principal who mostly kind of restricts our bathroom usage.
>
> (Elvira, Interview 2, District 1)

> We got a new principal and she kind of thinks she can change anything and everything because she is a new principal. She said we could no longer take

food onto the campus even if it is in a lunch box. She wants everyone to eat school lunches; I don't know why. The dress code has changed a lot. Pants used to go from mid-thigh, now they are all the way – they went to the knee for this year because people were disobeying the mid-thigh one. Now she is completely getting rid of shorts and capris. There are a lot of things she has changed just because she is now in power – being principal.

(Ashlee, Interview 2, District 2)

The girls apparently viewed the conduct of school administrators as weak in relational as well as rational leading practice, and therefore engaging in conduct un/becoming. It is one thing to look at nationwide or even school-wide data and see the problems associated with inconsistency in how discipline is practised and polic(i)ed, and another to look into the mirror at one's own involvement in the disciplining of youth.

Reflexivity Stage Two: Un/becoming findings

The unit of inquiry in this reflexive stage shifts from leading practices in schools to leading practices in researching about discipline in school. Herein we highlight events and, through reflection and critique of theoretical and methodological issues, consider these subsequent questions in terms of our researcher practice: What conduct is un/becoming? What conducts un/becoming? This critical reflexive inquiry takes seriously the idea that "there can never be a final, accurate, complete representation of a thing, an utterance or an action. There are only different representations of different representations" (Denzin, 2013, p. 354).

In addition to the multiplicity of representations that come from this study and reflection upon it, there are "certain things we can build our new practices around" (Denzin, 2013, p. 355):

(1) We have an ample supply of methodological rules and interpretive guidelines.
(2) They are open to change and to differing interpretation, and this is how it should be.
(3) There is no longer a single gold standard for qualitative work.
(4) We value open-peer reviews in our journals.
(5) Our empirical materials are performative. They are not commodities to be bought, sold and consumed.
(6) **Our feminist, communitarian ethics are not governed by Institutional Review Boards (IRBs).**
(7) Our science is open-ended, unruly, disruptive (MacLure, 2006; Stronach, Garratt, Pearce, & Piper, 2007, p. 197).
(8) Inquiry is always political and moral.
(9) Objectivity and evidence are political and ethical terms (Denzin, 2013, p. 355).

Although most of these "things" apply across all phases of our study, number six (bolded font) is most relevant to the planning phase of the study. We intend to

Conduct un/becoming 179

highlight ways in which the study was pregnant with moments in which disciplining, conducting and leading were entangled with power, people and things. In continuing with the support of vital matter in assemblages, we continue into this reflexive stage to further elucidate the pragmatics (or schizoanalysis) of leading and researching discipline as a machine with alternatives, jumps and mutations (Deleuze & Guattari, 1987, pp. 146–147).

Planning the study: Framing girls of colour

In designing the study we initially reviewed literature on discipline and gender (girls of colour) that characterised them as being aggressive (Bright, 2005) and/or fighting (Brown & Tappan, 2008). Our search of literature (2003–2013), using key terms such as *discipline* and *girls of colour*, resulted in an abundance of literature that helped to frame the initial proposal we submitted for IRB approval. The headings we submitted in the research proposal were bullies, beauties and resistance. As such, the emphasis was on relational aggression, sexuality and abuse – mainly on how the behaviour of girls' of colour was tantamount to subjecting themselves to disciplinary procedures.

Overall, the literature suggested to us that girls of colour were being disciplined for misbehaviour even if it was because they were responding to abuse or resisting cultural insensitivity. However, after initial interviews, it became apparent to us that the girls in our study were not living out the stereotypes about girls of colour being (hyper) aggressive or sexual. They did not describe experiences of fighting, feelings of hostility toward students or educators or infractions related to sexual expression. Although one out of the six girls had been expelled from school (though later reinstated), it was an unusual circumstance that did not involve aggression, harm, abuse or sex.

Instead, we were learning from the girls how discipline in the school carried into their homes, such as how the dress code policy informed their morning preparation and weekend shopping excursions. Both activities involved deliberation about what clothing to select, and whether or not it would meet the school criteria related to coverage once on their bodies. The absence of infractions involving aggression, coupled with the daily incursion of the student code of conduct into their lives outside of school, urged us to re-search the literature – as is typically done in case study research (Flyvbjerg, 2006). In re-searching the literature we found work on identity types (Gee, 2000) which seemed more aligned with the girls' ways of negotiating how discipline was enacted in their schools and a point to which we will return shortly on the topic of social group identifiers.

IRB meets Y-PAR: Disciplining desire in research design

Some scholars claim that Youth Participatory Action Research (Y-PAR) affords students an opportunity to become youth researchers and to position them as participants in inquiry about institutions that shape their lives (Cammarota & Fine, 2008; Cook-Sather, 2002; Oakes & Rogers, 2006). In addition, youth participation in research provides an outlet for their expression of agency or agentic potential – or voice. With regard to studies of discipline among students, we were also familiar with the idea that student self-reports of school discipline may be more valid than the data reported by individual schools, districts and perhaps even states, given that schools may underreport the level of violence and discipline statistics to avoid the loss of funding or being labelled a dangerous place (Wallace, Goodkind, Wallace, & Bachman, 2008).

The assumptions we held about the effects of Y-PAR on students (rather than researchers), such as the validity of data and the influence of the IRB, were not automatically evident to us in the planning phase. Instead, they were un/becoming evident through writing, critical questioning and self-assessing. Initially, when designing this study, we envisioned the research design would be youth participatory action research (Y-PAR). However, we recognised early on that the IRB process posed limitations for designing a strong version of Y-PAR. For instance, consent forms were needed in order to engage students – or that was how we interpreted the IRB process, as primarily about the internal ethical concerns associated with obtaining informed consent (from parents of students and students under age 18). Furthermore, two of the three co-principal investigators (authors), professors in the Educational Leadership and Policy Studies program (ELPS), were leading the research team, which included two doctoral students in their program. Thus, there was a layer of teaching/mentoring that heightened our sense of responsibility to lead a study that was ethical internally (IRB guidelines) and externally (researchers' axiology concerning engagement with participants and co-principal investigators). Instead of the original version of Y-PAR we envisioned, with girls co-designing the study, we settled on their participation using an alternative form of the focus group. The focus group approach, and how student participants revised it, is described in detail below in the section on conducting and leading the study.

Conducting interviews: Eliciting social group identifiers

Others have inquired into youth identity development in secondary education, such as racial identity formation (Flory, Edwards, & Christerson, 2010; Staiger, 2004) and gender identity (Erarslan & Rankin, 2013). More recently, arts-based approaches such as assemblage have been incorporated into research on youth identity formation (Drouin, 2015). However, the following observations by Rodino-Colocino (2010) about research with youth concern both Y-PAR and youth identity. According to Rodino-Colocino (2011), there are tendencies among researchers when conducting research with or about youth. Researchers tend to:

- reduce youth to broad categories of identity (i.e., girls of colour);
- present stereotypical portrayals of youth (i.e., agents or victims); and
- present coherent and linear narratives about youth.

While we use broad categories of identity to characterise the girls as girls of colour and as either African American (four participants), Black/Latina (bi-ethnic) (one participant), or White/Latina (bi-ethnic) (one participant), the girls did not automatically use these labels in their process of self-definition. Additionally, the notes (i.e., outtakes) and journal reflection entries researchers recorded after each interview session included questions about what it means to self-identify. As researchers we were working within a pre-established set of identity markers (i.e., IRB demographic table) and an academic language we often use. Some of the girls' responses to questions to describe themselves are captured in the journal reflections of five of the seven researchers, indicating that at times they were "leading" the girls to describe themselves using social group identifiers instead of, for instance, personality characteristics.

For instance, Researcher D (District 1) wrote about one of the girls, "In terms of her identity she began with characteristics that had nothing to do with race, gender, religion or sexual orientation. She began by [describing herself as] being nice and not fitting into any one particular group". Additionally, Researcher B (District 1) wrote, "It was only through prodding that they gave their answers". Last, Researcher A (District 2) questioned, "Why did we push them to define themselves by the categories we work under/with? Left to their own devices the girls seemed quite confident describing themselves according to their personality traits, although we pressed them to redefine themselves using broad categories of race and gender".

Additionally, socioeconomic status was another group identity marker that was eventful, at least for us:

Interviewer: How would you describe your social class?

Elvira (District 1, Interview 1): What do you mean, like my social status?

Interviewer: . . . Well I said social class, but you can tell us about that.

Elvira (District 1, Interview 1): Hmm, I am kind of miscellaneous – sort of. I hang out with all different types of people, like, there is no general, like, classification.

As researchers we were unfamiliar with this self-characterisation, "miscellaneous", and uncertain as to whether Elvira was using it as an adjective, a noun or both. She initially defied being classified as a member of a group given that she "hangs out with all different types of people". This claim is supported by an entry in Researcher B's (District 1) journal describing how Elvira responded when asked to describe herself during the second interview: "I conducted the second interview with Elvira. She continues to identify as a nice person, etc. (very similar to last time). This time she also described herself and her academic standing". Eventually, when asked to imagine the researchers conducting the interview were aliens, and unfamiliar with her and her name, Elvira described herself as Black and Mexican, Puerto Rican, Haitian, Native American and African American.

Here we came to understand how the interview process was a site of leading as researchers "prodded" (Researcher B, District 1) and "probed" girls to state their identity (Researcher C, District 1). As Researcher C wrote in her journal, "It was as if she were reluctant to identity herself in terms of race, ethnicity, social class, etc". Our desire to have the girls identify as particular types of girls, namely as girls of colour (by race and/or ethnicity) became salient during interviewing, an event through which becoming moved in an eternal and productive return to difference (Stagall, 2010). Simultaneously, our desire to have the girls verify that they fitted the sampling criteria, as "girls of colour", illustrated a tendency among some researchers conducting research as Y-PAR: reducing youth to broad categories of identity (Rodino-Colocino, 2011).

As professors and educators concerned with racial disparities in education, whether based in the curriculum, pedagogy, assessment, policies or practices, or across several of these areas (i.e., discipline), researchers recorded journal reflections that spoke to the perpetuation of racial stereotypes of inferiority by some of the girls and their limited awareness of racial disparities related to discipline. Regarding racial stereotypes, Researcher E (District 2) wrote about one girl, "I was shocked that she associated being Black with having little or no intelligence and speaking Ebonics". Additionally, Researcher C (District 1) wrote:

> I too am curious about the identity questions, their response, our response, and their lack of making a racial/ethnic designation, even when they were able to articulate some of the racial/ethnic differences related to discipline in school. It's curious to me that the girls were aware of difference in terms of treatment by gender and race but did not 'see' (my interpretation) their race/ethnicity as a salient factor.

The girls' constancy in describing their individual qualities rather than social group positionalities was similar to that of the clerk in Melville's *Bartleby the Scrivener*, who responded to all requests with the phrase, "I would prefer not to". This phrase has often been cited as an act of resistance to that which attempts to domesticate someone (Taubman, 2009). We read these engagements (between researchers and participants, women and girls) regarding identity, positionality and self-identification as socialisation events involving claims about being and involvement in one another's becoming as researchers, participants and members of broader social groups.

Post-interview debriefing sessions: Researchers, mothers and mentors

After being interviewed and starting to exit the room, Gorgeous commented that as a form of punishment her mother had removed her bedroom door from its hinges. Researcher B (District 1) shared this comment as part of the debriefing session with other members of the research team who had conducted interviews in other rooms. This comment prompted three of us researchers (professors) to reflect on the disciplining practices we used with our children, which included withholding affection and giving children the "silent treatment" as well as spanking them *and* removing doorknobs. There were tensions between the researchers over which disciplinary measures were abusive or not in the discussion, which bordered on naming what we viewed as un/becoming of a mother. Through the reflective dialogue we considered what cultural norms were operating in how we, as researchers from different racial/ethnic backgrounds, disciplined our children and how varied those practices can be depending on whether we are private or public.

Later, Researcher B, District 1 entered a reflection into her journal about how she was reminded of the news that the door had been removed when she and a student/co-researcher entered the home of Gorgeous to conduct an interview with her mother:

> Gorgeous said her mother took the door off the hinges! I did not know what to do with that bit of information. I considered questioning her mother about it, but I was afraid to ask after she said she was raised on a military base. I did not want to provoke a 'drill sergeant episode' response to my [perceived] questioning of her "single-parent child-raising skills".
>
> (Researcher B, District 1)

We understand this journal entry as including the researcher's desire to avoid the backlash that she imagined could erupt if the mother had sensed she was being judged. Also intertwined in this desire was the fear of the military, a fear based on images of controlled training being used to discipline soldiers.

Gorgeous' statement served as a starting point – a thing involving relationships between people (her and her mother), objects (hinges, a door) and action (removal of the door). What was at the time a statement Gorgeous made in passing was a statement that had repercussions for us. It prompted us to reflect on their experiences with discipline as an aspect of parenting and entered the assemblage of desire as a creative force to dislocate our thinking about leading/following. We shifted in our roles from being personally detached to personally invested leaders (influential figures) to leaders~followers, and saw the girls become similarly personally invested followers~leaders. By taking Gorgeous' statement as a point of reflection and re-engaging with it self-reflexively we have come to understand it as a shaping force that led us to reflect differently. In addition to reflecting on the study we have been helped to re-imagine ways of becoming mother(s)~researcher(s) who also discipline children and youth in ways we (and others) may find unattractive or unbecoming.

Gorgeous' comment helped us to raise a mirror to our practice as researchers, a mirror that distorted our sense of what we knew about conducting research, including how we were becoming knowledgeable about the research participants. Ironically, we did not capture the comment by Gorgeous with the digital recorder since the interview ended and the recorder was stopped. Neither did we capture the interview with Gorgeous' mother since a researcher (professor) did not press the record button with sufficient force. Even this reflection is a reminder of the importance of the middle as the most interesting area between beginnings and endings (Deleuze & Parnet, 1987) or (in research terms) what happens between data generation and data analysis. While we knew better (i.e., how and when to start and stop the recorder), we did not practise what we knew (perhaps for the better). We contend that discipline practice in schools can suffer from the same lapses in judgement and might also benefit from the mirrors students would hold up if invited to openly participate in dialogues as leaders~followers.

Focus group

The focus group was developed as a role-play activity that asked the girls to imagine themselves in our roles, as researchers, and collaboratively design a similar study. The purpose of this activity was to inform the girls about the significance of the current study and the significance of the one they were to design from the research question they would ask to the participants/informants they would invite to participate.

To inform their design, we provided them with statistical data on discipline across districts in the US. More specifically we provided the data on disproportionality across race and gender (e.g., Blake, Butler, Lewis, & Darensbourg, 2011). In the first instance (District 1), only two of four girls showed up so that our group was instead a dyad/pair. They proceeded to brainstorm and deliberate over the study they would design. Then, just when we thought we were "leading from a shared vision" (a popular phrase depicting leading practices in K-12 school literature), our plan to conduct a focus group in another district (District 2) was revised by two siblings participating in the study.

After reviewing the nationwide report on discipline-related disparities by race and gender that we provided to the siblings, instead of following the research outline we offered, they proceeded to communicate using arts-based modalities by drawing on whiteboards as they narrated their observations and interpretations of how girls are entangled in discipline at schools. The focus group we imagined was revised as the participants' and researchers' desires commingled and became entangled with the agency of objects, like whiteboards and cell phones, that hail users by often simply being present and performing as they were designed to do. The focus groups served as events that dislocated our sense of control as researchers who were "leading a study" and "conducting focus groups". In planning we thought about what they are and would be rather than what they could become in the context of students' lives.

Conclusion

According to Deleuze and Guattari (1983), "desiring-machines work only when they break down, and by continually breaking down" (p. 8). In this concluding reflection we note that what broke down in the desiring machine of researching discipline was the design of the study: envisioning it as Y-PAR, re-viewing of relevant literature, imposing labels for students, restructuring the focus groups.

Also, what broke down in the desiring machine of leading discipline in schools was consistency: the gap between teachers and administrators, the logic of the demand for noise reduction at a pep rally and the inconsistency in the degree of punishment enforced for students of colour when compared to white students. Assemblages operate through desire and a wide range of flows (Deleuze & Guattari, 1986). What might be perceived as a desire for power is only one's fascination with the gears of the overall machine. It is either a desire to make sure the gears operate, a desire to be a gear and/or a desire to be treated as material used by a gear (the finger that presses the button on the walkie-talkie button, the finger that presses too softly or fails to press the button on the audio recorder).

Machines that break down can provide opportunities for problem-solving, reimagining problems of practice and inquiry and leading practice that is responsive to what girls of colour experience. The continual breaking down of research about discipline and the implementation of discipline in schools allowed us to probe events and take notice of multiple, transitional and divergent meanings of conducting and leading. To the question of *what conduct is un/becoming?* we found that entanglements of power, people and things exposed how unsteady the relationship between discipline and education was playing out for girls of colour. Instruction emphasising adherence to rules versus instruction emphasising growth seemed to be in constant competition for primacy in the cultures of the schools. Thus it seems a great task before those in educational leadership roles, especially those directly or indirectly influencing students' lives on a daily basis (i.e., teachers, school administrators), to recognise the inharmonious chord that can be struck when leading to discipline *and* leading to educate.

There is growing attention to the adoption of restorative justice in schools to reduce race-related disparities and exclusionary practices associated with discipline (as punishment). Attempts to take up a restorative justice approach to discipline in school offers those in educational leadership positions an opportunity to dialogue with students on the Indigenous philosophical roots undergirding restorative justice practices (Zehr, 2008), including how power, people and things are in constant flux yet fueled by desires for consistency – among others. However, as Lustik (2015) noted, researchers and educators (i.e., school administrators) should have as their goal to understand when opportunities for student voice are technologies of pastoral power that reproduce the racially disproportionate outcomes educators seek to mitigate. Restorative justice practices can offer opportunities for students to make decisions and then provide rationales for those decisions (Gregory, Clawson, Davis, & Gerewitz, 2014; Wachtel, 2012). Y-PAR might then be a precursor to restorative justice, for it is guided by the ethic of justice and an emancipatory relationship between members of society regardless of age, gender, rank or race. Though as we have illustrated, equity and parity in research or leadership are not automatically produced through the adoption of a practice.

This critical and self-reflexive praxeological approach challenged our comfort with qualitative research that generates data and analyses it as if disconnected from the processes of conducting and reflecting upon it. It also poses a challenge to traditional constructions of leadership in schools as it repositions leading practices within an entanglement of power exchanges between people, objects (walkie-talkies, whiteboards) *and* places (offices, pep rallies). Through our entanglement with people, power and objects in the research process we were afforded mirrors through which to consider how research is disciplined and how we as researchers responded to the various desires associated with planning, leading and conducting research related to discipline.

By exploring some unexamined assumptions that underpinned research methodology and theoretical frameworks used to examine educational leadership practices (leading in schools, leading research with students), we are perhaps be/coming more skeptical of research on the experience of girls of colour with discipline, even when conducted with emancipatory interests and guided by frameworks informed by critical and postmodern perspectives. At least we are more sympathetic to administrators who are enmeshed in the desiring machine without plentiful opportunities for critical self-reflection yet with abundant opportunities to be observed and critiqued for how they conduct themselves and others. After all, we are also enmeshed in a desiring machine of wanting to know through research that is weighted with assumptions and imaginations about the ideal conditions under which it will be conducted and consumed – and by whom.

References

Alloway, L. (1961). Junk culture. *Architectural Design, 31*(3), 122.

Bennett, J. (2010). *Vibrant matter: A political ecology of things.* Durham, NC: Duke University Press.

Blake, J. J., Butler, B. R., Lewis, C. W., & Darensbourg, A. (2011). Unmasking the inequitable discipline experiences of urban Black girls: Implications for urban educational stakeholders. *The Urban Review, 43*(1), 90–106.

Bright, R. M. (2005). It's just a Grade 8 girl thing: Aggression in teenage girls. *Gender and Education, 17*(1), 93–101.

Brown, L. M., & Tappan, M. B. (2008). Fighting like a girl fighting like a guy: Gender identity, ideology, and girls at early adolescence. In M. Azmitia, M. Syed, & K. Radmacher (Eds.), *The intersections of personal and social identities: New directions for child and adolescent development* (pp. 120, 47–59). San Francisco, CA: Jossy-Bass. doi:10.1002/cd.212

Cammarota, J., & Fine, M. (Eds.). (2008). *Revolutionizing education: Youth participatory action research in motion.* New York: Routledge.

Cook-Sather, A. (2002). Authorizing students' perspectives: Toward trust, dialogue, and change in education. *Educational Researcher, 31*(4), 3–14.

Deleuze, G., & Guattari, F. (1983). *Anti-Oedipus: Capitalism and schizophrenia* (R. Hurley, M. Seem, & H. R. Lane, Trans.). Minneapolis, MN: University of Minnesota Press.

Deleuze, G., & Guattari, F. (1986). *Kafka: Toward a minor literature* (Trans. D. Polan). Minneapolis, MN: University of Minnesota.

Deleuze, G., & Guattari, F. (2004). *A thousand plateaus: Capitalism and schizophrenia.* London: Continuum.

Deleuze, G., & Parnet, C. (1987). *Dialogues II* (H. Tomlison & B. Habberjam, Trans.). London: Continuum.
Denzin, N. K. (2013). The death of data? *Cultural Studies ↔ Critical Methodologies, 13*(4), 353–356.
Drouin, S. D. (2015). Assemblage: Raising awareness of student identity formation through art. *Multicultural Education, 22*(3–4), 59–61.
Erarslan, A. B., & Rankin, B. (2013). Gender role attitudes of female students in single-sex and coeducational high schools in Istanbul. *Sex Roles, 69*(7–8), 455–468.
Evans, G. (1988). Those loud Black girls. In D. Spender & E. Sarah (Eds.), *Learning to lose: Sexism and education* (pp. 183–190). London: The Women's Press.
Flory, R., Edwards, K., & Christerson, B. (2010). *Growing up in America: The power of race in the lives of teens.* Stanford, CA: Stanford University Press.
Flyvbjerg, B. (2006). Five misunderstandings about case-study research. *Qualitative Inquiry, 12*(2), 219–245.
Fordham, S. (1993). 'Those loud Black girls': (Black) women, silence, and gender 'passing' in the academy. *Anthropology & Education Quarterly, 24*(1), 3–32.
Gee, J. P. (2000). Identity as an analytic lens for research in education. *Review of Research in Education, 5,* 99–125.
Gratton, P. (2010, July 26). *Bennett, vibrant matter* [Web log post]. Retrieved from https://philosophyinatimeoferror.com/2010/04/22/vibrant-matters-an-interview-with-jane-bennett/
Gregory, A., Clawson, K., Davis, A., & Gerewitz, J. (2014). The promise of restorative practices to transform teacher-student relationships and achieve equity in school discipline. *Journal of Educational and Psychological Consultation, 25*(1), 1–29. doi: 10.1080/10474412.2014.929950
Heck, R. H., & Hallinger, P. (2005). The study of educational leadership and management: Where does the field stand today? *Educational management Administration Leadership, 33*(2), 229–244.
Koonce, J. B. (2012). 'Oh, Those Loud Black Girls!': A phenomenological study of Black girls talking with an attitude. *Journal of Language and Literacy Education, 8*(2), 26–46.
Lustik, H. (2015). Administering discipline differently: A Foucauldian lens on restorative school discipline. *International Journal of Leadership in Education, 15*(1), 1–15. doi:10.1080/13603124.2015.1100755
Maffie, J. (2014). *Aztec philosophy: Understanding a world in motion.* Boulder, CO: University of Colorado Press.
Morris, E. W. (2007). 'Ladies' or 'Loudies'? Perceptions and experiences of Black girls in classrooms. *Youth & Society, 38*(4), 490–515.
Oakes, J., & Rogers, J. (2006). *Learning power: Organizing for education and justice.* New York: Teachers College Press.
Reckwitz, A. (2002). Toward a theory of social practices: A development in culturalist theorizing. *European Journal of Social Theory, 2,* 245–265.
Rodino-Colocino, M. (2011). Getting to 'not especially strange': Embracing participatory-advocacy communication research for social justice. *International Journal of Communication, 5,* 1699–1711.
Schmidt, R. (2010). Re-describing social practices: Comparison as analytical and explorative tool. In J. Niewöhner & T. Scheffer (Eds.), *Thick comparison: Reviving the ethnographic aspiration* (pp. 79–102). Boston, MA: Brill.

Skiba, R. J., Michael, R. S., Nardo, A. C., & Peterson, R. L. (2002). The color of discipline: Sources of racial and gender disproportionality in school punishment. *Urban Review, 34*(4), 317–342.

Stagall, C. (2010). Event. In A. Parr (Ed.), *The Deleuze dictionary* (pp. 89–91). Edinburgh: Edinburgh University Press.

Taubman, P. M. (2009). *Teaching by numbers: Deconstructing the discourse of standards and accountability in education.* New York: Routledge.

Wachtel, T. (2012). *Defining restorative.* Retrieved from http://iirpds.pointinspace.com/pdf/Defining-Restorative.pdf

Wallace, J. M., Goodkind, S., Wallace, C. M., & Bachman, J. G. (2008). Racial, ethnic, and gender differences in school discipline among U.S. high school students: 1991–2005. *Negro Educational Review, 59*(1–2), 47–62.

Wise, J. M. (2005). Assemblage. In C. Stivale (Ed.), *Gilles Deleuze: Key concepts* (pp. 77–87). Trowbridge, CA: Cromwell Press.

Zehr, H. (2008). Doing justice, healing trauma: The role of restorative justice in peacebuilding. *South Asian Journal of Peacebuilding, 1*(1), 1–16.

11 Left out

Gender and feminism in the educational leadership curriculum

Michelle D. Young, Catherine Marshall and Torrie Edwards

Introduction

For decades there have been calls for reforms in educational leadership preparation programs (ELPPs) (Griffiths, Stout, & Forsyth, 1988; Marshall, 2004; Murphy, Moorman, & McCarthy, 2008; Young, Petersen, & Short, 2002). Critics have argued for redeveloping curricula and learning experiences responsive to changing United States' demographics; developing an integrated, relevant knowledge base, including practical field-based programs; and developing a critical mass of faculty with an appropriate blend of academic preparation, theoretical understanding and administrative experiences (Young et al., 2002). As important as the above issues are, they give short shrift to the lived experiences of over 50% of educational leadership candidates in the United States: women.

Roughly more than half of the US student population is female, and the majority of teachers, school counselors, librarians, elementary school principals and other educational personnel are women; yet, it is rare to see gender or women's issues take centre stage within education research, policy or preparation discussions. Why are women's and gender issues consistently left out of important conversations and initiatives focused on improving the preparation of current and future educational leaders?

Consider the challenges schools and universities have experienced in protecting young women from sexual harrassment and abuse and in attracting and retaining females in science, technology, engineering and math fields. Consider the consistently low percentages of women taking leadership positions in US school districts, major corporations and the government. If the rate of change in district leadership positions from 1999–2011 remains on course, parity between men and women in superintendent positions will not be achieved until at least 2040 (Glass, 2000; Kowalski, McCord, Peterson, Young, & Ellerson, 2011; Marshall & Johnson, 2015).

Much feminist literature in educational leadership urges the inclusion of readings on women leaders in ELPPs as one strategy for addressing the trends impacting women in education (e.g., Marshall, 2004; Young & McLeod, 2001). According to Marshall (1995), including such literature is important because "leadership theory was developed by white males doing observations of white males holding leadership positions" (p. 486). Others have suggested the inclusion of feminist literature and theories that highlight gendered hierarchies, divisions of labors and micropolitics that reify male dominance in leadership positions (Blackmore, 1999; Marshall & Young, 2013). However, it is unclear whether or to what degree educational leadership faculty have adopted these strategies or attempted to address gender issues through program content and experiences. A review of relevant scholarship revealed little evidence that school leaders are being prepared to understand, much less disrupt, the gender hierarchy in leadership or to develop the knowledge or skills needed to interrupt gender-discriminating practices.

In this study, we investigated how aspiring principals and other educational leaders in the United States are prepared to support gender equity. Like O'Malley and Capper's (2015) investigation of the inclusion of lesbian, gay, bisexual, transgender, intersex and questioning (LGBTIQ) issues in ELPPs, our research operates from the perspective that

> because social justice is defined by its concerns with margins a principal preparation program's social justice commitment might be measured by the extent to which the program addresses identities that are minimally represented within the social justice research literature.
>
> (pp. 291–292)

Thus, the research reported in this paper seeks to understand the degree to which and how women's perspectives, women's experiences in educational leadership and feminist themes are integrated into the content and learning activities used to prepare educational leaders for their roles in schools and district offices.

Perspectives from the inside: Three authors' experiences

We begin this chapter by sharing slices of our experiences, in hopes that we might provide some insight into our purposes in this chapter and our hopes for work of this nature.

Michelle: Daughter, big sister, student, officer, professor, leader . . . Each role had its own set of gendered (as well as class, racial, ability) expectations, and I worked hard to meet them, judging goodness of fit and aligning to standards. Theory, and in particular feminist poststructural theory, provided a framework and language to understand my experiences. It is powerful to discover oneself, others, organisations and systems through new lenses – to develop new and different ways of thinking, to find problems and possibilities in the most unlikely places. Educational leaders not only deserve the opportunity to experience the power of feminist (and other) frameworks; in some cases, the effectiveness of their practice may depend upon it. The 'real work' of leadership is based upon the very stuff that theory troubles and shakes. It is time that ELPPs educate future leaders in the transformative power of theory.

Catherine: "When do I get to teach about gender issues?" This has been my persistent question during three decades as a professor of educational administration in three US research universities, during which time I persistently pursued gender issues in education in my research and dissertation advising, leading to my being an international 'name' in feminist critical policy analysis. The answer is, "We need you to teach the courses required for research methods and for licensure requirements". My next question then is: When will I see administrator licensure clearly designating that gender issues in school programs, leadership and policy must be part of ELPPs? 'Social justice' and 'cultural diversity' could be a start, but, without clear designation and without empowered feminist faculty, gender will not be an emphasis in those courses.

Torrie: As a high school English teacher, I marveled at how little attention was paid to gender in public schools. No one took issue with the disproportionate number of higher-level courses being taught by male teachers, the inequitable application of the dress code policy to female students or the seepage of managerial norms into our classrooms. Later, I endured two years of gender-neutrality in my doctoral program where educational inequities such as re-segregation and the discriminatory distribution of school resources were emphasised under the umbrella of 'social justice', while gender was not. Not once did I have a course that discussed feminism, feminist policy or feminist issues in education, that included feminist readings or focused on girls' or women's experiences in education. My exposure to feminism has been a result of my own initiative. This gap has been disappointing. How can there be a strong emphasis on intersectionality in social justice language without a clear focus on gender in education?

As feminist poststructuralists, we consider beliefs, values and practices associated with gender and the very notion of gender to be constructed, and we hold that constructions like gender and educational leadership can be reconstructed through language and practice (Alcoff, 1988). Our experiences and our perspectives have led us to a common concern: leadership preparation may be, albeit unwittingly, participating in the reproduction and reinscription of beliefs and practices that foster inequality and exclusion. As explained by Wilkinson and Bristol in the introduction to this volume, "educational leadership as a discipline remains firmly gripped by positivist and functionalist paradigms", paradigms that drip with ethnocentrism. In this project we seek to understand whether US ELPPs are contributing to or interrupting status quo understandings and the systems of exclusion and power that result by examining if and how gender and feminist issues are taught with US ELPPs. After reviewing related scholarship and our methods, we present the findings from a survey of US ELPPs and discuss those findings in light of their potential to support gender equity.

Perspectives from research

From accumulated research we know much about the problematic situation faced by women who are and who aspire to be educational leaders (Young,

Mountford, & Skrla, 2006). However, we know very little about the types of leadership development content and strategies used in ELPPs to support educational leaders in altering systems that perpetuate gender inequities. To inform our study we reviewed three pertinent areas of the literature: (1) literature on the preparation of educational leaders; (2) literature on standards and licensure policies; and (3) literature concerning the development of curriculum relevant to gender equity. We complement this section with a review of scholarship on different feminist perspectives.

Research on leadership preparation

Research on the education of school leaders has significantly enriched our understanding of effective preparation (Young, Crow, Murphy, & Ogawa, 2009). Not only have scholars identified a clearer set of program features that contribute to candidate effectiveness (e.g., cohort structures and internships), but research has also identified important elements of preparation curriculum, pedagogies, practical experiences and university and district partnerships (Darling-Hammond, LaPointe, Meyerson, & Orr, 2007). Hackmann and McCarthy's (2011) study of the educational leadership professoriate complements program research by providing insight into those who are designing and teaching in ELPP programs. Women ELPP faculty numbers have increased overall; tenured female faculty members have increased from 12% in 1986 to 45% in 2008; and the proportion of women "tenure line professors more than doubled between 1994 and 2008" (Hackmann & McCarthy, 2011, p. 62). These authors also found significant differences in faculty perceptions. For example, women reported placing higher value on social justice, inclusion and diversity; they reported higher levels of work-related stress and felt greater pressure to publish. Hackman and McCarthy also found that women continued to be underrepresented in administrative positions and overrepresented in terms of service commitments.

Recent meta-analyses of research on preparation (Crow & Wideman, 2016; Lumby, Crow, & Pashiardis, 2008; Young et al., 2009) call for more research on who is participating in ELPPs and their career intentions and choices, how to recruit and select the kinds of leaders schools need to ensure equity and excellence, and how to structure powerful learning experiences that allow candidates to transfer knowledge and skills into their leadership positions. However, this literature says very little about the preparation of women leaders, gender issues or preparing leaders to support gender equity. Although the literature speaks generally to the notion of excellence and equity, it has yet to engage with the preparation of leaders for social justice broadly or gender equity specifically (O'Malley & Capper, 2015).

Standards and licensure policy

As noted above, the general literature on educational leadership preparation pays minimal attention to the issue of preparing leaders to support social justice, and gender equity is hardly addressed at all. Like other authors who are concerned about the development of equity-minded leaders, we argue that this is not terribly surprising given that leadership for social justice is not a central theme within the efforts to develop standards and licensure policy (Davis, Gooden, & Micheaux, 2015; Fuller, Williams, Nash, & Young, 2016). Clearly, leadership preparation does not exist in a vacuum but in a context that has both internal and external forces. Crow and his colleagues (2012) argue that such forces influence the types of studies and the attention given to different program elements, and, from our perspective, these same forces influence the policy and professional discourses shaping the development of standards and licensure policy.

Of the many contextual changes influencing preparation in the US, the most significant is accountability and the resulting keen focus within educational policy on assessment and outcomes. This focus has shaped a set of standards that emphasises measurable forms of student achievement and teacher and school performance. As many before have argued, these ideas are derived from business management, and while there is value in holding educators responsible for the impact they have on students, the notion of accountability is not the same as the professional value of holding oneself responsible for fostering equity and social justice.

Additionally, while there are specific standards that speak to ethics, community and care for all children, these are given less attention within the discourses of educational policy and educator evaluation. Furthermore, gender equity is ignored: It is left out (CCSSO, 2015). The fact that national and state standards and state licensure requirements lack gender-related language reflects the values and beliefs of the greater US society that consistently deny the fact that gender inequity continues to plague our society, demonstrates the low priority placed on gender equity for educational leadership, and reinforces the worldviews of most faculty and practicing leaders who are blind to issues of gender equity.

Curriculum development

Since 1997, when the ISLLC standards were first introduced, the curriculum of ELPPs has become increasingly standardised. Coursework has concentrated around the six ISSLC standards, which include an emphasis on school vision, instructional leadership, organisational culture, school management, community engagement and the political, legal and ethical dimensions of leading schools (Kottkamp & Rusch, 2009). Scholars of leadership for social justice, however, argue that student learning outcomes are dependent upon a variety of factors that extend beyond these widely established content areas, and, as a result, hold that ELPP curriculum should reflect the complex practical realities of achieving excellence and equity in schools as well as the theoretical constructs that enable leaders to grapple with and make meaning of such realities (Capper, Theoharis, & Sebastian, 2006; Jean-Marie, Normore, & Brooks, 2009; Marshall & Oliva, 2010; Pounder, Reitzug, & Young, 2002; Theoharis, 2007).

Importantly, a growing number of ELPPs' mission statements include a commitment to social justice. However, research on preparing leaders for social justice has found that different identities within the umbrella of social justice are given uneven emphasis in preparation programs (Capper et al., 2006; O'Malley & Capper, 2015). Specifically, identities given high emphasis included "race/ethnicity (95.4%), socioeconomic status (94.9%), and culture (93.8%)" (pp. 306–307). Identities given frequent emphasis included "dis/ability (79.7%) and language (78.5%)" (p. 307), and identities given less emphasis included gender (58.2%), "sexual orientation (48.6%) and religion/belief (45.1%)" (p. 307). O'Malley and Capper (2015) found that, while more than 85% of "social justice" oriented programs reported being effective at preparation for developing anti-harassment/bullying policies, only 50% asserted effectiveness for addressing anti-harassment of LGBTIQ students. Further, they found that LGBTIQ issues were only marginally integrated. As Marshall and Young (2013) point out, it is significant that a field made possible by a predominantly female workforce places such minimal emphasis on gender issues.

According to Marshall (2004), "Professors have the power and the privilege to reproduce and reify whatever discourse they choose in classrooms and in research... [which is] primarily maleocentric" (p. 23). This doesn't bode well for the teaching of gender issues in ELPPs. Rusch (2004), for example, found "gender issues are definitely left up to the women in the department" (p. 35), though men, more than women faculty, reported a high frequency of engaging in discussions about race and gender issues, though their discussions included comments like "lip service" and "not part of the reward system" (p 29). Similarly, among students' self-reports on student-initiated classroom discourse in ELPPs, women more often speak of "contentious, personalized dialogue" (p. 37).

A few scholars have been explicit in their publications calling for specific focus on gender and/or feminist insights in ELPPs (Poplin-Gosetti, 1995). However, such calls for inclusion are much more plentiful than scholarship examining or discussing the inclusion of feminist and gender issues in the classroom. One study, which focused specifically on the impact of incorporating a set of readings focused on issues of gender, diversity, leadership and feminist thought into the curriculum, sought to determine whether having a chance to critically reflect upon and communicate about various gender and feminist topics might shift pre-existing assumptions, biases and paradigms (Young et al., 2006).

After a year's exposure to readings and written assignments about gender and its intersection to other diversity issues, however, Young et al. (2006) found few students had undergone significant transformations in their thinking, while a significant number demonstrated resistance. For example, some students viewed "-isms" (i.e., racism, sexism) as existing only at the individual level, believing that institutions like schools or policies could not be homophobic or sexist. Although some were willing to focus on oppression and how it operates to the disadvantage of certain groups, they were less willing or unwilling to discuss how oppression advantages other groups, particularly groups of which they were members. Another example involved protecting the dominant group. One of their participants, Dorothy, expressed discomfort about the focus on gender bias and sexism because of the way it made the men feel. Some went as far as denying that sexism exists and describing men as the real victims of discrimination in today's society. Another example of resistance involved the invalidation of course content or the teacher. Nine of the 13 students, who expressed negative opinions about having to read about issues of gender bias and sexism, suggested they had a problem with the course materials and/or the person presenting the material. One student, Clark, questioned studying gender issues in a leadership course and suggested that it was a faculty member's agenda being pushed.

In summary, like O'Malley and Capper (2015), we found that the literature on teaching for social justice was not well or evenly developed. Moreover, if the literature is a lens into how researchers think about social justice, then it appears ELPP scholars are not terribly concerned with gender equity.

Feminist frameworks

In the survey we administered to university representatives, which will be discussed in detail in the next section, we asked respondents to identify the type(s) of feminisms that their university ELPP taught, including Black, cultural, liberal, postcolonial, postmodern/poststructural, radical and socialist/Marxist feminisms. To aid the reader in understanding what we mean by these different terms, we define (albeit simplistically) these types of feminist thought in the paragraphs that follow.

Black feminism emphasises Black women's experiences, as told by those who themselves live it (Arya, 2012; Collins, 1996). Black feminism pushes against second wave feminism's universalisation of women's experiences as white and middle class (Arya, 2012); it challenges the ideological underpinnings of traditionally white feminism that has excluded women of colour and the unique experiences of these communities (Collins, 1996); and it requires Black women to reflect on their own views of racism and sexism. Black feminism has also been called "womanism", although there is contention within the Black feminist and womanist communities about the interchangeability of the terms, as womanism has traditionally been associated with Black nationalist movements that are not interested in "foster[ing] interracial cooperation among women" (Collins, 1996, p. 11). Both terms refer to women of colour who struggle against racism and sexism in support of Black women's "self-definition and "self-determination" (Collins, 1996, p. 10).

Cultural feminism recognises and utilises "women's essential differences from men". In the larger body of literature, cultural feminism posits that there is an "essential female" and focuses on "the ideology of a female nature or female essence" (Alcoff, 1988, p. 408). Cultural feminists reject the notion that men can define women's essential characteristics. Cultural feminism is, thus, a reclamation of femininity by women and a means to reverse the valuation of the male and the devaluation of the female (Taylor & Rupp, 1993).

Liberal feminism focuses on legal action and "practices that demand gender equity". Liberal feminism is defined more broadly as addressing women's "general or universal positions" (Enslin & Mary, 2004, p. 504) and treatment under the law. As the "liberal subject" is identifiable by its "primary political mechanism" of "equal rights", liberal feminism calls for structural action to ensure legal guarantees (Kotef, 2009, p. 500). It is liberal feminism that has been credited with large gains in women's equal political, social and legal rights such as suffrage, property rights, equal pay initiatives and anti-discrimination law (Epure, 2014).

Postcolonial feminism focuses on "women's experiences in non-Western cultures, indigenous societies, or developing nations" (Suleri, 1992, p. 760). Postcolonial feminism focuses on women in postcolonial contexts who occupy a space at the intersection of race, history and gender. It works to understand how Western feminist discourse examines the "Third World Woman" in a way that is itself a colonialist activity, one in which the Western feminist remains in control and the Third World Woman never rises above her object status (Suleri, p. 760). Like in Black feminism, in postcolonial feminism, there is a question of authenticity; that is, who can speak for whom in regards to the lived experiences and realities of the postcolonial woman?

Postmodern/poststructural feminism emphasises "that gender and sex are constructed, and can be reconstructed, through language and other discursive practices" (Alcoff, 1988, p. 415). The main tenet of poststructural feminism is that there is no "self-contained, authentic subject" beneath socially constructed, external identities (Alcoff, 1988, p. 415); this notion is itself a social construct. Postmodern/postructural feminists argue that there is no essential woman and that social discourse and cultural practices that force such binary identities also provide a space for women's resistance to these dichotomous categories. Postmodern/poststructural feminists focus largely on the ways in which language is used to construct knowledge and meaning not through a formal, logocentric system of sign and signified, but rather through social struggle and a constantly shifting social context (Ebert, 1991; Lather, 1992; St. Pierre, 2000).

Radical feminism focuses on "systematic restructuring that eliminates male supremacy in any and all contexts" (Epure, 2014). It is defined in the literature as focused primarily on removing itself from mainstream feminisms that work within existing systems to make changes. Instead, radical feminism works to change the central ideology of social thought. In their challenge to patriarchal dominance, radical feminists privilege womanhood and fight against sex-based oppression (Epure, 2014). In this system, women and women's bodies are supreme; sexual liberation is key. However, in some radical feminist thought, sexual pleasure and sexual activity (including maternity) that tie women to heterosexual and heteronormative, patriarchal institutions are dangerous for women's true freedom from subjugation (Epure, 2014).

Socialist/Marxist feminism works toward the elimination of capitalist practices that do not compensate for or undercompensate women's labor (Epure, 2014; Weeks, 2011). Socialist and Marxist feminism focuses on women's position in society relative to economics and labor; to bring about true equality between the genders, Socialist/Marxist feminists argue for the abolition of the capitalist system (Epure, 2014). These feminists argue that capitalist systems privilege men's work over women's work by rewarding those who engage in productive (waged) labor and excluding unpaid labor, the work done by women in domestic arenas. Socialist/Marxist feminists are interested in establishing a system of labor that "accommodates its entire working force" and redefining what is "productive labor" to include the significant work done in the "domestic sphere" (Weeks, 2011, p. 32).

Our inclusion of the above frameworks in our survey of educational leadership preparation design, curriculum and pedagogy was intended to both help us understand what kind of feminist frameworks were included in ELPPS and to educate those unschooled in feminist thought about variations within the umbrella term "feminism". Each of the frameworks raises different questions about women, relationships, leadership and reality and has much to offer the preparation of educational leaders who work within complex realities.

Methods

Data for this research project was collected through a cross-sectional survey (Fraenkel, Wallen, & Hyun, 2012; Patton, 1990), administered in the summer of 2015 via an emailed hyperlink to leadership faculty working in University Council for Educational Administration (UCEA)[1] member institution preparation programs. The survey invitation asked institutional representatives to either complete the survey or forward it to the program coordinator for completion. Faculty from 46 of the 98 universities responded to the survey, indicating participation in the survey from approximately 46% of UCEA institutions.

The survey consisted of 27 questions focused on program gender demographics, faculty preparation, curricular content and pedagogy. Reflecting our review of the literature, survey questions were grouped into five categories: (1) the emphasis placed on gender issues; (2) the inclusion of gender and feminist themes in courses; (3) the resources used to teach about gender and feminist issues; (4) the emphasis placed on feminism within the program; and (5) institutional factors, such as climate, feminist faculty and feminist scholarship. Although we did not specifically ask about how programs addressed combinations of oppressions, gender is inextricably linked with other demographic variables like race and social class, which undeniably impact program structure, pedagogy and leadership practices. Furthermore, intersectionality undergirds several of the feminist frameworks we included in the survey (e.g., Black feminism).

Importantly, the findings and implications presented below must be considered in light of the study's limitations. First, our study only included UCEA program faculty as participants because we valued the participation of programs that voluntarily engaged in a consortium like UCEA, which is focused on quality leadership preparation. The study is also limited by the perspective and knowledge of the individual filling out the survey. In some cases, the respondent may have been well informed; however, the opposite may have been true as well. Third, the survey included primarily closed-ended responses to allow comparability across programs; however, this limited the richness of participants' responses. Fourth, the survey data provides only a snapshot of the participating preparation programs. As such, the data are illustrative of certain patterns evident across our sample rather than definitive of all ELPPs.

Findings and discussion

Survey findings indicated that women's perspectives, women's experiences in educational leadership and feminist themes are only marginally integrated into US educational leadership preparation programs. Most respondents reported that their ELPP courses on cultural diversity and/or social justice did have one or more readings or activities that addressed gender issues in school systems. However, only a small percentage claimed a semester-long required course on issues related to gender and women in leadership, and an even smaller percentage of programs claimed open engagement with questions of women in leadership. In the following subsections, we provide further detail on these and other findings from our survey.

Course content

We examined the inclusion of gender and feminist perspectives in educational leadership program content in two ways: first, by the programs' general content and second, by programs' specific course offerings and a gender focus. With regard to general content, six respondents (13.33%) reported their program places high emphasis on gender, while 42.22% reported that their programs placed high emphasis on race/ethnicity and another 51.11% reported placing high emphasis on socioeconomic status. Additionally, one respondent who provided a write-in comment explained that "gender issues are largely ignored".

These findings are particularly interesting given findings from O'Malley and Capper's (2015) survey of UCEA leadership preparation programs. Specifically, they found that 82.1% of the programs identified social justice as a core program dimension, and of those programs gender was emphasised in only 58% as compared to race (95.4%), socioeconomic status (94.9%) and culture (93.8%). According to O'Malley and Capper "social justice discourse that normalizes attention to particular aspects of identity while legitimizing layers of silence vis-à-vis others carries the risk of devolving into an alternate mechanism of colonization" (p. 319).

With regard to specific course offerings, respondents were asked how frequently gender was incorporated in program courses. Table 11.1 shows results concerning courses that focused most on gender issues. Eight courses are listed in order from those in which gender is most frequently included. In contrast, Table 11.2 displays the courses in which faculty reported focusing the least on gender issues. It is worth noting that several additional courses were identified as not focusing on gender in any way: student services, instructional leadership, leadership and the principalship. Specifically, gender was reported missing by 40% of faculty (2 of 5) who taught Student Services, 36.84% of faculty (7 of 19) who taught Introduction to Instructional Leadership, 33.33% of faculty (5 of 15) who taught Leadership and 30.77% of faculty (4 of 13) who taught the principalship.

Although certain classes do seem to lend themselves to focusing on gender issues more easily than others, it is difficult to distinguish clear patterns in the courses listed. One might assume, however, that the above findings are the result

Table 11.1 Courses in which gender is most frequently discussed

Course Content	Frequency
Human Resources/Personnel	90% (9 of 10)
Introduction to Educational Leadership	81.82% (9 of 11)
Communication	75% (6 of 8)
Contemporary Issues	72.73% (8 of 11)
Ethics	70% (7 of 10)
Social Foundations	66.67% (4 of 6)
Continuous Improvement	63.64% (7 of 11)
Community Relations	62.5% (5 of 8)

Table 11.2 Courses in which gender is least frequently discussed

Course Content	Frequency
School Finance	100% (6 of 6)
Strategic Planning	100% (4 of 4)
Facilities/Environment	85.71% (6 of 7)
Curriculum	66.67% (6 of 9)
Program Evaluation	62.5% (5 of 8)

of individual faculty taking responsibility for the inclusion of gender, rather than the program as a whole being planned with the full range of social justice identities and issues in mind, which is what O'Malley and Capper (2015) found in their research on the inclusion of LGBTIQ issues within the curriculum.

Aside from the specific courses taught, respondents also supplied information on their programs' effectiveness in delivering gender-related content. Survey participants were asked about their effectiveness in five areas: (1) exposing leadership candidates to effective methods for eliminating barriers to women's access to leadership; (2) exposing leadership candidates to research on women's leadership; (3) exposing leadership candidates to research on the effectiveness of women leaders; (4) exposing leadership candidates to literature on issues affecting girls and women in education; and (5) exposing leadership candidates to feminist theories, including different types of feminisms and frameworks. In each case, respondents were critical of their programs' effectiveness in preparing students with regard to gender issues in education. For example, just under 39% of respondents described their program as minimally effective in exposing leadership candidates to literature on issues affecting girls and women in education and 36% of respondents described their program as minimally effective in exposing leadership candidates to research on women's leadership. Similarly, 38% of respondents indicated that their program was minimally effective in exposing leadership candidates to research on the effectiveness of women leaders.

With regard to specific knowledge and skill sets, we asked participants about their effectiveness in preparing future leaders to develop anti-harassment policies, deliver empowering programs and curricula for girls and to provide effective staff development focused on gender issues. The findings were moderately promising. Twenty-four respondents (55%) indicated that they agreed and another 13.64% strongly agreed (for a total of 68.64%) that their program prepared future leaders in these areas, while 18% disagreed and 6.82% strongly disagreed. Over 63% agreed or strongly agreed that their program prepares leaders to create empowering programs and curricula for female students and staff. Another 25% disagreed and 4.55% strongly disagreed, indicating that they either do not teach about these issues or they do not teach about them well.

The survey questions focusing on the inclusion of feminist perspectives yielded generally disappointing (though not surprising) results. Less than 39% of respondents said their programs were even moderately effective in exposing leadership candidates to feminist theories, including different types of feminisms and frameworks, and just under 20% indicated that their programs did not discuss or include feminism in their ELPP in any way. Table 11.3 displays the types of feminisms shared by the respondents' institutions, listed from most to least frequently. In the comments section of the survey, one respondent noted the inclusion of Chicana feminism in his or her ELPP coursework. Additionally, three other respondents explained that feminism is addressed directly with candidates but is not included in coursework, though in one case it was included as part of a transformative paradigm, which was shared with students but not "promoted".

We find the lack of emphasis on feminist perspectives and feminist research to be troubling. The lenses that are used to define "good" leadership, teaching and educational practice typically reflect the legacy of white male hegemony, whereas feminist perspectives offer opportunities to see with new and different eyes these same phenomena (Marshall & Young, 2013). Feminist scholarship asks questions that research from traditional frames will not. For example, feminist scholarship asks: How do educational decisions affect women and girls? What power arrangements have been amassed? What is privileged? Who benefits and who loses? Addressing such questions enables leaders to practice

Table 11.3 Types of feminisms included by respondents' institutions

Type of Feminism	Number of Respondents Who Felt Their Program Supported This Feminism	Frequency
Liberal Feminism	22	22 of 36 (61.11%)
Cultural Feminism	14	14 of 36 (38.89%)
Postmodern/Poststructural Feminism	12	12 of 36 (33.33%)
Black Feminism	7	7 of 36 (19.44%)
Postcolonial Feminism	6	6 of 36 (16.67%)
Socialist/Marxist Feminism	5	5 of 36 (13.89%)

in more reflective and equitable ways. Feminist scholarship has other benefits as well, such as: (1) "giving voice" to women respondents and highlighting their experiences; (2) challenging hegemonic notions of practice; (3) expanding the range of acceptable issues to consider and ways of thinking about those issues; (4) pointing to the emotional, subjective, personal or "non-academic" aspects of education; (5) correcting the canon; (6) pointing out how gender is a social construction; and (7) providing tools for pushing back against stereotypes.

Resources and pedagogy

The resources and learning experiences that faculty use when teaching course content can also provide insight into how an educational leadership program prepares its students around gender issues in education. Table 11.4 shares the pedagogical methods used by respondents who reported that they taught feminist theories and topics in their courses. As the table indicates, the most common resource and method of teaching involved having students read theoretical, philosophical or historical analyses, whereas the least commonly used resource was actual data on women leaders and female students. The limited use of data, and for that matter using women leaders as guest speakers, is surprising and disheartening given the opportunities such resources provide for making concrete connections between theory and practice. According to Young et al. (2006), it is important to authentically engage adult learners in the acquisition of knowledge and skills and the development of complex understandings about the effective use of knowledge and skills.

Table 11.4 Teaching feminist theories and topics

Resource/Pedagogy	Number of Respondents Who Used These Methods	Frequency of Using These Methods for Teaching
Required Readings (Theoretical, Philosophical, or Historical Analysis)	41	53.66% (22 of 41)
Required Readings (Empirical Studies)	41	43.9% (18 of 41)
Case Studies	41	43.9% (18 of 41)
Instructors' Personal Experiences	41	43.9% (18 of 41)
Current Events	41	34.15% (14 of 41)
Women Leaders as Guest Speakers	41	39.02% (16 of 41)
Data:		
On Women Leaders	41	29.27% (12 of 41)
On Female Students	41	24.39% (10 of 41)

Institutional climates

In addition to exploring whether and how gender and feminist issues and perspectives were included within ELPP curriculum, our survey also gathered information on respondents' institutional climates. Several questions were structured to collect information on institutional climate both directly and indirectly.

Of the respondents, just under 46% said their program was very effective in creating a supportive environment for female students, families and/or staff, and another 37.84% reported that their program was moderately effective in creating a supportive environment for females. Additionally, just under 39% of respondents said their program was very effective in demonstrating a model of equitable gender dynamics among its faculty and another 11% indicated that their program was effective in doing so. As noted above, 27 of the respondents were female and 14 were male; furthermore, according to these respondents, a majority of their faculty colleagues were women. Specifically, of the 40 respondents, only 7.5% reported that less than 25% of their full-time tenured and tenure-earning faculty members were women, while 27.5% reported that 25% or more were women, 37.5% reported 50% or more were women and 27.5% reported 75% or more were women. These numbers reflect a strong female presence among full-time tenured and tenure-earning faculty. The same appears to be true among non-tenure-earning faculty. Specifically, 45% of respondents reported that women made up 75% or more of non-tenure-earning faculty in their program. Thus, the fact that 84% of the programs provided supportive environments for females is significant. That only 50% reported equitable gender dynamics, however, indicates that more work is needed. Indeed, one respondent, who provided a write-in comment, described how women in educational leadership are perceived in her university:

> [E]ven among our university colleagues and bosses, those of us who are women and in educational leadership are called "aggressive" and "intense" and are described as complex to work with. We believe that if we were men, we would be called strong leaders. We notice that our colleagues who are from cultural backgrounds that have historically oppressed women have an exceptionally hard time working with the women faculty who are strong leaders.

Another interesting finding concerns the lack of work on gender or feminist issues. Results indicated that although women made up a large portion of faculty positions, relatively few engaged in feminist work. Specifically, of the 41 respondents, 14 (34.15%) replied that there was one full-time/tenured faculty member in their department doing feminist/gender-related work, 12 (29.27%) reported two to three and eight (19.51%) reported zero. It does appear, however, that feminist work is taking place in 26 of these 41 programs (in most cases by a lone faculty member); moreover, 46.34% strongly disagreed that a feminist perspective would negatively influence tenure decisions. Still, it appears that responsibility for engaging students in learning and thinking about gender issues and challenging them to view education and leadership issues through a feminist lens is placed on a single faculty member in most programs, which can weaken the legitimacy of such content among the student body. Hawley and James (2010) and O'Malley and Capper (2015) found similar patterns with the inclusion of race and LGBTIQ issues.

Conclusions and implications

Although critical research focusing on gender issues in educational administration has been conducted for more than two decades, there has been virtually no research that has examined, in depth, the inclusion of women's issues and perspectives within ELPPs. Our research, which begins to address this deficiency, reveals that gender issues and feminist perspectives are one of the least attended to issues in leadership preparation. As such, our findings indicate that ELPPs are doing little to interrupt hegemonic notions of educational leadership that unproblematically present leadership as a masculinist and Eurocentric practice.

The sharp divisions along gender, racial and social-class lines, "are clearly associated with exclusion, marginalization, and other negative outcomes, including unequal educational opportunity and achievement" (Allen, Jacobson, & Lomotey, 1995, p. 297). As Wilkinson and Bristol assert in their introduction to this book, it is critical that ELPPs interrogate status quo understandings of leadership, leadership theory and leadership preparation as culturally neutral and apolitical as such ideas make obscure and silence the experiences and ideas of 'other' leaders.

In addition to shedding light on the absence of feminist and gender-focused content and theory, our research offers several major conclusions. First, one would expect our study sample, UCEA institutions, given they are research institutions and their faculty are research-active and committed to excellence in leadership preparation, to lead the way in breaking down status quo understandings and developing critical leaders who are able to foster equitable educational environments. However, this is not what we found. As Blackmore (1999) asserted, our field "has remained relatively quarantined from the more critical impulses of the new social movements . . . responding to external pressures by looking inward to produce better mechanisms of control" (p. 49). It appears that most ELPP students' education is limited to more traditional scholarship and issues, reflecting dominant discourses – discourses that assume all knowledge is masculinist – and that "women's only alternatives are to speak in a masculine voice, construct a new language, or be silent" (Sawicki, 1991, p. 1). UCEA and other ELPP programs have an opportunity to change this situation, however. By including non-hegemonic identities and discourses that emphasise intersectionality in ELPPs, faculty can impact the future of leadership practice through their programs.

Second, our research revealed that in most programs, the responsibility for exposing students to content and theories related to gender and feminism (and apparently other social justice identities and issues) is placed on one or two faculty members, as opposed to the faculty as a whole taking responsibility. This signals the need for at least two steps: First, we recommend that universities provide faculty with professional development concerning gender and feminist issues and how to teach about them intersectionally. Second, research has demonstrated the importance of intentionality and planning in the development and delivery of ELPPs (Darling-Hammond et al., 2007), indicating that ELPP faculty should work together to identify the gender issues they will address and how they will address them. Not only is such an approach more intentional, but by engaging the whole faculty in an effort to integrate feminist frameworks and gender issues into the ELPP curriculum holistically, such issues are less likely to be marginalised as 'someone else's' agenda.

The assumptions people hold about gender and the ability of women to lead poses a problem for women aspiring to and serving in educational leadership roles (Bell & Chase, 1993; Blackmore & Kenway, 1997; Hackmann & McCarthy, 2011; Marshall, 2004; Marshall & Kasten, 1994; Ortiz & Marshall, 1988; Skrla, 2000; Young & McLeod, 2001; Young et al., 2006). After more than three decades of research showing the barriers to women's ascent up the career in school leadership and decades of research demonstrating women's leaders' particular leadership strengths, it is time that ELPPs work to eliminate barriers that are still impacting girls and women in education. The preparation of educational leaders can and should work to influence status quo assumptions, and more importantly, they should provide the knowledge and skills for leaders to fight against gender-related biases and oppressions as well as other wrong-headed and misinformed belief systems that make schools and society inequitable.

Note

1 UCEA is a consortium of higher education institutions committed to advancing the preparation and practice of educational leaders for the benefit of schools and children (UCEA, 2015). UCEA programs are committed to excellence in leadership preparation and engage in ongoing program evaluation and continuous improvement efforts.

References

Alcoff, L. M. (1988). Cultural feminism versus post-structuralism: The identity crisis in feminist theory. *Signs*, *13*(3), 405–436.

Alcoff, L. M. (1997). The politics of postmodern feminism, revisited. *Cultural Critique*, *36*, 5–27. doi:http://doi.org/10.2307/1354498

Allen, K., Jacobson, S., & Lomotey, K. (1995). African American women in educational administration: The importance of mentors and sponsors. *Journal of Negro Education*, *64*(4), 409–422.

Arya, R. (2012). Black feminism in the academy. *Equality, Diversity and Inclusion: An International Journal*, *31*(5/6), 556–572. doi:10.1108/02610151211235523

Bell, C., & Chase, S. (1993). The under representation of women in school leadership. In C. Marshall (Ed.), *The new politics of race and gender* (pp. 141–154). London: Falmer Press.

Blackmore, J., & Kenway, J. (1997). *Gender matters in educational administration and policy: A feminist introduction*. London: Falmer Press.

Capper, C. A., Theoharis, G., & Sebastian, J. (2006). Toward a framework for preparing educational leaders for social justice. *International Journal of Educational Administration*, 44(3), 209–224.

Collins, P. H. (1996). What's in a name? Womanism, black feminism, and beyond. *The Black Scholar*, 26(1), 9.

Crow, C., & Wideman, R. (2016). Effective preparation program features: A literature review. *Journal of Research on Leadership Education*, 1–29. doi:10.1177/1942775116634694

Crow, G. M., Arnold, N. W., Reed, C. J., & Shoho, A. R. (2012). The complexity of leveraging university program change. *Journal of Research on Leadership Education*, 7(2), 172–194.

Darling-Hammond, L., LaPointe, M., Meyerson, D., & Orr, M. T. (2007). *Preparing school leaders for a changing world: Lessons from exemplary leadership development programs*. Stanford, CA: Stanford Center for Opportunity Policy in Education.

Davis, B. W., Gooden, M. A., & Micheaux, D. J. (2015). Color-blind leadership a critical race theory analysis of the ISLLC and ELCC standards. *Educational Administration Quarterly*, 51(1), 335–371. doi:0013161X15587092.

Ebert, T. L. (1991). The 'difference' of postmodern feminism. *College English*, 53(8), 886–904. doi:http://doi.org/10.2307/377692

Enslin, P., & Mary, T. (2004). Liberal feminism, cultural diversity and comparative education. *Comparative Education*, 40(4), 503–516.

Epure, M. (2014). Critically assess: The relative merits of liberal, socialist, and radical feminism. *Journal of Research in Gender Studies*, 4(2), 514–519.

Hackmann, D. G., & McCarthy, M. (2011). *At a crossroads: The educational leadership professoriate in the 21st century*, UCEA Leadership Series. Charlotte, NC: Information Age Publishing.

Hawley, W., & James, B. (2010). Diversity-responsive school leadership. *UCEA Review*, 51(3), 1–5.

Jean-Marie, G., Normore, A. H., & Brooks, J. S. (2009). Leadership for social justice: Preparing 21st century school leaders for a new social order. *Journal of Research on Leadership Education*, 4(1), 1–31.

Kotef, H. (2009). On abstractness: First wave liberal feminism and the construction of the abstract woman. *Feminist Studies*, 35(3), 495–522.

Kottkamp, R. B., & Rusch, E. A. (2009). The landscape of scholarship on the education of school leaders, 1985–2006. In M. D. Young, G. M. Crow, J. Murphy, & R. T. Ogawa (Eds.), *Handbook of research on the education of school leaders* (pp. 23–85). New York: Routledge.

Kowalski, T. J., McCord, R. S., Peterson, G. J., Young, I. P., & Ellerson, N. M. (2011). *American superintendent: 2010 decennial study*. Lanham, MD: Rowman & Littlefield Education.

Lather, P. (1992). Critical frames in educational research: Feminist and post-structural perspectives. *Theory into Practice*, 31(2), 87–99.

Lumby, J., Crow, G. M., & Pashiardis, P. (Eds.). (2008). *International handbook on the preparation and development of school leaders*. New York: Routledge.

Marshall, C. (2004). Social justice challenges to educational administration: Introduction to a special issue. *Educational Administration Quarterly*, 40, 3–13.

Marshall, C., & Johnson, M. (2015, April). *A feminist critical policy analysis of patriarchy in leadership*. Paper presented at the annual meeting of the American Educational Research Association, Chicago, IL.

Marshall, C., & Kasten, K. (1994). *The administrative career: A casebook on entry, equity, and endurance*. Thousand Oaks, CA: Sage.

Marshall, C., & Young, M. D. (2013). Policy inroads undermining women in education. *International Journal of Leadership in Education*, *16*(2), 205–219.

Murphy, J., Moorman, H. N., & McCarthy, M. (2008). A framework for rebuilding initial certification and preparation programs in educational leadership. *Teachers College Record*, *110*, 2172–2203.

O'Malley, M., & Capper, C. (2015). A measure of the quality of educational leadership programs for social justice: Integrating LGBTIQ identities into principal preparation. *Educational Administration Quarterly*, *51*(2), 290–330.

Ortiz, F., & Marshall, C. (1988). Women in educational administration. In N. Boyan (Ed.), *Handbook of research on educational administration* (pp. 123–142). New York: Longman.

Patton, M. Q. (1990). *Qualitative evaluation and research methods*. Newbury Park, CA: Sage.

Pounder, D., Reitzug, U., & Young, M. D. (2002). Preparing school leaders for school improvement, social justice, and community. *Yearbook of the National Society for the Study of Education*, *101*(1), 261–288.

Rusch, E. A. (2004). Gender and race in leadership preparation: A constrained discourse. *Educational Administration Quarterly*, *40*(1), 14–46.

Sawicki, J. (1991). *Disciplining Foucault: Feminism, power and the body*. New York: Routledge.

Skrla, L. (2000). The social construction of gender in the superintendency. *Journal of Education Policy*, *15*(3), 293–316.

St. Pierre, E. A. (2000). Poststructural feminism in education: An overview. *Qualitative Studies in Education*, *13*(5), 477–515.

Suleri, S. (1992). Woman skin deep: Feminism and the postcolonial condition. *Critical Inquiry*, *18*(4), 756–769.

Taylor, V., & Rupp, L. J. (1993). Women's culture and Lesbian feminist activism: A reconsideration of cultural feminism. *Signs*, *19*(1), 32–61.

Theoharis, G. (2007). Social justice educational leaders: Toward a theory of social justice leadership. *Educational Administration Quarterly*, *43*(2), 221–258.

Weeks, J. (2011). Un/re-productive maternal labor: Marxist feminism and chapter fifteen of Marx's capital. *Rethinking Marxism*, *23*(1), 31–40. doi:10.1080/08935696.2011.536327.

Wilkinson, J. (2015, January). Unpublished communication.

Young, M. D., Crow, G., Murphy, J., & Ogawa, R. (2009). *The handbook of research on the education of school leaders*. New York: Routledge.

Young, M. D., & Laible, J. (2000). White racism, antiracism, and school leadership preparation. *Journal of School Leadership*, *10*, 374–414.

Young, M. D., & Maguire, G. D. (2002). The national commission for the advancement of educational leadership preparation: An introduction. *Educational Administration Quarterly*, *38*, 130–136.

Young, M. D., & Mcleod, S. (2001). Flukes, opportunities and planned interventions: Factors affecting women's decisions to enter educational administration. *Educational Administration Quarterly*, *37*(4), 430–462.

Young, M. D., Mountford, M., & Skrla, L. (2006). Infusing gender and diversity issues into educational leadership programs: Transformational learning and resistance. *Journal of Educational Administration, 44*(3), 264–277.

Young, M. D., Petersen, G. J., & Short, P. M. (2002). The complexity of substantive reform: A call for interdependence among key stakeholders. *Educational Administration Quarterly, 38*(2), 137–175.

12 Commentary

Leadership as a relational practice in contexts of cultural hybridity

Jill Blackmore

The new millennium policy discourse of knowledge economies promotes innovation, interdisciplinarity, institutional triple bottom line and a global orientation as being critical to our shared survival as individuals, institutions and nation states. Such discourses intersect with aspirational discourses about the need for greater gender, cultural and racial diversity of leaders together with diversity in leadership practices. Organisations, including schools and universities, are expected not just to be more flexible, adaptable and responsive to their clients' needs but also to be more representative of the diversity of their clients. Racial, gender and cultural diversity in and of leadership is, the discourse goes and research shows, a good thing for organisations, national economies and societies generally. Paradoxically, at the time when diversity of students is increasing, multiple reports and studies in many advanced economies and democratic societies indicate how organisations lack gender and significantly, racial and ethnic diversity in leadership. Scholars therefore continue to critique the marginalisation of those of a different gender, race or ethnicity who are still considered to be 'unfit' rather than 'best fit' in organisational cultures that continue to privilege white, masculinist and heteronormative notions and images of leadership. This point is well made in Wilkinson's discussion (Chapter 4) regarding the disconnect between well-intended but unreflexive school leadership and how white male leaders address student diversity.

Educational leadership, as this collection of research studies illustrates, is about unequal relationships of power informed by multiple intersectionalities of gender, race, class, ethnicity, religion and sexuality and enacted into practice that is situated within a conjuncture of particular historical, social, political and economic moments. There is no universal or specific model of leadership that can ignore context. Nor is there a leader-follower dichotomy so often assumed in the conventional or hero-leadership imaginaries but rather a constant re/negotiation of leadership as a collective social practice immersed in relations of interdependence and intersubjectivity and under conditions not of any leader's own making. Recognising the differential positioning of leaders relative to others by drawing on theories of intersectionality is highly relevant in the complex contemporary world of education. This text addresses this complexity and in so doing challenges the dominant mindset of the educational leadership field and policy most evident in the globalising influence of school effectiveness and improvement studies as outlined in the early section of the text.

Together, these studies not only challenge the field of educational leadership but require researchers and practitioners in the field to undertake self-assessment as to how key issues for the 21st century are to be meaningfully addressed. The text provides some key indicators as to future ground work that has to be done in the field. First, it illustrates how schools are at the macro/micro socio-political interface as it foregrounds the significance of understanding national contexts and the specificity of location, revealing that education is indicative of the changing relationship between the nation state, the individual, society and the economy. The focus on the socio-political and cultural contexts of practice highlights how the role and nature of the state, historical legacies, cultural practices and belief systems inform local leadership practices and possibilities. The changing nature of education, informed by constantly reconfigured interaction between the government, national identity and the economic, social and political impact of global forces, is illustrated in a number of ways. Haiyan, Walker and Jiacheng's review of the English print literature (Chapter 6) recognises the hybridity of cultural contexts and leadership practices arising from the localised mix of Western and Chinese policies, local context and traditional attitudes, values and practices. It explains the mixture of cultural components in China affecting the definition, practice and development of successful principalship. As an authoritarian one-party state, Communist ideology could be expected to permeate institutional practices at every level. But there is no homogeneity. Due to rapid and massive social and economic transitions, China is moving from a largely closed system to one more open to external influence as well as internally generated education reforms seeking to address 21st-century needs. There is no unitary culture, as different values, beliefs and symbols are represented, creating "a hybridity of traditional, socialist, enterprise and patriarchal aspects of culture across the Chinese education system" (see Chapter 6 in this volume). This results from the intermingling of a top-down meritocratic culture based on Confucian obedience to class ordering and authority. We see this being played out in the context of a rapidly globalised city such as Shanghai, which is experiencing education reform as it aims to be globally competitive by encouraging creativity and innovation. School leaders, as principals and party secretaries, are both state employees and usually Communist Party members. They embody this tension as they constantly re/negotiate pressures for Western-oriented individualism and the collective socialist norms of communism.

In the democratic contexts of Sweden, Finland and Australia, leaders and teachers are also positioned within cultural belief systems as to the value of education and recognition of professional expertise, as explicated in three case studies analysed through the lens of "practice architectures" by Wilkinson, Rönnerman, Bristol and Salo. The Nordic countries have shared cultural traditions around the role of education within democratic welfare states as a Scandinavian democratic ethos permeates school leadership (Moller, 2009). Within this Scandinavian cultural framing, there are differences. Although Sweden adopted neoliberal reforms of school choice with Free Schools during the 1990s, the Swedish Early Years example illustrates how the Nordic tradition of *folk enlightenment* and study circles provided a mindset conducive to creating research circles as part of the wider cultural value of *bildung* or education for and of the whole person. The Finnish educational culture has a greater reliance on a conservative trust in individual research-based professionalism and personal responsibility in combination with loose educational standards and flexibility within a consensus valuing school reform.

The Australian case by contrast shows how different national "practice traditions" frame how researchers, teachers and leaders work together collaboratively as there are preconditions of professional *and* public trust. But in the competitive climate of Australian schooling resulting from an assemblage of national standardised assessments, online individual school data on the *MySchool* website and a large government-assisted private school sector, this trust is being quickly depleted (Lingard et al., 2016). These examples highlight the historical conjuncture of culture-discursive, material-economic and socio-political arrangements (practice architectures) that infuse cultural attitudes towards education and teachers and which create a receptiveness of teachers and leaders to undertaking action research. These examples show how favourable conditions of work impact on teachers' sense of agency to develop practices conducive to student learning more broadly.

Second, the text foregrounds issues of how religion, gender and culture intersect in terms of the possibilities for leadership practice within specific cultural contexts. Whereas China is a secular state, and therefore offers greater equality for women in many instances in school leadership, Pakistan is a religious state premised upon Islam. Religion, government and cultural identity coincide. Culture, Shah argues in Chapter 5, as religion, is a "frame of meaning", which produces particular habitus and dispositions towards those with different belief systems. Shah's five female vice chancellors of women's Pakistani universities epitomise how female leadership is contentious because female leadership signifies fundamental cultural change in social, political and economic arenas in a faith-based nation state.

Women are positioned in leadership within an all-encompassing cultural and religious patriarchal frame that informs not only everyday aspects of daily life but also higher education practices that are taken for granted. The traditional social order historically constituted through the family and religion is ingrained into notions as to what counts as legitimate educational leadership and cultural practices. As in secular states, patriarchal leaders use discourses of 'tradition' and cultural practices to maintain male privilege. Regardless of more open and progressive possible readings of scripture that refer to equal rights, the women leaders in Pakistan in this chapter could mobilise their authority only within the 'safety' of female-only contexts. Because these women wished to maintain the intimacy of interpersonal and familial relations by being perceived as 'a good Muslim woman', they were disciplined by narrow readings of the Quran. While their institutional role suggests they were powerful women, their reality was different, producing a form of symbolic violence. Brown, Esnard and Bristol's story (Chapter 8) similarly shows how cultural relations and norms set up young (female) principals in Trinidad and Tobago to fail. Imparting real power to women leaders to step out of traditional roles outside the educational institution is symbolic of wider cultural and religious progressivism. Culture shapes leadership practices, and changing the social relations of gender in ways that reduce male power, regardless of culture, is symbolic of, and therefore challenges, traditional (often faith-based) values and practices. Culture, class and sexuality work in particular ways to position some women as more acceptable than others. Women in leadership can, but do not necessarily, symbolise and embody cultural change.

A third provocation to the field is that the text offers a comparative framing which foregrounds sameness as well as difference. While a nation state's jurisdiction is geographically bounded, policies flow transnationally. A subtext of these studies, but no less important, is that of the increasing influence of the universalising and decontextualised approaches to school reform that arise from the adoption of travelling policies of school effectiveness and improvement, teacher quality, professional standards and international and national testing regimes such as PISA. Globally, while the numbers of women are increasing in school and university leadership with the feminisation and casualisation of educational work, despite the diversity of student populations, there is little indication of greater cultural diversity in leadership at the executive level of schools and systems. Likewise, policy actors in the influential global policy networks are predominantly Western and male. So there is a narrowing, not a broadening, of the framing of leadership representations and practices through globalising processes of quantification, standardisation and comparison. Professional discretion and judgement locally is being compromised at the very moment that more nuanced theorisations and practices are required to unpack the implications of edu-capitalism as it re/constitutes the rapidly changing context of educational leadership. Teachers and leaders struggle to translate these top-down policies to create meaningful networks that are conducive to professional learning while meeting increasingly more stringent external accountability demands.

These chapters indicate the power of hegemonic policy discourses and show the impact of new forms of privatised provision and practices that are circulating globally. Thus Brown, Bristol and Esnard (Chapter 8) indicate how "leadership practices in Trinidad and Tobago have not escaped external, socio-historical, political and internationalized norms" with the "international connection between leadership development, school improvement, and cultures of excellence". Not surprisingly, Haiyan et al's review of the leadership literature (in English) with regard to China identifies Western notions of what constitutes successful principalship, as these case studies were associated with a project across 20 countries and were framed by Western assumptions and mindset(s). More worrying is what Sahlberg (2010) has referred to as the Great Education Reform Movement (GERM) and what Thomson, Gunter and Blackmore (Blackmore, 2016) characterise as the transnational leadership package that circulates globally through policy actor networks. School provision, improvement, leadership and professional learning have become an edu-business which multinationals such as Pearson, consultants such as McKinsey and philanthro-capitalists such as Gates are now actively reconfiguring for profit across Africa, South America and Asia (Hogan, Sellar, & Lingard, 2015). What responsibility does the field of research in educational leadership have to address issues of social justice at the transnational level?

A fourth provocation to the field is the relational perspective of leadership which focuses on practice. Education policy is what is enacted in practice and not merely what is circulating in global discourses or in the policy text. Teachers, principals and parents adopt, adapt and reject policies and practices. Narrative is a key way in which leaders learn to position themselves proactively, to reject particular values, to promote shared understandings of how to work collaboratively with others, although not without difficulty. Narrative is also how researchers illuminate leadership practices. Through the stories of early career leaders, Brown et al. show how the "established rituals of professional socialisation and habits of leadership performances – the practice landscape" – connected social sites (schools and communities), social projects (education and socialisation) and practices (leading and learning to lead). Storying is also a key element of how researchers reflected on their own positionality relative to those they researched, and how they came to negotiate the research relationship.

The text thus captures the sociological move towards theorising an epistemology of practice (e.g., Bourdieu's logic of practice and Ball's policy enactment) and what that means methodologically in the field of educational leadership. In this instance it draws on Kemmis and Grootenboer's (2008) theory of practice architectures. Focusing on practice means studying not just what is said but studying what is happening through social interaction in "intersubjective spaces", while recognising the material conditions which enable, constitute and discourage different forms of leadership practice (as elaborated in Chapter 9). This gets beyond the self-reporting of individual leaders so common in leadership research – whether it be teachers or those in positional leadership. Leadership is a set of social practices and processes that we recognise. Leadership is relational: It is about processes, shared understandings and communicative practices; reflection on, in and for practice as a professional community; and instilling and drawing on the values of recognition, respect and trust important to professional communities.

A fifth provocation to the field of educational leadership is how the collection requires us to consider how subjugated knowledges have been ignored, sidelined or co-opted by the mainstream. The Australian example of Indigenous leadership by Ma Rhea entitled, *Indigenist holistic educational leadership* (Chapter 7) indicates how the nation state and processes of colonisation have excluded Indigenous people from recognition and sustainability of cultural identity. Ma Rhea refers to the struggle for Indigenous leaders with "colonial, habituated legacies embedded within contemporary organisational structures". Her narrative indicates how subjugated peoples on their traditional lands need to call upon the discourse of human rights at the international level and the United Nations' *Declaration on the Rights of Indigenous Peoples*, to which nation states are increasingly expected to accede, in order to claim Indigenous people's distinctive economic, linguistic and cultural rights within complex, globalised, postcolonial education systems. Ma Rhea argues for a holistic approach to leadership that brings together Indigenous and non-Indigenous leadership from an Indigenous rights-based perspective. She therefore challenges the colonialist mindset that has dominated and continues to be scaled up through the global circuit of neoliberal policy actors promoting a universal solution to local problems.

The text therefore challenges the field as Wilkinson and Bristol claim. It interrogates leadership practices in culturally specific contexts and how gender, class, culture, race, sexuality and location intertwine in terms of how leadership is represented, perceived, practised and understood. Young, Marshall and Edwards in Chapter 11 illustrate how leadership programs in the US exemplify the lack of recognition of issues of gender. In particular, they emphasise how American values and beliefs infuse national and state standards and state licensure requirements that in turn "lack gender-related language" as US society and universities refuse to accept gender inequality exists in leadership. Their analysis of professional learning programs in the US provides further evidence as to why the domesticated notion of diversity now endemic in equity discourses is more a descriptor than a powerful driver towards understanding how inequality works in practice, and is inadequate in terms of providing substantive discourses to inform purposeful leadership for socially just education (Ahmed, 2009).

The unproblematised whiteness of educational leadership and the programs that 'develop leaders' with their lack of professional reflexivity is most evident in Wilkinson's Australian example of a school leadership team (Chapter 4). While well intended, the team sought to enable a more positive cultural recognition of student ethnic diversity at a school-wide level. Yet ethnic diversity was considered to be the property of 'them' (refugee students) and not 'us' (taken-for-granted white, male leaders). Indigenous as postcolonial theorists reject this infantilisation of 'the other' as being in need of 'help' and who are different from the male norm, and offer viable alternatives that foreground belonging, place and two-way learning. School leaders in Australia, as elsewhere, are inducted via programs focusing on financial and personnel management, marketing, the media, communication, risk management and so on, neglecting over 30 years of feminist, anti-racist or postcolonial research on leadership. Reflexivity on a leader's positioning (class, race, gender, ethnicity, religion) and understanding institutional discrimination are starting points for professional learning in leadership.

All of this raises issues around epistemology, methodology and the ethics of researching leadership. Brown, Bristol and Esnard (Chapter 8) in their study excavating leadership in Trinidad and Tobago indicate that "our assumptions and practices as researchers highlight a potential colonising relationship between theory, practice and context". Their use of collective narratives allows the "intersubjective relationship between the *sayings*, *doings* and *relatings* to unfold against a backdrop of cultural assumptions of and for authority". Positioning the researcher, understanding their cultural background (coloniser, postcolonial), experiences and assumptions and addressing our ethnocentrism are therefore critical starting points in undertaking leadership research. The theme of reflective practice is a constant reference throughout the text: reflection on the self as an ethical subject, on practice and on purpose and on leadership as a social and relational practice that is context-specific.

The tension underpinning many of these studies is about what can inform leaders as to how to conduct moral and ethical leadership when one's position is always tenuous within performative systems. Leaders are confronted by ethical dilemmas and conflicts that are highly situated in terms of how they are positioned with regard to those who wish to protect and those who wish to change cultural norms in a rapidly changing social, economic and political context, taking into account who can and should speak for whom, when and about what. Moral, cultural and ethical orders are contested. While Shah's female vice chancellors call upon their faith, the leadership discourse in the secular Western societies focuses on ethical leadership as one that seeks to enable social justice. From a secular perspective, Keddie and Niesche in Chapter 3 draw from Foucault's conceptualisation of four elements of ethics that are significant for leadership in terms of how leaders through their values, reflect on practice and through purposeful approaches constitute themselves as ethical leaders. This and another Australian case study exemplify how difficult leadership for social justice is when principals in schools in disadvantaged communities have to manage politically, materially and emotionally the tension between doing what is best in terms of their diverse student needs in order for students to achieve, and national contexts where they are pressured by a narrow range of externalised decontextualised performative outcomes demanded by high-stakes tests (Lingard, Thompson, & Sellar, 2016).

From a Foucauldian perspective, Niesche and Keddie's contrast of an Australian and English school mobilises Foucault's notions of advocacy, truth-telling and counter-conduct. It offers a capacity to analyse and understand how principal subjectivities are formed and informed by thinking about moral and ethical issues as they reflect on their own position and identity relative to others in the relationships and practices that are leadership. The context acts as a "mode of subjection but also allows freedom to act according to a particular telos of social justice". These leaders require significant self-governing behaviours and repertoires, positioning themselves as self-responsibilising with regard to their work as "autonomous, self-determined and self-sustaining subjects who are solely responsible for successfully working within its parameters". Other examples echo how being a leader is always about being and becoming, an ongoing reflection on self and relationships with others.

This text further challenges the field of educational leadership by offering multiple theoretical perspectives of understanding the complexity and nature of how social justice is worked through in everyday practices by inclusive and collaborative nature of research with teachers as co-participants through a reflexive "praxeological approach" as researchers work with principals and teacher leaders. The mentoring of novice researchers models the type of practice critical to leadership. Agosto and Karanxha in Chapter 10 identify the absent voice in educational leadership research. Utilising Deleuze and Guattari's tools, they unpack how discipline is practised in an analysis of school administrators and student relationships. How students view school administration provides new insights into why and how they respond to disciplinary strategies with regard to their mis/conduct. This study indicates how administrators communicate both through policy but also illustrate how inclusionary/exclusionary interpersonal interactions lead to mis/readings between students and leaders and shape student attitudes to schooling. Such a discussion raises issues for school leaders about to whom does a school belong. School leaders often use terms such as "my school", which excludes many students from feeling they belong. The micro-analytics of inquiry based on relational leadership provides more nuanced explanations regarding student responses to schooling.

The theoretical mix of the chapter offers new ways of seeing, doing and researching leadership. It draws from Deleuze and Guattari and the ever-present non-human technologies' capacity to enhance or detract from practices and possibilities and thereby "provoke discussion of the power, people, bodies and 'things'" or the objects of research. Leadership is necessarily embodied and located within material conditions shaped by time, space, technology and place. Such a perspective demands recognition of the unequal distribution and allocation of material goods (e.g., technologies) that are becoming more significant in shaping pedagogical practices. It also demands recognition of the opportunities and aspirations of students, and how leadership is about enabling teachers and students by capturing, mobilising and using resources to enhance possibilities.

The diversity of the theoretical and methodological approaches also provokes thinking about the unpredictability of research (in contrast to the claimed predictability of randomised control trials) because it deals with the human. No matter how carefully designed, all research requires researchers be adaptive, reflective and cautious in terms of the processes and relationships we seek to develop and the assumptions brought to any person or place. Those whom we research with/on are often troublesome, and our 'subjects' (who provide 'the data') have agency in their refusal to be readily categorised or just by not turning up, thereby limiting our research. The objects we use in our research are equally problematic – recorders that do not record and spaces that make it impossible to concentrate. This prompts us to realise that our 'subjects' are not invested in our research and they are 'gifting' us with their time and stories. Research relies on a gift economy – voluntary participation based on respect, recognition and trust. It therefore demands, as these chapters indicate, a degree of empathy with those who offer their time and knowledge, rather than just being the critical observer who can always leave the situated messiness of schools where time to reflect is difficult to obtain and in which there are no ideal circumstances.

The collection of studies is revealing of what have been undercurrents of scholarly work within the field of educational leadership but which are increasingly foregrounded in contemporary times. It unpacks and puts on display the institutionalised and systemic nature of exclusionary and discriminatory practices. It challenges the claims and orthodoxies of what constitutes leadership for organisational effectiveness and improvement as well as their economic, epistemological and political assumptions. It does so at the very moment these orthodoxies are being promoted by a transnational leadership project to promote particular versions of leadership, organisational effectiveness and provision, whether it be charter and free schools, visible learning, psychometric evaluation of prospective teachers, professional standards or privatisation of provision in the name of entrepreneurialism. Discourses of re/form which circulate globally ignore (unless they have use value for edu-capitalism), culture, ethnicity, gender and class at the macro (transnational), meso (State) and micro (school and university) levels. These chapters forewarn progressive movements as to how education will continue to be the site of value contestation, but in a much more troublesome global context in which there is a rise of extreme social conservatism. This conservatism, together with market neoliberalism mixed with emergent xenophobia (e.g., Trump, Brexit, Le Pen and Hanson) challenge hard-won gains for those who are 'different'.

The empirical studies of leaders – principals and teachers – indicate tensions between modernist transnational discourses of education reform (flexibility, innovation, creativity, school autonomy, transformational leadership, community partnerships) and the colonial, secular and religious state-driven bureaucracies (hierarchical meritocracies) to which they are held responsible. They indicate tensions between how these are mediated through research (largely Western school effectiveness research). The practice orientation of the studies is invaluable as it points not just to the discursive context but also to the materiality of leadership practices and relationships. The nature of the state (secular or faith-based, democratic or authoritarian) informs discourses about social justice, how education is valued, the role of professionals and how one makes claims upon the state for social justice. Each of these provocations signals the need for rethinking not just educational leadership but also the purpose and promise of education in the 21st century.

References

Ahmed, S. (2009). Embodying diversity: Problems and paradoxes for Black feminists. *Race, Ethnicity and Education*, *12*(1), 41–52. ISSN: 1361-3324.

Ball, S., Maguire, M., & Braun, A. (2014). *How schools do policy: Policy enactment in secondary schools*. London: Routledge.

Blackmore, J. (2016). *Educational leadership and Nancy Fraser*. London: Routledge.

Deleuze, G., & Guattari, F. (2004). *A thousand plateaus: Capitalism and schizophrenia*. London: Continuum.

Hogan, A., Sellar, S., & Lingard, B. (2015). Network restructuring of global Edu-business: The case of Pearson's efficacy framework. In W. Au & J. Ferrare (Eds.), *Mapping corporate education reform: Power and policy networks in the neoliberal state* (pp. 43–64). London: Routledge.

Lingard, B., Thompson, G., & Sellar, S. (Eds.). (2016). *National testing in schools: An Australian assessment*. London: Routledge.

Moller, J. (2009). Approaches to school leadership in Scandinavia. *Journal of Educational Administration and History*, *41*(2), 165–177.

Index

Note: Italicized page numbers indicate a figure on the corresponding page. Page numbers in bold indicate a table on the corresponding page.

Aboriginal and Torres Strait Islander communities 120–1, 126–8
Aboriginal education 17
Aboriginal teachers 60–1
advocacy 44–5, 47–9
age and cultural authority 144–6
Anglo-American knowledge 153, 166
Anglo-Australian ethnicity 58, 60–1, 65–6
Anglocentric educational leadership 166
Anglophone leadership scholarship 13–14
Applied Critical Leadership (ACL) 11
assemblages and discipline context 172–3
asset-based approaches to leading 26
asylum seekers 65
Australian educational leadership 162–5, 167, 210, 213
Australian Professional Standard for Principals 11, 57, 69
autonomy of schools 42

belief systems, impact on leadership 77–8
bildung tradition 156, 166, 167, 210
Black feminism 195
Black women in leadership 26

Chicana feminism 200
China *see* principalship success studies in China; school leadership in China
collaborative leadership practices 158–62
colonist mindset 119–22
colour-blind approach to education 64

communist values in school leadership 99, 109, 209
community of leadership model 9, 17–18
Confucian values in school leadership 98–9
counter-conduct notion 45, 47–9
cross-cultural value systems 13–15
cultural authority 143, 144–8
cultural belief systems 209, 211
cultural competence 26
cultural-discursive arrangements 140–1, 155, 157, 160–1, 163–4
cultural diversity 57
cultural embeddedness 76–8
cultural feminism 195
cultural hybridity 208–16
cultural instrumentalism 31
culturally irrelevant leadership 55
culturally varying empirical sites: cultural turn in leadership 30–2; introduction to 3, 23–4; as organizing mechanism for leadership 26–30; the 'othered' in leadership research 30–2; subjugated knowledges 23, 24–6; summary of 34–6; transferability challenge 32–4
cultural pride 126–7
cultural safety 127–8
cultural turn in educational leadership: cross-cultural value systems 13–15; ethnically diverse schools 11–12; female leaders 12–13; Indigenous bodies of literature 8–11; introduction to 2–3, 7–8; structural paradigms 30–2; summary of 18–19; theoretical frameworks 15–18

"developing famous principals" (*mingxiaozhang*) study 107–9
discipline context: assemblages 172–3; debriefing sessions 182–4; findings on 173–8, *175*; focus group on 184; inconsistency with 177–8; introduction to 171; leading discipline 173; racism in 177, 179; social group identifiers 180–2; student/administrator contact 175–7; summary of 184–6; teacher/administrator boundaries *174*, 174–5; theoretical framework 171–3; un/becoming findings 173, 178–84; Youth Participatory Action Research 179–84; inconsistency with discipline 177–8; incorporeal transformation of bodies 172
diversity and educational leadership: educational leadership as coded white 56–8; ethnic and cultural diversity 57; introduction to 4, 54–6; methodology of 58–67; race equality and 29–30; recognitive justice for refugee students 62–7; student/teacher links 60–2; summary of 67–70

educational leadership: as coded white 56–8; collaborative leadership practices 158–62; community of leadership model 9, 17–18; cultural embeddedness and 76–8; cultural hybridity 208–16; curriculum development 193–5; hegemonic leadership 26, 30, 139; introduction to 1–3, 152; methodological critiques 152–4; othering ideology 30–2, 141–2; overview of 3–5; practice architectures 154–65; school-based leadership 4, 160; summary of 165–8; *see also* cultural turn in educational leadership; diversity and educational leadership; feminism and leadership; principalship success studies in China; school leadership in China; Trinidad and Tobago educational leadership
Educational Leadership and Policy Studies program (ELPS) 180
educational leadership preparation programs (ELPPs) 189–204

English as a Second Language (EAL/D) 58, 59, 63–7
English-language Chinese principalship 96
ethnically diverse schools 11–13, 57, 68

"famous principal" (*ming xiaozhang*) context 101, 104
"famous principalship" (*ming xiaozhang lingdao*) context 101
female Muslim leaders: belief systems, impact on leadership 77–8; cultural embeddedness and 76–8; discussion about 88–90; honour (*izzat*) concept 87–8, 90; introduction to 4, 12–13, 75–6; overview of 80–8, 210; patriarchal assumptions 79, 80–6; segregated systems/spaces 85–7, 90; 'good Muslim woman' discourse 82–3; honour (*izzat*) concept 87–8, 90; patriarchal assumptions about Muslim women 79, 80–6
feminism and leadership: course content 198–201, **199**, **200**; critical approaches to 18; curriculum development 193–5; exclusion of 153; experiences of 190–1; findings and discussion 198–203; framework of 195–7; Indigenous women leaders 10, 17; institutional climates 202–3; introduction to 189–90; methodology 197; research perspectives 191–5; resources and pedagogy 201, **201**; standards and licensure policy 192–3; liberal feminism 195–6; Marxist feminism 196–7; postmodern/poststructural feminism 196; radical feminism 196; socialist feminism 196–7
Finnish leadership case study 158–62, 167, 210
folk enlightenment 153–4, 156, 166, 210
Foucault, Michel 41, 43–6, 50, 62

gender and ethnicity 13
gender and feminism in leadership *see* feminism and leadership
gender-discriminating practices 190
gender equity 193
globalisation 27, 34

hegemonic leadership 26, 30, 139
holistic education *see* Indigenist holistic educational leadership

Indigenist holistic educational leadership: case study 122–4; colonist mindset 119–22; cultural pride 126–7; cultural safety 127–8; emergent themes in 124–31; ensuring permanence 130–1; humility of white administrators 124–5; introduction to 4, 118–19; multiple viewpoints on 128–9; proper way of 129–30; role modelling of trust 125; summary of 131–2
Indigenous Australian women leaders 10–11, 17
Indigenous bodies of literature 8–11
Indigenous Hawaiian educational leaders 9, 17–18

leading practices in secondary education 162–5
lesbian, gay, bisexual, transgender, intersex and questioning (LGBTIQ) issues 190, 194, 199

masculinity constructions 11–12, 18
material-economic arrangements 140–1, 155, 157–8, 161, 164
Muslims: belief systems 77–8; 'good Muslim woman' discourse 82–3; leadership 14; male leadership in Islamic society 88–9; Pakistan religious ideology 78–80; segregation in Islam 85–7, 90; *see also* female Muslim leaders; male leadership in Islamic society 88–9

neoliberal principles 16, 209–10

organisational culture 28–9
organizing mechanism for leadership 26–30
othering ideology 30–2, 141–2

Pakistan 78–80
Pakistani women leaders 13, 80–8; *see also* female Muslim leaders
"people's educators" *(renmin jiaoyujia)* study 107–9
political subjectivity 44, 48–9

postcoloniality 139, 153, 196
practice architectures: collaborative leadership practices 158–62; cultural belief systems 209; introduction to 154–5; leading practices 155–8, 162–5
practice landscape 142–3
principals: Australian Professional Standard for Principals 11, 57, 69; "developing famous principals" study 107–9; early career principal 138; English-language Chinese principalship 96; preparation programmes 4; school leadership in China 102–9
principalship success studies in China: defined 102–4; development of 107–9; "famous principal" *(ming xiaozhang)* context 101, 104; "famous principalship" *(ming xiaozhang lingdao)* context 101; introduction to 102; practices of 104–7; "successful principal" *(chenggong xiaozhang)* context 101; summary of 110
principal-teachers 160–1

Quran 81–2, 87, 88

racism: Black feminism 195; in discipline 177, 179; social justice and 194
recognitive justice for refugee students 62–7
refugee students 59, 62–7
religion and educational leadership 13, 77; *see also* female Muslim leaders; Muslims
researcher stance 32–3

school leadership in China: communist/socialist values 99, 109; Confucian values 98–9; introduction to 4, 14, 95–7; principalship studies 102–9; review process on 100–9, **101**, **102**; successful research on 97–100; traditional and contemporary context 98–100; understanding implications of 109–10; Western philosophies 99–100, 110
segregation in Islam 85–7, 90
sex and cultural authority 147–8
sex-segregated education in Islam 86
socialist values in school leadership 99, 109

Index

social justice in leadership: advocacy 44–5, 47–9; counter-conduct notion 45, 47–9; feminism and 191, 193–4; forms of elaboration 43, 44–5; Foucault, Michel, ethics of 41, 43–6, 50; introduction to 4, 40–3; summary of 49–52; telos of leading 43, 46–7; truth-telling 44, 47–9
social-political arrangements 140–1, 155, 158, 160, 164–5
societal culture and leadership 28–9, 76
subjugated knowledges 23, 24–6
"successful principal" *(chenggong xiaozhang)* context 101
sui generis rights of Indigenous peoples 118
super diversity 8, 153

teachers: Aboriginal teachers 60–1; boundaries with discipline *174*, 174–5; diversity concerns 60–2; learning practices 156–7; school leadership practices 160–1
telos of leading 43, 46–7
Trinidad and Tobago educational leadership: age and cultural authority 144–6; challenge of context with 139–42; discussion of 148–9; introduction to 137–8; practice landscape of 142–3; presentation of data 144–8; sex and cultural authority 147–8; study overview 138–9; Trinidad and Tobago Unified Teachers' Association (TTUTA) 139
truth-telling (parrhesia) 44, 47–9

un/becoming, defined 173
un/becoming findings 173, 178–84
United Nations Declaration on the Rights of Indigenous Peoples (UNDRIP) 118–21, 131, 212–13
University Council for Educational Administration (UCEA) 197, 198, 203

Western philosophies of school leadership 99–100, 110
Western theoretical concepts of leadership 15
whiteness constructions 11–12, 213
women/girls-only *(zanana)* institutions 85, 86
women's experiences of leadership 8; *see also* feminism and leadership
women vice chancellors in Pakistan 78–80

xenophobia 216

youth identity development 180–2
Youth Participatory Action Research (Y-PAR) 179–84